The Queen's True Worth

THE QUEEN'S TRUE WORTH

DAVID McCLURE

LUME BOOKS

LUME BOOKS

First published in 2020 by Lume Books
30 Great Guildford Street,
Borough, SE1 0HS

ISBN 978-1-83901-213-6

Typeset using Atomik ePublisher from Easypress Technologies

www.lumebooks.co.uk

Table of Contents

Foreword

When monarchs grow old a blind eye is often turned to their money. Such was the case with the ageing Queen Victoria who saved a fortune from her public grant under the noses of a succession of compliant Chancellors of the Exchequer and so too it was with the Queen Mother whose extravagant expenditure on racing and entertaining in her nineties was indulged by palace courtiers with barely a murmur. Today, something similar is happening to the nonagenarian Queen who now receives far more revenue than she can possibly spend without anyone seeming to notice or care.

This partial-sightedness by the public and parliament alike is convenient since historically money is the monarchy's weakest link: Charles I lost his head over it when he tried to bypass parliament to fund his military ventures; William III had to agree to be a constitutional monarch in order to get a steady stream of it from the state; and George III was obliged to give up all his Crown lands to secure a set sum of it each year. Money forces sovereigns to interact with parliament when they would much prefer to stay above the political fray.

The public, though, have recently got a glimpse of the monarch's wealth through popular television series like "The Crown" from Netflix and "Victoria" from ITV. Some of the glittering jewellery and sumptuous palaces have also been on display to viewers in two 2018 weddings at Windsor Castle – Prince Harry's spectacular ceremony with Meghan Markle in May and his cousin Princess Beatrice's more modest affair in October. Both caused controversy over the cost of security and raised questions whether the bill could have been paid by the royal family from their own private resources.

If today the public find it hard to follow the money of the monarch, it is because the royal finances are shrouded in fog. The sovereign and her heir enjoy a multitude of information privileges that prevent outsiders from penetrating their coffers. Their wills and the value of their estates are not made public unlike the case with ordinary citizens. Their official papers at the National Archives are kept secret for 50-100 years in contrast to the normal release time of 20-30 years. Their official communications with government are immune from Freedom of Information requests whereas other state institutions are obliged to allow the public to see what happens in their name.

This book is an attempt to shine some daylight on the Queen's foggy finances. It is the product of three years of truffling in the archives (including the private papers of many cabinet ministers as well as the more public National and Royal Archives and the English and Scottish Land Registries), talking to contemporary actors on both sides of the palace gates (including dozens of courtiers, royal correspondents, parliamentarians, financial advisors and professional valuers) and visiting royal residences (including Buckingham Palace, Clarence House, Windsor Castle and Sandringham House as well as the Royal Palace in Stockholm).

It is also the result of a decade of researching the royal finances which has helped to produce a range of television programmes, radio broadcasts, books and newspaper articles. The form of media may change but the same questions keep coming up. How rich is the Queen and where did her wealth come from? Was it inherited or derived from tax privileges or savings from the public grant? What part was played by her highly profitable ancestral estate, the Duchy of Lancaster? And what about her private residences – Balmoral and Sandringham – and her official ones – Buckingham Palace and Windsor Castle? Are they partly public and if so, how should they be included in her private assets? Similarly, are all the treasures in the Royal Collection – from Old Masters to Crown Jewels – hers or ours?

In short, what is the Queen's true worth?

Prologue:

Monetising the Monarchy

It felt as if the tectonic plates had suddenly shifted at the palace. In early 2020 the Queen's plans for a smooth handover of power to Prince Charles – and with it a frictionless transfer of the Windsor wealth and the priceless royal brand to the next generation – were thrown into disarray when her grandson lobbed a hand-grenade into the forecourt of Buckingham Palace. Prince Harry's bombshell announcement on January 8 that he and Meghan, the Duchess of Sussex, wanted "to step back" as full-time working royals and lead a life of financial independence in North America rocked the foundations of the House of Windsor. Up until then, no senior royal had been allowed to combine carrying out public engagements and earning a private living. The two were a toxic mix. On hearing the news, the Queen who had been given no written warning as to what the Sussexes were proposing, was said to be "hurt" and "disappointed" – an astonishingly overt and disparaging comment from the head of an institution that never washed its dirty linen in public.[1]

Five days later on January 13[th,] there was an attempt at a compromise at the so-called "Sandringham Summit" when all the competing parties including the Queen, Prince Charles, Prince William and Prince Harry (but not Meghan who was away in Canada looking after little Archie) convened in the Big House on Her Majesty's Norfolk estate. At the end of a long day, she issued another remarkably personal statement expressing her desire to accommodate the couple's aim to forge a new "progressive

1

role" within the family: "Although we would have preferred them to remain full-time working members of the Royal Family, we respect and understand their wish to a live a more independent life as a family while remaining a valued part of my family." But ultimately after a further week of negotiations between courtiers from both camps, the circle could not be squared. You could not both be a working royal and do paid work. The only answer was a clean break.

The announcement came mid-evening on Saturday January 18th – just in time to make the Sunday papers. Harry and Meghan would be allowed to go to North America and pursue their financial independence, but they would have to step down from all public duties. They would not be able to use their HRH titles – so that henceforth they would be known simply as Harry, Duke of Sussex and Meghan, Duchess of Sussex, without the style "Royal Highness" – and they would be denied any financial support from the taxpayer-funded Sovereign Grant. Most personally wounding for Harry was that he would be stripped of almost all of his formal connections with the army for which he had served for almost a decade, rising to the rank of captain and holding honorary titles in all three armed forces. In effect, he was abdicating.

The news was historic. There had been nothing quite like it since the abdication of Edward VIII in 1936. Camilla Tominey, the royal reporter who first broke the story back in 2017 that Harry was secretly dating Meghan, said "this separation of powers, this divorce, if you like, from the royal family is unprecedented in the modern era," while Alastair Bruce, a royal protocol expert with impeccably close ties to the palace, called the agreement "a seismic announcement... This is an abdication... No more representing the Queen on great occasions. No more being part of the royal and ceremonial royal family, no more military involvement and no more public money."[2]

In truth, the Queen's announcement about the Sussexes' new status raised a number of sensitive financial issues that had bubbling under the surface during the handover process but had yet to be fully resolved. What was the price of a slimmed down monarchy? How many working royals were really necessary? How far down the line of succession could you be before you were permitted paid employment? What sort of commercial activities should be allowed? Would cashing in on the family name damage the royal brand and by extension undermine the authority of the sovereign?

But the most expensive financial issue concerned security. Royal protection had long been the elephant in the room that no one discussed in detail but whose huge costs overshadowed the budget for the monarchy. The total cost for the whole family was thought to be well in excess of £100m a year but the government refused to give a precise figure as it might compromise security by giving information to potential enemies of the state about whether the level of funding was going up or down. In the recent past, several junior royals had quietly had their protection removed or downgraded but their names had never been revealed. When it came to the Sussexes' protection, all the Queen's statement would say was: "Buckingham Palace does not comment on details of security arrangements. There are well established independent processes to determine the need for publicly funded security."

But others *were* commenting on the cost of security – most notably taxpayers in Canada who were up in arms about the prospect of paying for the extra protection costs of the couple residing in their country. Ten thousand citizens soon signed a petition demanding that they foot the bill themselves – or at least get the UK government to compensate its Canadian counterpart – and the public rancour grew more heated after one independent security expert estimated that the cost for Canada alone could be as high as £4-6m a year.[3] Eventually the Canadian government announced that it would stop paying for Harry and Meghan's security and they decided to relocate to California. Once they settled in Los Angeles, President Trump also made it clear that the United States would not pay for their protection.

It is impossible to get hard and fast figures but reliable estimates suggest that before their exit the Sussexes' total security bill with a team of around six bodyguards was just under £1m a year and that once they went to North America with the security detail swelling to ten officers it could rise to over £5m.[4] Faced with such an embarrassingly large figure, the couple let it be known that they planned to repay the taxpayer for security on private business engagements with no royal connection (the payment model might be similar to the one for former prime minister Tony Blair who has earned millions travelling the world doing deals but has reimbursed the state for his commercial costs). But this of course does not cover their non-commercial activities and given that as former senior royals they will need protection for the rest of their lives (with Harry being particularly vulnerable having served in Afghanistan) and that they are unlikely to be able to afford £5m annually for the next 40 years, the UK taxpayer will have to foot a huge bill.

The other embarrassing item of expenditure which had to be paid for from the public purse was the refurbishment of Frogmore Cottage which cost an eye-watering £2.4m from the Sovereign Grant in 2019. The Grade II-listed Windsor property which had been a wedding gift from the Queen would now lie empty for long periods of the year while they were in Canada and the United States. When the Sussexes announced their departure plan and with it their desire to keep their official residence, there was an immediate public backlash. Why could they not return it to the Queen or give it to the state? Why should the public bankroll the official residence of two royals who do no public duties? To quell the growing storm, the couple agreed to pay rent and to refund the costs of the refit. But how could they suddenly find £2.4m when they had yet to make serious commercial money?

In theory the Queen could have come to the rescue since it was her original gift and she did already help other close family members – like Princess Anne and Prince Edward – with the hefty costs of running their country residences. But in the end, it was Prince Charles who stepped in since up until then he had been funding their public duties – and the odd private cost like their wedding – from his Duchy of Cornwall revenues. Charles was understood to have agreed to finance their new life for at least a year, including providing up to £2m for their security, although it was made known that the pot of cash was "not inexhaustible."[5]

The Frogmore refurbishment costs, it later emerged, would be paid for via a surcharge on their rent.

What was most revealing about Charles's intervention was the suggestion that this time the funding would not come from the Duchy of Cornwall, his semi-public ancestral estate, but from his own private investment income. This was a rare admission that he had a source of funding separate from the Duchy. The only other occasion when his private portfolio of investments had been publicly discussed was back in 2004 when his former financial advisor disclosed in a newspaper interview that the prince had had to liquidate all his shares to pay for the £17m divorce settlement from Diana.[6] Clearly if he was able to fund his son to the tune of several million pounds a year, he must have been able in the intervening two decades to rebuild his private shareholdings to rude health. So, where did the investment money come from?

Previously, Charles was not believed to have huge savings. According to his biographer Jonathan Dimbleby who was given access to his private papers in 1994, he had amassed a personal fortune of some £2m,[7] while by 2001 the *Mail on Sunday's Royal Rich Report* estimated that "Charles had about £4m outside the Duchy."[8]

Although it is possible that he received some money from family trusts and the odd private bequest, the ultimate source of his investment money in 2020 was almost certainly the Duchy of Cornwall. If you drill down into his 2018-2019 annual review of expenditure and income – which was nearly totally derived from the Duchy – you can see that he paid a total of almost £4.7m in income tax at the top rate of 45%.[9] After factoring in his £11,850 personal allowance and the lower rate on his first £150,000 of income, that would mean that his total taxable income was around £11m. When you deduct from this gross sum his stated non-official expenditure of £3.16m (which unlike his official expenditure of £8.6m was taxable) along with the tax of £4.7m you arrive at a figure of £3.14m. No doubt there were a few other non-disclosed items of expenditure and perhaps some other personal costs that were not tax deductible, but even allowing for that by this rough calculation he would still be left a surplus of well in advance of £2m to give to Harry and Meghan or invest in his private shareholdings.

No one knows what sort of investments he has because like the Queen's private ownership of shares it is shrouded in a fog of pea-souper impenetrability, but a clue was given in the Paradise Papers data leak in 2017 which revealed that the investment portfolio of his Duchy of Cornwall included significant holdings in an ecologically friendly company called Sustainable Forestry Management which traded in carbon credits in Bermuda. So, given his lifelong commitment to environmental issues, it would come as no surprise if some of his investments were green or ethically friendly and if he wanted to keep them private, perhaps in companies located overseas. As we show in Chapter 2, one of the attractions of investing offshore is that it can provide greater confidentiality.

Harry and Meghan, of course, have their own private wealth and investments but they are unlikely to be as large or as liquid as Charles's. What we do know is that Harry inherited £6.5m from his mother's estate which was reinvested in a trust fund and that he was also left an undisclosed sum from the Queen Mother in another family fund which may be worth up to £20m but is spread among half a dozen of her great grandchildren. Meghan had a successful acting career in the hit TV series *Suits* where she was reportedly paid £38,000 an episode and once she retired after seven seasons she was believed to be worth (when you added on her endorsement earnings) in the region of £3m, but some of that money may already have been eaten up by her affluent transatlantic lifestyle.

When they announced their decision to become financially independent, it sparked off a frenzy of speculation about the value of the Sussex brand. Some PR analysts suggested it might be worth £500m a year. "They are going to be the most famous brand in the world – the Beckhams, Obamas, Bill Gates," said Andy Barr, a retail price expert, "they are going to far surpass them."[10] They had already taken steps to protect their own image and identity. In June 2019 they applied to trademark the Sussex Royal brand which features a monogram of H and M entwined. The long list of products covered included books, calendars, clothing and charitable fundraising.

Palace insiders immediately wondered if this was a prelude to them launching their own line of branded products. What caused most concern was the use of the word "royal" in the Sussex Royal brand. At first sight it seemed incompatible with the Queen's January 18th statement that "while they can no longer formally represent the Queen, the Sussexes have made clear that everything they do will continue to uphold the values of Her Majesty." Those values are enshrined in the royal brand which stands for duty, diligence and not to put a finer point on it, dullness, in the sense that family members are supposed to behave and not make waves. Since the monarchy is all about image and has little formal power, its most valuable asset is its reputation for dutiful behaviour – something that Princess Elizabeth on her 21st birthday famously pledged to honour: "I declare before you that my whole life whether it be long or short shall be devoted to your service and the service of our great imperial family to which we all belong."

In the end – after another round of negotiations with the palace – the Sussexes were forced in late February to accept that they could not use the brand name Sussex Royal as it broke long-standing government rules about the commercial exploitation of the term "royal." But this was done with a degree of reluctance (with them pointing out that although they would respect it, technically the UK ban did not apply overseas) and there still remained the risk that the couple might tarnish the Queen's carefully nurtured brand with some tacky merchandising.

There was no shortage of business options on offer. Clothing and beauty was one obvious commercial avenue given that Meghan was already well connected in the fashion industry after Givenchy had designed her £300,000 wedding dress and she had guest-edited the September edition of British *Vogue*. There she wrote of "her love of writing" and another option was writing books and following the example of her friend Michelle Obama who had recently made a fortune from her memoir "Becoming," with the joint book deal with Barack said to be worth £48m. The Obamas also make serious money from speaking engagements and the lucrative US lecture circuit so beloved of former UK prime ministers like Tony Blair and John Major could be another income stream for the Sussexes. And indeed their first step was taken in June 2020 when they signed with the same Harry Walker agency that represents the Obamas. But with it comes the elephant trap of straying into overt politics and compromising the political neutrality of the monarchy that the Queen has diligently observed. One could only guess at the public reaction if one of their talks turned out to be sponsored by a US tobacco firm or a bank with a dubious reputation.

A safer course for a former actress and a prince who was a natural on screen was film and television work. Well before the January 8th bombshell announcement, Meghan had already signed a deal with Disney to voiceover a movie and Harry had teamed up with Apple TV to make a series of documentaries on mental issues with Oprah Winfrey. Other television companies were quick to get in on the act and when Ted Sarandos, Netflix's chief content officer, was asked if he would be open to working with them, his reply came at a shot "who wouldn't be interested?"[11] Almost inevitably the Sussexes were then dubbed "the Duke and Duchess of Netflix."

"How do you do this and how do you do it tastefully?" one veteran adviser to the royals told the *Financial Times*. "The real risk will be that the wrong people will be throwing money at them and they will have to resist it. We saw what happened to Prince Andrew and Sarah Ferguson."[12] The danger of independent royals doing it the wrong way was soon clear when just a few days after the Queen announced a clean break with Harry, it was revealed that her grandson had apparently been using his Windsor connections to sell milk to China. A Chinese television advertisement showed Peter Phillips, the son of Princess Anne, promoting Jersey milk from a state-owned dairy firm with the line "It's fresh and it's what I want." He was presented as a "British Royal Family member" and shown in various regal settings despite the fact that he had never been a working royal nor held a royal title. The promotion, according to the *Daily Mail* who broke the story, "could be worth tens of thousands of pounds" for the former RBS banker.[13] Was he – as Windsor watcher Ingrid Seward put it – "absolutely entitled to do what he likes because he is not a member of the royal family" or was he simply cashing in on his connections?[14]

But, of course, royals have more stardust than simple celebs, enabling them to open doors and thus making them especially valuable to businessmen. Even if they forsake their royal titles and pursue financial independence, they can never totally shake off the glitter. Sometimes despite their best efforts it is impossible *not* to appear to be benefiting from their famous name. When Princess Margaret's son David Linley (now the second Earl of Snowdon) was appointed Chairman of Christie's UK in 2006 with comparatively little experience in the auction world despite a successful career in the furniture business, there were inevitable mutterings about how he was able to land such a lucrative job. He declined to disclose his salary when pressed by an interviewer but it could be argued that it was Christie's who did best out the deal.[15] At a time when the auction world had been rocked by a series of price-fixing scandals, its international image could only be enhanced by the cachet of the royal association. After all, who among their many foreign clients wouldn't be impressed by a call from the Queen's nephew?

So, it would appear that everyone – from the sixth in line like Harry to other royals further down the pecking order – is not averse to monetising the monarchy. The most recent controversy over cashing in may have removed some of the lustre from the royal brand that has been so carefully polished and buffed by the Queen over her long reign but if there is one thing that is crystal clear from the fallout of Harry and Meghan's exit it is that the Windsors are much wealthier than they would have us believe.

Chapter 1:

Handing over Control of the Purse Strings

They were changing the guard at Buckingham Palace in the winter of 2017. Some called it a palace coup. On December 19th the Queen granted a final audience to Sir Alan Reid who after 15 years as her treasurer was now, as the Court Circular grandly put it, "relinquishing his appointment as Keeper of the Privy Purse." Out too was Sir Christopher (now Lord) Geidt who following 12 years as the sovereign's private secretary had decided to go by October. Also waiting in the departure lounge was Samantha Cohen, her assistant private secretary and palace aide for more than 16 years, who made it known that she would be gone by April – although she would in fact stay on several extra months to assist the transition of the then Meghan Markle into the royal family.

Within the space of a few months, three of the Queen's most trusted courtiers had announced their departure. Was this just a coincidence? Or could it be part of the handover of control of the purse strings to Prince Charles? And if so, was it in any way related to the fall-out from that winter's embarrassing disclosures from the Paradise Papers which revealed that the Queen had £10m invested in two offshore tax havens?

To add to the rumour mill, in the subsequent summer it emerged that Sally Osman, the director of royal communications for the previous five years, and Steve Kingstone, the Queen's media secretary of three years' standing, would also be leaving soon. Later, in March 2020 Lord Peel, the Lord Chamberlain for the previous 14 years, also announced that he would be leaving at the end of the year.

When the sovereign's private secretary declared his surprise exit, Buckingham Palace was awash with whispers that he might have been pushed out. "Queen's aide Sir Christopher Geidt ousted in palace power struggle" ran a well-sourced story in *The Times* that claimed that his departure came after complaints from Prince Charles and Prince Andrew about his management of the handover.[1] Clarence House had apparently objected to the brusque way he had told the royal household in May of the retirement of Prince Philip as consort to the Queen, while the Duke of York was unhappy that his daughters had been excluded from the new slimmed-down monarchy. Andrew also harboured a resentment about Geidt's control over his expenditure and the part the courtier had played in forcing him to step down in 2011 as trade ambassador after his controversial friendship with the convicted American sex offender Jeffrey Epstein. According to this account, the Lord Chamberlain, the head of the royal household, had to tell Sir Christopher that his position was untenable. It was the first time that the Queen had got rid of her private secretary. Geidt denied that he was forced to go and others pointed out that 10 years was about par for the course for such a high-octane job. But the consistency of the message coming from different palace sources did suggest that he left unwillingly. Multiple reports said he felt "bruised" and the normally circumspect BBC royal correspondent seemed closest to the truth when he described the whole episode as a "bloodless coup."[2]

At first sight, the departure of Sir Alan Reid was not directly prompted by the "coup" against Geidt or indeed the embarrassment caused by the recent Paradise Papers disclosures since he had announced in July 2016 that he would be gone by the end of 2017. Nevertheless, those two events would not have encouraged him to reconsider or seek an extension. But regardless of whether their leaving was voluntary or forced the overall effect of Reid, Geidt and Cohen going within a few months of one another was to leave Prince Charles with more control over the direction of travel of the monarchy and its money.

In passing it is worth noting in the wake of the Jeffrey Epstein sex trafficking scandal which forced Andrew to withdraw from royal duties in November 2019 that Geidt's judgement in wanting the wayward prince to play a diminished role was largely correct and indeed vindicated by subsequent events. One of the ironies of the whole affair is that if Geidt was forced out of office by internal palace pressure, then the same fate was to befall Andrew two years later. Some commentators have even argued that if Geidt with his safe pair of hands had still been on the scene in 2019, then whole matter would have been handled more adroitly and the palace might have sidestepped a highly damaging episode.

Reid had been the Queen's man and someone who had stamped his personality on the job. Although educated at Scotland's elite private school Fettes and then St Andrews University before setting up home in the heart of rural Berkshire, he did not fit the bill of the tweedy upper-class courtier who might make up the numbers as a country house guest and partake in field sports on the Balmoral estate. In an interview with the former royal correspondent of *The Guardian* he admitted to a surprise choice of reading matter: "in my village, everyone assumes I must be a *Telegraph* reader, holding this position. Actually, I have always read *The Guardian*."[3] As an employee of an institution renowned for obfuscation, he became famous earlier in his career for a campaign to promote plain English and outlaw mumbo jumbo from boardroom announcements. Not unsurprisingly he was well-regarded by royal reporters: one described him as "small, precise, grey-haired and bespectacled, he is charmingly accessible," another summed him up as "he is a really nice man… he has been great fun over the years to deal with."[4]

Part of the fun and games was the media briefing on the royal finances that he hosted every year. This would take place at Buckingham Palace in early summer when he would make a series of on the record comments and then more interestingly answer some questions off the record. But a few royal correspondents pointed out that the information was only released "in a very controlled way."[5]

In the summer of 2018 this control was achieved by holding the open day at the very time when almost all of the royal press pack were abroad.

On June 27th most royal reporters were in or around Amman covering the historic trip of Prince William to Jordan, Israel and the occupied territories. This meant that when the media briefing began at 9.30 am in the Centre Room at Buckingham Palace the new Keeper of the Privy Purse, Sir Michael Stevens, would have been subject to less expert questioning. The resulting coverage in the next day's papers was less critical than previous years which might have been because the news was simply less bad or because the royal reporters had to send non-specialist nominees in their place. Many were far from content with the arrangement which mirrored what had happened in 2015 when the briefing took place when the press pack were in Berlin covering the Queen's state visit to Germany. Incidentally, when this author inquired whether he might also be accredited, the answer from the Queen's media secretary was a polite but firm no: "The press briefing is only for the small group of Royal Correspondents that we work with on a continuing basis, so I am afraid we won't be able to sign you up to attend."[6]

The message is also controlled by swamping the press pack with a tidal wave of financial information. The royal family used to have separate briefing days for the accounts of Buckingham Palace and Clarence House but when the new public funding system of the Sovereign Grant was introduced in 2012, a decision was taken that it would be better to do it all on one day. Now there are three briefings within the space of a few hours: first at breakfast time the Crown Estates meeting to release details of how much money is going to the Sovereign Grant; then at early morning the Buckingham Palace briefing to explain how much the royal household has been spending from the grant; and finally at midday the announcement at Clarence House to give details of the accounts of Prince Charles and his household.

"At the end of the day your head is spinning" is how one royal correspondent described the experience, mindful that the main story was usually what came out of the accounts of the royal household and not the other two briefings. "Now they just take one hit while they used to take many more."[7] Reid would have known about management – whether of the news agenda or business affairs – having previously worked as a management consultant. Indeed his first taste of court life came around the millennium when he was invited to give a talk at the palace on the need for modern business practices in the royal household (he soon discovered that Buckingham Palace had no external computer links and it took three days to communicate with the outside world.)[8] At the time he was chief executive of the management consultancy arm of the accountancy firm KPMG, which he joined in 1982 as a tax expert and left in 2002 as its UK Chief Operating Officer.

KPMG are part of the DNA of the royal family. Before Klynveld joined Peat Marwick and Goerdeler they were for many decades the auditors of the palace accounts (as well as the books of the Royal Collection). Reid's predecessor as Keeper of the Privy Purse, Sir Michael Peat, who was the great-grandson of the firm's founder, while his successor, Sir Michael Stevens, was a senior manager at KPMG for more than 15 years before becoming managing director of the Royal Collection Enterprises in 2002 and then deputy-Keeper of the Privy Purse.

Discretion is clearly one of the requisites of the job of being in charge of the Queen's pocket money. He – and so far there has never been a "she" in control of the purse strings – handles the revenue that comes to the monarch from her private ancestral estate, the Duchy of Lancaster and for that reason the Keeper of the Privy Purse always has a seat on the board of the Duchy as its Receiver-General. Since his job spec entails a meeting with the Queen at least once a week, it would be expected that during one of the sessions he would brief the monarch about the amount of cash going into her private coffers – known as the Privy Purse – but it is not clear whether he offers any advice on how any of it should be invested subsequently – which is probably handled by an independent financial advisor.

The job itself is well remunerated. In his last full year in office (2016-17), Sir Alan Reid was paid more than the Prime Minister with his total salary package coming to £150,000 when the £32,000 pension contribution is added to the basic wage of £128,000 (in 2018-19 his successor, Sir Michael Stevens received a salary package of £156,000). His main responsibility concerned the financial management of the royal household. Since this is paid by public money through the Sovereign Grant, he had to account for almost every penny spent through an annual report submitted to the Treasury. When it comes to official events at the palace, he had to cost everything – down to calculating, for example, which meals should go under the budget of the Foreign Office and which are charged to the Sovereign Grant.

Being responsible too for the official state apartments he can on occasion generate income. In 2010 the Disney Corporation contacted Sir Alan's office to see whether they could hire official rooms in Kensington Palace for the launch of their new movie *Rapunzel* which was part of the lucrative seven-film Princess franchise. He took the idea to the Queen, Her Majesty green lit it with a brisk "it seems like a good idea" and the result boosted the royal coffers by an estimated £10,000. Not all Keepers of the Privy Purse have been so financially flexible. Traditionally the post has been filled by former soldiers who, according to Reid, were not always top cadre: "someone in their second career is not the best pilot for change. They have done the dramatic stuff. They want to run a safe ship."[9]

The Queen's first Keeper of the Privy Purse was Brigadier-General Charles Tryon DSO. His nineteen years at the wheel was a case of steady-as-we-go – symbolised by his one rare public appearance in 1971 when in the course of an hour-long session before the Select Committee on the Civil List he barely uttered a word, leaving everything to Lord Cobbold, the Lord Chamberlain. He had sat similarly tight-lipped a month earlier in a confidential meeting at Downing Street with committee chairman and Chancellor of the Exchequer Anthony Barber when Cobbold had agreed that the palace would be represented by just the two of them which in practice meant Cobbold, who as a former longstanding Governor of the Bank of England was an experienced political infighter.

Tryon's predecessor but one Clive Wigram was a decorated army captain who had fought on the North West Frontier with the British Indian army and in the second Boer War in South Africa with Lord Kitchener's Horse. This should have proved a useful training for the frequent skirmishes he encountered during the brief reign of Edward VIII – although he survived only six months before handing over the purse strings to Sir Ulrick Alexander, a retired major.

Much like Edward VII before him, Edward VIII chaffed at being unable to exercise the same amount of control over the Duchy of Lancaster as he had over its sister estate the Duchy of Cornwall which funded all his expenditure when he was heir to the throne. Edward VII, the official historian records, was "not only disappointed but also hurt" and so took "little interest in the Duchy of Lancaster for the rest of his reign" – although just before his death in 1910 he agreed that the cash from people dying in the Duchy without a will and an heir should go into a special No Kin Investment Fund.[10] The capital would be retained for future claims, while the income would be immediately available to the sovereign. With claims relatively few in the interwar period, the capital had grown to £38,000 by 1936 – when Edward VIII decided to raid it.

In June the yet-to-be-crowned monarch informed Clive Wigram that he intended to reduce the Duchy reserves to £10,000 and dispose of the remaining £28,000 as he so wished. The Keeper of the Privy Purse immediately appealed to the Chancellor of the Duchy of Lancaster, Sir John Davidson, arguing that the new king was acting in a way which his predecessors would have deplored and which was unfair to his successors. Davidson who knew the estate better than any modern holder of the office due to his six years' tenure decided that the monarch was acting within his legal rights. Apparently the Duchy had an archaic claim to the estates of those who died heirless and intestate dating back to a 1377 statute.

Despite this ruling, the Chancellor may have secretly harboured reservations about what the king was up to. When his diaries and private papers were published in 1969, their compiler noted: "One incident in particular rather dismayed Davidson, but as it occurred in a meeting between himself and the King and concerned the affairs of the Duchy of Lancaster he does not wish the details to be revealed."[11] Reading between the lines it is clear that he did not trust the monarch and "was becoming increasingly perturbed about the delicate situation created by the personality of the king."

Edward VIII had aroused suspicions when on May 6th he travelled to the London offices of the Duchy – the first visit by a reigning monarch since the 16th century. Next he tried to get Davidson to set aside £250,000 for a trust fund for his private purposes and when this failed he attempted to obtain two years of revenue in advance of future profits – again unsuccessfully.[12]

The suspicion has always been that Edward VIII was trying to raid the royal piggy bank in anticipation of his abdication and his expected new life with the twice-married American socialite Wallis Simpson. The possibility of a truncated reign may have been a factor – although until the divorce of Mrs Simpson came through on October 27th there was little urgency to make a final decision – but equally important may have been the drop in his Duchy revenues. In 1935 when he was Prince of Wales he received £108,000 from the Duchy of Cornwall, almost a fifth more than the £85,000 that went to the monarch from the Duchy of Lancaster in the same year.

In recent times the differential between the two duchies has narrowed. If Prince Charles had become king in 2017 he would have taken a 7% pay cut with the Duchy of Lancaster profits £1.5m lower than those of the Duchy of Cornwall. But unlike some of his predecessors, Charles has prepared for the switch. In February 2017 he held a meeting with representatives of the Duchy of Lancaster and over the previous few years he has provided Prince William specific training in both the college classroom and in the field on how to run the Duchy of Cornwall after the handover.

People close to Charles have also been dropping strong hints that when he is king he may not wish to move into Buckingham Palace. In September 2017 *The Sunday Times* reported that he had been discussing plans to turn it into a more business-like "monarchy HQ."[13] According to a palace insider, "I know he is no fan of 'the big house', as he calls the palace. He doesn't see it as a viable future home or a house that's fit for purpose in the modern world. He feels its upkeep, both from a cost and environmental perspective, is not sustainable." Another source noted that he was "very comfortable" at Clarence House where he had been living since the death of its previous resident the Queen Mother in 2002. A spokesman for the prince later responded that "Buckingham Palace will remain the official London residence of the monarch" although it should be pointed out that that the current monarch prefers to spend much time away from the palace at the more homely Windsor Castle and indeed that is where she decided to quarantine herself during her lengthy coronavirus lockdown.

This news of residing in Clarence House – if remotely true – would have come as a surprise to the Keeper of the Privy Purse. Sir Alan Reid had been responsible for negotiating with the Treasury a £369m financial package for the ten year refit of Buckingham Palace which included a major refurbishment of the sovereign's private apartments beginning in April 2019. If King Charles decided not to live there, then a vast amount of public money would have been wasted.

Chapter 2:

Trouble in Paradise

Less than two months before Sir Alan Reid left his job as treasurer, the royal household was shaken by an unwelcome piece of financial news coming out of the Caribbean. In November 2017, after hardly putting a foot wrong during her 65 years on the throne, the Queen trod on a nasty sea urchin hidden offshore. "The royal pain," screamed *The Sun* headline and "one's cash is orf-shore" came the punning howl of outrage from *The Daily Mirror*, while "Queen's £10m tax haven scandal" was the *Daily Mail*'s verdict and "if you are looking after the money of the monarch you have to be cleaner than clean" was the reaction of one senior MP on the BBC News website.[1]

The source of the monarch's discomfort was the disclosure that her private estate the Duchy of Lancaster had invested £10m in the offshore tax havens of Bermuda and the Cayman Islands. The news was first revealed in a wide-ranging investigation into tax avoidance by the BBC current affairs programme *Panorama* which aired on November 5th, Guy Fawkes Night. "I do remember when it [the date] was agreed a couple of us said to each other 'there will be fireworks' which we thought was much funnier than it actually is," joked its assistant producer Tim Robinson, although he took deadly serious the task of keeping all the details secret before transmission: "only a very small part of the *Panorama* team knew about it and only a small part of the BBC, and people do not tell their families... so you do not talk to anyone about it apart from people on the team which is quite frustrating."[2]

The terrier-like Robinson who had come to the flagship programme from BBC regional news was part of a team led by an equally determined producer James Oliver who worked on the investigation – and nothing else – for more than a year. His first inkling of a story came from a tip from a pool of reporters known as the International Consortium of Investigative Journalists (ICIJ) who had previously worked with *Panorama* and who had now obtained a data leak of 13.4 million documents. "Someone said to me there is another one. I worked on a project called the Panama Papers which was the previous leak and then I was told there was another leak… So very quickly it became apparent that this would be a story – as in we would be making a film – the question was how big?"[3] The story soon grew like Topsy, taking them round the world to the Caymans and Bermuda as well as to the Isle of Man and Munich where there was a secret conference of some of the 95 ICIJ press partners in order to pool their information and decide who should pursue which story and when it should be published. Disclosure day was set for Bonfire Night, November 5th.

The meeting took place in Munich because the ICIJ had originally received the data leak from the German newspaper *Süddeutsche Zeitung* which was based in the Bavarian capital. The material became known as the Paradise Papers as the two reporters who obtained it, Bastian Obermayer and Frederik Obermaier, were also responsible for releasing in 2016 another embarrassing data leak, the Panama Papers. Ten other reporters were assigned to the Paradise project and for reasons of secrecy they were not allowed to discuss their work with their newsroom colleagues or even mix with them in the canteen. "We were always going to get lunch very early," team-member Mauritius Much told a *New Yorker* reporter. "We were going at 11:30 am, and everyone was thinking, what the hell are these guys doing?"[4] To which Obermayer commented dryly: "This is very German." In order to reinforce security, they stored all the 1.4 terabytes of data in a roomful of computers that were never connected to the internet and in order to search through the material they employed a special database and search engine developed with the ICIJ.

Obermayer, who won with Obermaier the 2017 Pulitzer Prize for his investigative work and became an overnight international celebrity almost on a par with Woodward and Bernstein, remained as tight-lipped as Deep

Throat about the source of the massive data leak. "This time, with the Paradise Papers, we were so happy when we found many US names," he said in a reference to the Panama Papers where he was attacked for being an American stooge who only revealed anti-Russian material. "Because we knew OK we won't be accused of working for the C.I.A. Now they say K.G.B. Which is fine."[5] Beyond that he would say no more.

All we know for certain is that the cache of documents relating to the Queen came from Appleby, one of the world's leading offshore law firms with offices in the Cayman Islands, the Isle of Man, Jersey, Guernsey and all the main tax havens. They advise the wealthy – whether private individuals, global corporations or financial institutions – how to set up companies and trusts in overseas jurisdictions with low tax rates and high financial confidentiality.

After the mass data dump, Appleby insisted that it did not come from their staff: "our firm was not the subject of a leak but of a serious criminal act. This was an illegal computer hack." Then just before Christmas 2017 they began legal action against the BBC and its partner in the investigation the *Guardian* seeking to force disclosure of the source documents and damages from both organisations. After months of legal wrangling, a settlement was reached in May 2018 with both sides claiming victory. The joint statement explained that "without compromising their journalistic integrity or ability to continue to do public interest journalism the *Guardian* and the BBC have assisted Appleby by explaining which of the company's documents may have been used to underpin their journalism" and went on to clarify that "the vast majority of documents that were of interest in the Paradise Papers investigation related to the fiduciary business that is no longer owned by Appleby and so were not legally privileged documents."[6] But what was not made clear in the confidential settlement was whether the BBC and the *Guardian* had paid any damages.

For their part, the ICIJ always maintained that the documents were "obtained" not just from Appleby but from "a smaller, family-owned trust company, Asiaciti, and from company registries in 19 secrecy jurisdictions." But critics of the ICIJ speculated that only a national intelligence agency would have had the technical know-how to gain access to Appleby's database.

The legal firm has offices in Bermuda where one of the Queen's two offshore investments was initially located. In June 2004 the Duchy of Lancaster put £5m in the Jubilee Absolute Return Fund Ltd which invests in hedge funds and which was renamed Permal Absolute Return Fund after its move to Guernsey in 2006. In 2010 the Duchy redeemed its stake in the fund but the Paradise Papers offer no explanation why the investment ended or how much money, if any, was earned.[7]

The Queen's other offshore investment, in the Cayman Islands, is better documented and more controversial. In September 2005 the Duchy agreed to put $7.5m in the Dover Street VI Cayman Fund LP which invested in medical and technology companies. In September 2007 it was asked to contribute one sixth of that sum ($450,000) to five new investments called "Project Bertie." In charge of the venture was a London-based private equity firm called Vision Capital which two months earlier had bought a stake in two UK retailers: 75% in First Quench, the owners of Threshers, the off-licence chain, and 100% of BrightHouse, the rent-to-buy retailer.[8]

In October 2009 Threshers went into administration as a result of poor trading in the face of intense supermarket competition, leaving an unpaid tax bill of £17.5m and nearly 6,000 employees without a job. In October 2017 BrightHouse was ordered to pay £14.8m compensation to the 249,000 customers from its 270 stores by the UK regulator, the Financial Conduct Authority after being reprimanded for not acting as a "responsible lender." The company charged interest rates of up to 94% on the initial rent of retail goods and in one case a freezer which cost £644 in the high street was acquired for £1,716. In March 2020, it collapsed into liquidation.

When the story broke in November 2017, the Duchy said that it was unaware of its 12-year investment in BrightHouse since it was not involved in fund investment decisions. Its chief financial officer Chris Adcock explained that "the Duchy has only invested in highly regarded private equity funds following a strong recommendation from our investment consultants." He also pointed out that the holding was now negligible, equating to £3,208 – although he did not say what was the size of the original stake in 2007 when the company's value was booming.

In late November 2017 when Prince Andrew was asked by the *Sunday*

Times about the offshore investments he jumped to his mother's defence: "First of all, the money's invested in a country in which she's the head of state… And the other aspect of it is that if any of the investments have benefit derived by the Queen, she pays tax on them. There's nothing wrong with it."[9] His arguments were supported in a discussion with the author by Crispin Blunt MP, the former chair of the Commons Foreign Affairs Committee: "I can't see what is remotely wrong with the Queen investing in a British overseas territory where she is head of state."[10]

At the time he was not aware that she also held investments in non-British jurisdictions. A spokesman for the Duchy later said that it "operates a number of investments and a few of these are with overseas funds," adding in another statement "it invests in a fund domiciled in Ireland."[11] The Queen, of course, has not been formally head of state of Ireland since its legal establishment as a republic in 1949. Since then it has transformed itself from a low corporate tax regime into a de facto tax haven attracting many of Appleby's clients including its near namesake Apple. In November 2017 a report by Oxfam concluded that Ireland should be blacklisted as a tax haven under European Union rules.

Did the Queen have any idea that the Duchy had investments in tax havens like Ireland and the Caymans or should the responsibility lie elsewhere? Graham Smith, the chief executive of the anti-monarchist campaign group Republic, argued that the buck stops at the top: "If you are in charge of an organisation you do not push the blame down the line… She ought to take responsibility for ensuring that it is done properly, ethically and in line with the law… rather than turn a blind eye."[12]

The Duchy in its 2017 annual report is very clear that it is "a private estate owned by Her Majesty" and that she takes a "keen interest" in the management of the property portfolio and financial investments. Traditionally, though, the sovereign has been permitted only an arm's-length role in the running of the estate, with formal powers of oversight being held by the Chancellor of the Duchy who is answerable to the monarch alone. But the office of Chancellor is nothing more than a sinecure for a member of the cabinet without a portfolio and in practice he or she devotes little time to Duchy matters. One former office-holder, Kenneth Clarke, recently wrote in his memoirs about the far from onerous workload:

"The Duchy was a largely ritual and nominal role and only took up Friday mornings… It was always followed by an excellent lunch at a place I came to call our Duchy pub [the Savoy Hotel]… bringing my working week in London to an extremely pleasant end before I headed back to my constituency."[13]

When it comes to asset management, the real powers of oversight rest with the Council of the Duchy – effectively its board of directors. Its eight members included at least four with specialist financial knowledge: the Queen's Treasurer Sir Alan Reid, the ex-Co-operative Group Chief Executive Martin Beaumont, the Duchy's Chief Executive and ex-Forth Ports Managing Director Nathan Thompson and its Chief Finance Officer Christopher Adcock. They meet four times a year to review the financial portfolio.

So, shouldn't they have spotted the potentially embarrassing offshore investments and alerted the Queen? "Even if her close advisers don't make the investments themselves, it is a question of oversight," one seasoned courtier argued. "There should surely be a mechanism to ensure that the ethical dimension to all the Queen's finances is strictly observed."[14] The royal correspondent Richard Palmer was also taken by surprise by the nature of the investments: "it was astonishing… most people would have thought that the royal family's financial vehicle would have been investments in legitimate, blue-chip British companies… I would have imagined they would invest ethically."[15]

The veteran MP Dame Margaret Hodge accused her advisors of tarnishing the Windsor brand: "I think the Queen herself would be completely shocked to find her advisers have used tax havens in which to invest their money and that her reputation has been sullied by the actions of the tax advisers."[16] Her Labour colleague Frank Field the then MP went one step further in demanding that the whole board resign: "We want a new board to safeguard the Queen by having new councillors who would not let this happen."[17]

In July 2018 when the new annual report came out the Duchy confirmed that there had been no resignations due to the Paradise Papers fall-out. In their defence, only one executive member of the current Council (Sir Alan Reid) was serving in 2005 when the initial Cayman Islands investment was made. The Duchy has also made it clear that the hands-on administration of the portfolio was largely delegated to Newton Investment Management, a long-established fund manager owned by the Bank of New York Mellon. The Duchy also used the City consultancy firm Stanhope Capital to keep an independent watch on the portfolio.

So, if the Queen probably did not know about the overseas investments but her city advisors did, was it for tax reasons that they decided to go offshore? Graham Smith from Republic would not go that far but insisted that "the Queen is responsible for her investments. She should have instructed her advisors to ensure her money was invested ethically, and that there was no tax dodging involved."[18]Both Bermuda and the Cayman Island have traditionally been attractive to UK-based investors because they charge no corporation tax and in December 2017 the EU put them on the so-called "grey list" of nations who need to reform their tax structures to avoid being classified a tax haven.

The Duchy's response to the suggestion of tax avoidance was to point out that that "the Queen voluntarily pays tax on any income she receives from the Duchy." Its spokesman also said that "tax strategy played no part in the estate's investment policy" and that "we are not aware of any tax advantages to the Duchy in investing in offshore funds."[19]

The Duchy's argument gained some traction in the financial press. *The Economist* concluded that the Queen's investment in the Caymans "appears to have carried no tax advantages,"[20] while the *Financial Times* observed that "offshore funds are often used to avoid double taxation and ensure tax neutrality if investors come from different jurisdictions."[21] Thousands of perfectly legitimate private equity funds, it pointed out, are registered in tax havens and many UK pension schemes, including the BBC's, have some of their capital tied up offshore.

If tax wasn't the main driver, then what was? The answer may lie in greater yields. When tax is taken out of the equation, the main attraction for institutional investors of offshore jurisdictions like Bermuda and the Caymans is that they enjoy minimal regulation. This does not just mean an absence of transparency rules ("if it had been open, I bet the Queen's money would never have been there," argued Margaret Hodge)[22] but also much greater freedom of investment. Many offshore firms are immune from diversification rules that operate in the European Union, with the result that they can run a more concentrated portfolio. They also attract more specialist (and more successful) fund managers and with light regulation meaning lower overheads, the end product is higher yields.

It has also been pointed out by the well-connected palace commentator Richard Kay that the timing of the initial investment in 2004-5 coincided with a change in the Duchy's fund managers which was apparently driven by a desire on the part of the Queen's advisors to improve the returns on her investment income which had been lagging of late.[23]

But the key factor forcing the Duchy's advisors to invest the money more profitably was probably the sheer volume of extra cash – mainly from land rentals – flowing into their coffers. In the decade before the initial investment, 1995-2005, annual payments from the Duchy to the Queen grew by £5.2m in real terms and if you look at the longer period, 2000-2016, they went up by an eye-watering £10.5m. What was missed in the Paradise Papers coverage which concentrated on the £10m being invested offshore was the extra £10m that the Duchy had generated in the first place. It was now a cash cow of extraordinary fecundity.

More than likely the Duchy's financial advisors did what any other city fund manager would have done in their place at a time when the UK stock market was performing badly: they went offshore for better returns.

It is worth stressing that the Duchy is today run in a highly commercial manner. Its modern, recently-refurbished headquarters overlooking London's Waterloo Bridge at the end of the Strand is close to the city and it pays its managers city salaries. In 2019 its chief finance officer Christopher Adcock received £160,000 with an allowance of £2,000 and a pension contribution of £21,000, while its chief executive Nathan Thompson took home a salary package of over £262,000, including a basic wage of £260,000, an allowance of £2,000 and a pension contribution of £31,000.[24]

Earlier in the Queen's reign the Duchy was run in a much less commercial manner. Up until the late fifties, its officials amazingly did not know how much the landed estate was worth, as its official historian and former clerk Sir Robert Somerville concedes: "in 1959 a valuation was attempted of the Duchy's property, something that had never been done before."[25] Even more remarkable was the admission that they did not charge the market

26

rate for land rentals. Speaking before a parliamentary Select Committee on the Civil List in 1971, Somerville's successor Ernest Wheeler who served as clerk and keeper of the records from 1970 to 1981 revealed how the Queen had personally intervened to give a helping hand to farmers: "At her wish the rents paid by sitting farm tenants are something like 10% below those operating in the open market."

When pressed by the committee on the overall gap between Duchy and market rent levels, he eventually let the cat out of the bag:

Ernest Wheeler: "I would say, and I hope it would not be quoted outside of the Committee because one's landlord friends would suspect possibly that we are moving to becoming a benevolent society, that it is 20 to 25% in real money that a Duchy tenant is better off than one outside the Duchy. There is real competition to become a tenant on the Duchy estate."

William Whitelaw: "I am not surprised."

Norman St John-Stevas: "How does one become a tenant?"[26]

Perhaps not surprisingly these comments were redacted from the final report published in 1971 and even today the official parliamentary database replaces his candid answers with asterisks.

It was not land rentals but the Queen's investment income that was most restricted in the early years of her reign. By statutes dating back to the 1920 Duchy of Lancaster Act and the 1925 Trustee Act, the estate could only invest in government securities like Treasury bonds and parliamentary stocks. Then, on 18th November 1957 Dr Charles Hill, its Chancellor and later more famously the BBC's "radio doctor," wrote a letter to Enoch Powell, the First Secretary to the Treasury and later more infamously the orator of "the rivers of blood" speech, requesting a relaxation of the rules. What was particularly unfair, he argued, was that its sister estate the Duchy of Cornwall was allowed to put its money in a wide range of investments other than gilts: "the least the Duchy of Lancaster would wish to secure is an extension which would put it on all-fours with the Duchy of Cornwall."[27]

Initially the Treasury was sympathetic to the request, but prevaricated due to domestic political pressure. It took a further three years of lobbying from the Duchy before an actual change in the law occurred with the 1961 Trustee Investments Act. This proved a breakthrough moment for the Duchy as it was now permitted to invest in the more lucrative domain of stocks and shares. These powers were extended in 2000 by the Trustee Act which for the first time allowed it to appoint investment managers and generally act like any normal investor. Without this act the Duchy could never have used an outside fund manager like Newton Investment Management to handle its portfolio. So overall the two new laws opened the investment sluice gates to allow the Duchy to voyage offshore.

It is unclear from the Paradise Papers what were the exact profits from the Duchy's investments in the Cayman Islands. A letter from June 2008 shows that it was entitled to receive $361,367 from the offshore Dover Street VI fund but since the fund was due to run until June 2014 it is quite possible that the Duchy realised its gain in smaller amounts spread over time so as to minimise the personal tax bill to the Queen (the tax liability only kicks in when you cash in the shares).[28] This may explain why in 2017 from a total investment portfolio of £70.5 million the Duchy made only £873,000 in finance income.

A better picture of the potential offshore profits on offer to the Queen is available by looking at what Prince Charles gained in Bermuda from his private estate, the Duchy of Cornwall. We know from the Paradise Papers that in February 2007 the Duchy bought shares in Sustainable Forestry Management Ltd for $113,500 and in June 2008 sold them for $325,000, almost tripling the investment.[29] It is not clear what caused the rise in the shares' value but the thinly-veiled suggestion in some reports was that Charles may have helped to ramp it up by his advocacy of ecological issues. For his part, the prince denied ever speaking on a topic simply because of a company the Duchy may have invested in.

According to the BBC *Panorama* team, Charles began campaigning for changes to two international environmental agreements "weeks after Sustainable Forestry Management (SFM) sent his office lobbying documents."[30] SFM traded in carbon credits as part of an international system that turned each western nation's emissions allowance into a voucher exchangeable on the market for cash if it went below the limit.

The difficulty with the argument accusing Charles of possible share ramping is that he had been campaigning on similar issues for decades.

While he seems not to have spoken specifically about changes to tropical carbon credits before 2008, "in the case of climate change," his spokesman pointed out, "his views are well-known, indeed he has been warning of the threat of global warming to the environment for 30 years," adding that he has "certainly never chosen to speak out on a topic simply because a company that it [the Duchy of Cornwall] may have invested in."[31] In his defence, it should also be noted that despite all the campaigning the two international agreements were never actually changed.

Where he is open to more legitimate criticism is in the lack of transparency in his political advocacy. In one revealing leaked minute from an SFM board meeting, "the Chairman thanked Mr van Cutsem for his introduction of the Duchy of Cornwall and the Board unanimously agreed that the subscription by the Duchy of Cornwall be kept confidential except in respect of any disclosure by law."[32]

The company director being thanked happened to be one of his oldest friends from Cambridge University, Hugh van Cutsem who owned a 4,400 acre estate near Sandringham, made a fortune in investment banking and company acquisitions and who, despite one notable falling out around the millennium, played – according to the prince's biographer – "the role of elder brother in Charles's life, a reliable source of guidance in whom he would confide his troubles."[33] He died from multiple sclerosis aged 72 in September 2013 and Sustainable Forestry Management Ltd closed in July 2011.

After the Paradise Papers revelations, the Duchy of Cornwall immediately issued a statement that the prince did not have any "direct involvement in investment decisions."[34] But given his well-known habit of stamping his green Wellington boots over every aspect of Duchy affairs, this begs the question: what *general* involvement may he have had? More specifically, when did he know that he had $113,500 invested in his friend's company? "I find it really difficult to believe that Prince Charles and the Queen did not know that those investments were being made. The keepers of the purse strings must have known," argued the royal reporter Richard Palmer,[35] while Dame Margaret Hodge had no doubt that "he wanted to put money into his friend's [firm] and he did not want anybody to know. They went to some lengths to try to create secrecy. I think that is not on."[36]

If Charles did know – and it seems likely that he must have been told at some earlier stage – then shouldn't he have declared in his speeches on carbon credits that he had a financial stake in the matter?

"There's a conflict of interest between his own investments of the Duchy of Cornwall and what he is trying to achieve publicly," argued Sir Alistair Graham, the former chairman of the Committee on Standards in Public Life, "and I think it's unfortunate that somebody of his importance, of his influence, becomes involved in such a serious conflict."[37]

Margaret Hodge went a step further in demanding he absent himself from the process altogether: "he should not get involved in the decision making around his own investments. He should just hand it over as people do when they put their stuff in trusts when they become ministers. He should not do it." When asked whether Charles's offshore dealings had tarnished the Windsor brand, she said: "it certainly has not helped his reputation."[38] According to a poll published a week after the Paradise Papers disclosures, his approval ratings slumped from 44% in April 2017 to 33%, while the Queen's numbers dipped from 72% to 66%.[39]

What this data suggests is that the two Duchies have become entwined. Just as we saw in Charles Hill's lobbying letter to Enoch Powell, what happens to the Duchy of Cornwall will often impact the Duchy of Lancaster which by extension may impact the Queen too. Following the embarrassing revelations about Charles's offshore investments, there were demands for both Duchies to be scrutinised by parliament. Hodge called for this to be done on a "regularised basis roughly every two years" by the Public Accounts Committee, the Commons' oldest and most aggressive financial watchdog which she chaired from 2010-15:

"I know they [the Queen and Prince Charles] have no choice in the matter but they are public figures and with that comes a different code of conduct."[40] Her successor as chair, Meg Hillier, told the BBC: "We need to see what's going offshore; if offshore was not secret then some of this stuff just couldn't happen… we need transparency and we need sunlight shone on this,"[41] but she was later unable to give a firm date when the PAC would next investigate the Duchy of the Lancaster.

If the Duchy sailed too close to the wind in some of its offshore dealings, then the Treasury is also open to criticism for being asleep at the wheel. Its job is to keep a close eye on the use and abuse of the public purse but Hodge feels that it bears some responsibility for the Paradise Papers embarrassment: "the Treasury should do its job properly… it ought to be vigilant on our behalf."[42] But as we shall see in subsequent chapters it has traditionally been loath to intervene in matters close to the Queen's personal finances for fear of provoking a public row – a reluctance which "is pretty shameful" according to Graham Smith: "Ministers and the Treasury need to be prepared to have a public row as they would have with anyone else." But they don't due to "their own deference to royalty" and "the major problem for politicians" of rebuking a public figurehead who is not ordinarily accountable or sackable.[43]

Given all these prickly issues, it's hardly surprising that both Whitehall and Westminster wanted the Queen's nasty sea urchin reburied deep under the sands. In July 2018 the Duchy quietly told media inquirers that it was getting out of offshore investments. It had disinvested in two funds and said it will be out of the remaining one by the end of the year.

But the Queen has other property nearer to home that is much harder to sell, most notably Buckingham Palace.

Chapter 3:

Is the Palace Public or Private?

If the Queen actually owned Buckingham Palace it would catapult her into a different class of wealth. Some crude valuations of her assets include it (along with the other official residences of Windsor Castle and Holyroodhouse Palace as well as the Royal Collection) and consequently they come up with astronomical figures. In 1989 *Fortune* magazine by adding on the Crown Jewels to the list calculated her wealth at £7b and in 2001 the *Mail on Sunday's Royal Rich Report* came to a figure of £1.15b by incorporating all the capital from the Duchy of Lancaster (£204m) with a generous assessment of what constitutes her private art collection (£150m).[1]

In recent years, valuers have become more sophisticated as the distinction between the private and public palaces has been factored into the calculus. In November 2017 *Fortune* revised downwards its valuation of the Queen's wealth to a paltry £360m. It seems likely that they took as their gold standard the calculation of the *Sunday Times Rich List* which reached exactly the same figure in May that year. Excluding the official palaces and the Crown Estates, the newspaper "only included her personal property such as Sandringham and Balmoral and similar residences."[2]

Since its inception in 1989 the *Sunday Times Rich List* has been valuing the wealth of the Queen along with that of Britain's 1,000 richest people. Philip Beresford who before becoming compiler from 1989-2016 had been editor of *Management Today* and industrial editor of the *Sunday Times* claims no inside knowledge of the royal coffers: "I am really no expert on the Queen's wealth. She was one of four or five thousand names I looked at, none in huge detail."[3] In 2011 he valued her art holding at the surprisingly low figure of £2m "because we don't count the £10m Royal Collection" even though it does include many privately-owned items.[4] His successor as compiler Robert Watts, the former deputy political editor of the *Daily Telegraph*, has explained that the original base year for the valuation goes back to 1989 "but the decision was taken – many years before my time on the List – to exclude the Crown Estate assets as the Queen does not have control over them. We do include Sandringham, Balmoral and smaller properties... There are other assets, including jewels, a stamp collection and other assets."[5] His grand total figure for 2020 was £350m.

Another commonly cited valuation of Her Majesty's money was published in November 2017 by the international marketing agency Brand Finance. In trying to put a price tag on the value of the monarchy as a whole rather than just the monarch, it ignored her private palaces ("they are not in public ownership and thus do not influence the profit and loss of the monarchy as a public institution") before coming to a sum of £67.5b. Interestingly it made a clear distinction between the monarchy's tangible assets of £25.5b (Buckingham Palace, Crown Estates and the Duchy of Lancaster etc.) and its more valuable intangible assets of £42b (the Windsor brand itself which was capable of generating billions of extra trade).[6] "It's Britain's most valuable brand," according to Konrad Jagodzinski, the agency's communications director. "This is higher than the £28b for Shell which is Britain's most valuable company brand." Contrary to what some republican groups argue, he believes that the existence of a reigning monarch physically residing in Buckingham Palace adds considerably to the brand: "It is far more interesting to see something where people are actually living. It is not just a relic."[7] As a result, his report concluded that "The appeal of pomp and circumstance set in living royal residences draws millions of tourists every year. We estimate that the overall uplift to the sector is a staggering £550 million, making the contribution to tourism the largest of the benefits generated by the Monarch."[8]

Of course a brand agency has a vested interest in vaulting the value of brands but Brand Finance's valuation – like that of the *Sunday Times Rich*

List – is more nuanced than some of the earlier calculations. They both grapple with the dilemma of where you draw the dividing line between private and public assets. What makes Balmoral a private residence and Buckingham Palace a public one?

The answer is alienability. The key test is whether the monarch could sell or dispose of the assets. The private residences can be sold – as was shown when Queen Victoria sold the Brighton Pavilion and Edward VII disposed of Osborne House after her death – while the official palaces have remained in place in perpetuity. In other words, they are inalienable.

The recent refit of Buckingham Palace affirmed its public status. When the government announced in November 2016 that £369m of public money would be spent repairing the crumbling old palace some politicians argued that since it was in part the Queen's private home and since she was one of the wealthiest women in Britain, then it was only right that she should pay part of the builder's bill. "I have always respected the fact that we have a royal family," said Alex Cunningham, the Labour MP for Stockton North, "but I know they also have vast wealth and I don't know what sort of contributions they will be making to this project."[9]

In the end, it turned out to be nothing as the taxpayer footed the entire bill through the publicly-funded Sovereign Grant. The government also decided to drop a plan to get the Queen and her family to relocate entirely from the palace during the building work – despite the fact that she is rarely there anyway.

It has been estimated that the Queen spends one third of her working year at Buckingham Palace and it is common knowledge that Windsor and not "BP" is her favourite home. In fact, when she acceded to the throne in 1952 there was some reluctance to relocate to Buckingham Palace. Prince Philip certainly dragged his feet about moving out of the more homely Clarence House which he had just helped to refurbish with a large government grant. He proposed that he and his wife should continue to live there and use the palace as an office.

"Prince Philip did not want to go to Buckingham Palace," admitted one member of the royal household "but all of the old codgers like Lascelles [the Queen's private secretary] said you must go."[10] In fact, Buckingham

Palace since it was first built by George IV in the 1820s has never been a particularly popular residence for monarchs: William IV declined to vacate Clarence House for it; Victoria much preferred Osborne House to it; and Edward VIII hated it and stayed mostly at Fort Belvedere near Windsor. As one former royal observed, it is like "living over a traffic island."

In July 1971 the Queen even issued a thinly veiled threat that she might move out of Buckingham Palace. The row arose over a plan proposed by Douglas Houghton, a Chancellor of the Duchy of Lancaster in the previous Labour government and then a member of the Conservative-led Select Committee reviewing the new Civil List public grant, which involved turning the royal household into a separate government department with civil servants deciding how Buckingham Palace was run and possibly choosing her staff. When the palace got wind of the scheme while the Queen was taking her annual Scottish summer vacation in Balmoral and Holyroodhouse Palace in Edinburgh, the official in charge of the royal household, the Lord Chamberlain, Lord Cobbold, immediately contacted the Chancellor of the Exchequer to express the sovereign's reaction. In a remarkable letter to Anthony Barber dated 30th June 1971, he did not mince his words about her displeasure:

"The Queen has confirmed her views to me in no uncertain terms. Her Majesty would see grave objection both on grounds of management efficiency and on grounds of wider principle, to transfer of the control of her household staff out of the hands of herself and her officers."[11]

He went on to say that even though he was unsure of the correct constitutional procedure he wanted the committee made aware of the "Queen's personal feelings." The implied threat to leave Buckingham Palace was spelt out more clearly in a later memo from a Treasury official:

"The whole scheme depends upon the willingness of the Queen and her Household to be reorganised along these lines, which Lord Cobbold indicated in evidence is unlikely... It is not clear for example that the Queen would wish to continue to occupy Buckingham Palace on these terms. If the Palace were in effect a government department she might well wish to live elsewhere in her personal capacity and appear at the Palace only for official functions."[12]

At the end of the day, the threat did not have to be carried out because the plan (which was by now Labour party policy) was rejected by the Conservative-dominated committee but the episode did demonstrate that even though Buckingham Palace was public property the sovereign regarded the appointment of its staff as her private domain.

Threats to leave the state palaces cut both ways. The Queen herself faced the possibility of being forced out of her official residences by the Chancellor of the Exchequer in March 1952. In what must rank as one of the most indiscreet memos ever issued by a cabinet minister about the royal finances, Rab Butler expressed his frustration about the "old-fashioned" arrangements to do with the palace: "it seems incredible that a young Queen should need to be saddled with all these massive buildings, their idle staffs and their upkeep... The Contingencies Fund indicates the immense size of the flunkey brigade and staff."[13]

He went on to argue for a change to Buckingham Palace which is still being seriously discussed today: "Could not Buckingham Palace be run in such a way that staff were imported for the great gala state functions rather than perpetually maintained? A sector of the Palace could be retained for London residence though I am sure that the Queen would prefer Clarence House." But his plan for her Windsor home was even more radical: "Might it not be suggested that Windsor Castle should be put on a National basis with all its treasures leaving a suitable sector for private upkeep and inhabitation?"

These ideas were more than just pie in the sky as he ordered his civil servants to investigate the matter and even offered to meet "anyone interested including the Treasurer of HM Household." It is not recorded how the Keeper of the Privy Purse, Ulrick Alexander, reacted to the news but in a March 6th letter to the Treasury he mentioned his concern about "some major retrenchment such as the closing down of Windsor Castle."[14]

Government pressure fell heaviest on the Ministry of Works which paid for most of the maintenance costs of the royal palaces. The matter became all the more urgent by the fact that a Select Committee was due to meet to set a Civil List for the new Queen and economies were needed to make up for a £30,000 funding shortfall. In a letter dated 21st May 1952 and marked "private and personal," Sir Burke Trend, the Under Secretary at the Treasury, counselled Sir Harold Emmerson, the Permanent Secretary at the Ministry of Works, on how best to brief his minister:

"I imagine that the questions he is most likely to be faced are, e.g. Is there any possibility of further economies in the administration of Buckingham Palace, Windsor Castle, etc. so far as the Ministry of Works are concerned?... Would there be any saving if, e.g. Windsor Castle ceased altogether to be a Royal Residence and became a sort of public museum."[15]

Should we take this radical proposal seriously or was it just an example of blue sky thinking of the sort that often takes place in Whitehall departments? The fact that Trend disclosed in the last sentence that his letter to the ministry was also being copied to the palace does suggest that it may have been at the very least a trial balloon:

"I imagine that you would wish to concert with the Palace your replies to questions of this sort, and I am accordingly sending Ulrick Alexander a copy of this letter for his information."

The Ministry of Works certainly took the idea seriously since a few days later on May 26th it drafted a lengthy brief for the minister David Eccles outlining possible economies in running the royal palaces:

"[Para] 18. It has been suggested that Windsor Castle might cease to be a Royal residence. To say exactly what the financial consequences of this would be would need careful study; generally, however, the cost of routine maintenance would be reduced and the Appropriations in Aid would be increased because of the admission of visitors; as against this the cost of warding would probably approximately equal the Appropriations in Aid. The main economy, however, would be in freedom from the necessity of modernising the engineering services. These are in many respects out of date and are likely to cost the Vote a good deal in the next 15-20 years.

"19. Unless, however, Her Majesty is willing to be content with Royal Lodge, Windsor, to close the Castle would seem to be straining the bargain referred to in Para 13 [i.e. the sovereign surrenders Crown property in return for a set revenue including the payment of running costs]."[16]

When Eccles went before the committee on May 27th, it is not clear how he handled the closure proposal as no oral evidence was transcribed but later when the Civil List bill was discussed in parliament Butler did confirm that the matter had been fully looked into: "If, say, Windsor Castle were transferred to votes and turned into a museum, I am assured on investigation I have made, that there would not necessarily be a saving of government money."[17]

There was no mention of the castle closure in the memo the Ministry of Works submitted to the committee but instead, it concentrated on the issue of staff costs and estimated the total wage bill for all the workers in palace maintenance down to the stove and flue attendant on £357.10s a year. After itemising all the costs, it concluded that there was no scope to make further savings from "the existing contributions."

Behind the scenes, the Ministry of Works were clearly rattled by Treasury plans to use its budget to plug the hole in royal household expenditure. Recently released files show that they were already annoyed about having to pay for some of the grace and favour apartments that went to courtiers *gratis* and a large slice of the heating bills at Sandringham and Balmoral when the Queen was in residence.

They had received a strong hint of what was afoot when on April 16th the Chancellor of the Exchequer, Rab Butler, wrote to Eccles suggesting that "the pay of the industrial staff engaged on the maintenance of the various Royal Establishments should be transferred to the Ministry of Works vote, the Civil List thereby being relieved to the extent of some £24,000 per annum." The minister responded bluntly on May 23rd that he "did not much like this."[18]

Eccles's reluctance to tow the Treasury line was based on more than simply defending his departmental turf. Never immodest about his own intellectual powers ("smarty pants" became his well-merited nickname) and ambitious to be President of the Board of Trade or even Chancellor, he saw himself in 1952 as a rival to Butler. They had both been Conservative Party modernisers but unlike Rab's vision of one nation Toryism (what later became known as Butskellism), he now favoured a minimalist welfare state, putting his faith in wealth-creation rather than wealth-distribution.

But on the issue of cross subsidising the royal finances, he eventually lost the battle between his ministry and Butler's. When the Select Committee

Report on the Civil List was finally completed in July 1952, it recommended that "the wages of the industrial staff engaged on the maintenance of the Royal Palaces should be transferred to the Royal Palaces Vote of the Ministry of Works." Eccles, however, did come out victor on two other royal issues. The argument of his ministry that there was little to be gained by the Queen leaving Windsor Castle appeared to have been accepted by the Treasury as the report said nothing on relocation. It was probably a complete coincidence but not long after parliament approved the report, Eccles was put in charge of stage managing the Queen's coronation ("The Earl Marshal is the producer – I am the stage manager… she is a perfect leading lady") and was knighted for this work in 1953.[19]

In the long run his ministry was also proved correct in warning that the fabric of the Windsor Castle needed "modernising." After the disastrous fire in 1992 that caused £35m of damage, it was found that the main building required complete rewiring and that there were hidden voids through which the blaze spread and no sprinkler system which would have contained it to one room.

More recently, the sight of scaffolding disfiguring Windsor Castle from early 2017 to the end of 2018 was testament to the enduring need to upgrade the building. It was decided that £27m was required to reconfigure the building's medieval state entrance and its Georgian entrance hall for better public access and to build a learning centre and a restaurant/cafe in the 14th century cellar and larder.

"We want everybody to have a proper sense of arrival, to be able to make choices about how they go about their visits," explained Jonathan Marsden, the then director of the Royal Collection Trust which administers the royal residence. "We will interpret the palaces and collections in new ways, open up new spaces to the public and we're going to create… purpose-built training centres." With this new education facility and visitor numbers surpassing those of the Royal Academy at 1.7m a year, the 1952 idea of turning Windsor Castle into "a sort of museum" is being realised by stealth.[20]

Windsor Castle is by far the most popular of the Royal Collection's residences, ahead of Buckingham Palace (552,000 visitors), the Palace of Holyroodhouse (439,000) and the Royal Mews (196,000) and the Queen's

Gallery (175,000). In 2018-19, it generated £25.1m from admission tickets and a further £5.9m from shop sales, helping the Trust to make a net profit of £8m. Not a huge figure given that the business had a gross income of nearly £72m.[21]

The reason why Windsor Castle could receive as much as £27m for a revamp was that the Royal Collection Trust was sitting on huge reserves of money. In 2018-19 it held an eye-watering £69m in additional cash (including the pension scheme surplus as part of its overall "Funds and Reserves Policy"). But is the best use of trust money to keep it all liquid in a vast reservoir of revenue? Wouldn't it be better to reinvest it in some high-yield, long-term fund or better still rechannel it in into improving the royal palaces?

The Royal Collection Trust argue that due to its special status as the custodian of the nation's treasures it is duty-bound to act prudently and set money aside for contingencies. A sudden rise in the value of sterling could seriously harm revenue from foreign visitors – and as it happened in March 2020 the sudden arrival of the Covid-19 virus did have a dramatic impact on the number of overseas tourists. In the 2019 annual report it also makes clear that it has earmarked £16m of the £69m reserves for future programmes.[22]

That still leaves at least £13m for a rainy day once you have deducted the cash going to make up for the pension deficit. In 2018-19 its new director, Tim Knox, benefited from a pension contribution of £19,000 on top of his basic salary of £129,000. The top brass of the Royal Collection are paid well: the nine members of the management board took home a total of £1.1m. Altogether the trust employs almost a thousand staff whose total payroll bill comes to £24.1m.

The Royal Collection Trust is a limited company but it pays no tax because it is registered as a charity. It was set up in 1993 in part as a response to the Windsor fire four months earlier which necessitated generating £40m in income from opening up Buckingham Palace to paying visitors to fund the five-year restoration programme. Even though it was a public palace, the Queen bowed to popular pressure by agreeing to meet 70% of the costs herself.

The Prime Minister John Major announced the change in status of the Royal Collection to a packed House of Commons on 11th February 1993: "The collection cannot be sold to generate private income or capital for the use of the Queen and the Queen does not benefit personally from the income generated by the collection. So, as to make the status of the Royal Collection clear, Her Majesty intends that the maintenance, conservation and presentation to the public of the Royal Collections should in future become the responsibility of a new charitable trust."

To some royal commentators – like Robert Hardman – this was a watershed moment in clarifying the public status of the collection: it was now clear to his eyes that the art did not in any way belong to the Queen and that future monarchs only owned it on behalf of the nation.[23]

But in the ensuing parliamentary debate Robert Sheldon, the Labour MP for Ashton-under-Lyne, put his finger on a key irregularity in the new arrangement: "why will the Royal Collection not be owned by the Royal Collection Trust?" It is worth quoting the prime minister's answer in full as he was clearly struggling to come up with a convincing explanation:

"It was thought more appropriate to establish trustees to deal specifically with the new arrangements for ensuring that the collection was generally available… There were detailed discussions as to the best method to achieve that, and the one chosen was the one I announced this afternoon… Certainly there is no doubt that the Royal Collection will be codified. Whether those elements of it that will be owned by the Queen will be set out in a separate pamphlet, I cannot immediately confirm, but I see no objection to that."[24]

More than a quarter of a century later, there is still no clear codification of what is the private property of the Queen under the care of the Royal Collection and what is the property of Royal Collection proper. The reason why it is impossible for an independent researcher to make such a distinction is that there is no comprehensive inventory of the Royal Collection available. Despite a costly 15-year programme to replace the books and card indexes with a computerised inventory, it cannot be fully accessed online by the public.

When asked to explain this in 2018 a spokeswoman said: "The internal computerised inventory of the contents of the royal palaces is used by

Royal Collection staff for the day to day care of the Royal Collection. For this reason it includes more detailed information than the public-facing online catalogue." She went on to state that the online catalogue contained around 260,000 entries – which amounts to only one quarter of the entire collection – although "each year several thousand entries are added."[25]

Disentangling private from public property remains a problem. When this author tried to find out whether the Monet painting "Le bloc" that the Queen inherited was actually part of the collection, he could find no record of it on the website and had to write to one of the officials to discover where it was located and whether it was on display to the public. The press office later explained that the painting was in fact private property bequeathed to the Queen from her mother and "as the late Queen Elizabeth's collection does not form part of the Royal Collection it is not included in the Royal Collection online."[26]

Referring to their internal system a senior curator had earlier stated that "there is a comprehensive inventory but no single comprehensive catalogue."[27] A more detailed catalogue would clarify the provenance of all of the one million items which would assist an accurate valuation of the collection as a whole. Estimates range from £2.7b in 2002 (the *Mail on Sunday's Royal Rich Report*) to £10b in 2011 (the *Sunday Times Rich List*) to the most recent in 2017 £11b (Brand Finance's *Monarchy* report). The Royal Collection's own annual report in 2019 gives no figure whatsoever and even the Treasury admitted that when it came to works of art and jewellery "it would be difficult to distinguish between those assets owned by the Queen in Her private capacity and those which are regarded as owned in right of the Crown and inalienable."[28]

We have to rewind to Tudor times to uncover the origins – and value – of the Collection. Henry VIII is seen as its founding father since during his thirty-eight-year autocratic reign he made a statement of his absolute power by amassing a treasure trove of art. He appointed as King's Painter the German Master Hans Holbein who crafted many monumental court portraits which today are worth millions. More expensive than the paintings were his huge tapestries – such as the magnificent Story of Abraham whose ten panels with gilt metal-wrapped thread still adorn the walls of Hampton Court.

An even greater connoisseur than Henry was Charles I who was dubbed by the television art critic Andrew Graham-Dixon as "the greatest art collector in the history of the royal family."[29] As one of the few British monarchs who actually travelled through Europe, he was able to add to his private art gallery the treasures of the Renaissance. When he visited Madrid in 1623, the king, Philip III, gave him several masterpieces from Titian and Veronese in the mistaken expectation that he would marry into the Spanish royal family. From the Duke of Mantua in northern Italy he purchased in 1632 nine magnificent canvasses "The Triumphs of Caesar" by Mantegna which were later supplemented by the paintings that he commissioned from Rubens and van Dyck.

We can put a price tag on the nominal value of artworks since after his trial and execution in January 1649 most of the collection was sold off on the orders of Oliver Cromwell. Records from the public auction at Somerset House in the form of work labels showing how much the pieces realised at sale were put on public display for the first time in the 2018 Royal Academy/Royal Collection exhibition "Charles I: King and Collector." "It was a political statement," said its curator Per Rumberg. "It was not only enough to chop his head off – the pictures had to go as well."[30]

From the meticulous bookkeeping of Cromwell's clerks, we know that a Rembrandt was sold for £6 whereas a Raphael went for the huge sum of £2,000. Many items were sold to the king's creditors who often demanded complicated trade deals. For example, a master plumber who was owed £903 for repair work to the royal palaces received £400 in cash before being permitted to pick up to £500 of paintings, including a Titian and Bassano's The Flood. In the same subversive spirit, a royal draper was given the tapestries.

It was not by chance that the sale was held in one of the former royal palaces – Somerset House. After 1,500 paintings and 500 sculptures had been sold, the coffers of the new Commonwealth were swelled by £185,000 – a not inconsiderable sum in 1650.

Even though a few artworks would be reinstituted after the Restoration through a mixture of threats and bribery, what the Somerset House auction showed was that the crown property of the sovereign was not in fact inalienable – it could be sold. If the monarchy went, so did its wealth.

The most emblematic expression of this was the destruction and dispersal of the Crown Jewels. In 1649 Cromwell's parliament issued an order that the royal regalia "be totally broken" on the grounds that as "monuments of superstition and idolatry" they symbolised the "detestable rule of kings." Most of the coronation regalia were melted down and the gold reminted into hundreds of coins. Some of the jewels were removed from Henry VIII's crown which was the most highly valued item at £1,100, but the only original piece to survive intact was the coronation spoon which had been used to anoint kings and queens since the 12th century. Mr Kynnersley, a yeoman of Charles I's wardrobe, bought it for 16 shillings but gave it back in 1661 so that it could be used in Charles II's coronation.

Today it is on display in the Tower of London along with the rest of the Crown Jewels that have been reassembled in the 360 years since the Restoration. The royal regalia might be regarded as the crown jewels of the Royal Collection since they are the prime draw for the 2.8m people who visited the Tower of London in 2018, generating more than £30m in revenue. Although they are cared for by the Royal Collection, the money they make goes to another registered charity, Historic Royal Palaces which runs the Tower along with Hampton Court Palace, Kensington Palace, Kew Palace, the Banqueting Hose and Hillsborough Castle. In 2018-19 it made £105m in income, with two thirds of revenue coming from admissions.

Supporters of the monarchy are quick to point out that charitable bodies like the Royal Trust are a boon to Britain and its taxpayers since they "lack public subsidy."[31] In sharp contrast to the public museums and galleries, they live or die on the money they generate from admission fees and merchandise sales.

But some of the Royal Collection's detractors question whether the public is really getting value for money. The art critic Robin Simon has in the past wondered if there should be far better access not just to Buckingham Palace which lets in the public for just two months in the summer but also to Windsor Castle which (excepting the Covid-19 shutdown) is open most of the year: "there are huge areas of the castle which remain private and yet are stuffed with treasures, the bulk of them from the Royal Collection."[32] Viewers of a 2018 BBC-4 arts documentary on the Trust would have been surprised to discover that the castle houses 600 drawings by Leonardo da Vinci which are acknowledged as being among the greatest works of art in Britain. The programme also shone a light on the 50 Canaletto paintings ("the greatest collection in the world") which are squirrelled away in other Trust-run palaces.

Six Canalettos are hung in Buckingham Palace's Picture Gallery along with a Vermeer, a Titian, two Rembrandts, two Claude Lorrains, half a dozen Van Dycks and several excellent Reubens. One single room holds dozens of Old Masters with an estimated total worth over £100m. The gallery is only open to the public for ten weeks of the year, although some paintings are occasionally loaned to other exhibitions.

So, should the Royal Collection be doing more to open up its treasure trove? According to its former press officer Dickie Arbiter, "a sizable chunk of the collection is put on public display." But some of the prized pieces are just not suitable for mass exposure: "The Leonardo drawings [and other items] are precious works of art… You cannot put everything out."[33]

But others disagree. "It is not a satisfactory situation," observed Robin Simon about the overall lack of public access. "The cynic or republican might suggest that everything is held in trust at least as much for the Windsor family as for the nation."

Chapter 4:

Stabilising Sandringham

Unlike the Royal Collection and the public residences, the Sandringham estate is privately owned. The Queen inherited the Norfolk property from her father George VI in 1952 after it had been passed down through the generations since 1862 when Queen Victoria purchased it for the future Edward VII with her own family funds.

But like the Royal Collection and the public residences, it is partially open to the public in order to provide an additional private income stream for the Queen. When she is not staying there (normally from the start of April until the end of October) or when it is not shut for reasons of the coronavirus pandemic (as happened from Spring 2020) any visitor can tour the house and grounds for the price of the £17.50 admission. The Big House is the most intimate of the royal residences: in its dining room, the sharp-eyed will spot that all the table mats bear pictures of her horses trained at the nearby Royal Stud and in the sitting room you can stroke the green baize table where the Queen does her jigsaw puzzles. "It is a family house," the guide explains, "and much smaller than a grand stately home." The scuffed carpets bear witness to normal family wear and tear.

For an extra £3.50 you can take a guided tour of the gardens and touch the oak tree planted by the Queen to mark her 80th birthday in 2006 and taken from an acorn planted by her grandmother Mary in 1947 to commemorate her own 80th birthday. It had been the old queen's grandson Edward VII – you will be told – who had reconfigured the layout with the help of over 100 gardeners. The lake was drained, reshaped and complemented by islands, streams and other water features.

If you fancy a longer stay, you can be one of the many who overnight in what is now a money-spinning caravan park or if you require greater comfort, you could rent one of the two holiday cottages (from £875 a week) and so get a real taste of country living. The cottages are surrounded by 6,400 hectares of agricultural land as Sandringham is very much a working farm. Over 200 people are employed on the estate – from gardeners and gamekeepers to foresters and farmers – growing a diverse range of crops including wheat, barley, oil seed rape, sugar beet and oats. Thanks to the combined revenues of farm income and visitor admissions Sandringham Inc. is today a going concern, returning – as best one can judge – a modest net profit to the sovereign. But it was not ever thus.

Historically the estate has haemorrhaged money – almost from the day it was first acquired for the Prince of Wales in October 1862. At a purchase price of £225,000 (£18m today), the future Edward VII with much help from Queen Victoria paid well over the odds for a property that contemporaries described as "very ugly, a whitewashed house with redbrick chimneys… and a fanciful brown porch" set in "6,000 acres of sand."[1] But his more cost-conscious father, Prince Albert, who had originally found the house, was no longer alive to beat down the price and "Bertie" (as everyone called him) was now flush with cash from the annual £60,000 (£5m today) he received on his majority from the Duchy of Cornwall and the contribution that Queen Victoria is known to have made from her ever-growing Duchy of Lancaster profits.[2]

He then spent another £200,000 demolishing the old house and building a neo-Jacobean mansion with new stables and gardens – as well as his own bowling alley. Soon it was a suitable venue for his lavish country parties, aided by the lure of some of the best game shooting in England. During his fifty-year tenure it has been calculated that about one million head of game were shot there.[3] Such extravagance shocked his financial advisors. When the assistant secretary to the Treasury, Sir Edward Hamilton, discovered in 1904 that "no less than £52,000" had been spent on Sandringham against an allocated budget of £30,000, he could not hide his despair in his diary:

"Last year there were some special items in connection with the installation [of electric light] but notwithstanding them the total is appalling."[4]

Like a poorly maintained thatched farm roof, the estate continued to leak money under George V even though he was by temperament less of a spendthrift than Edward VII. His only extravagance was shooting game. He became one of the best shots in Britain ("seven guns in four days at Sandringham killed 10,000 head" noted an envious Lord Lincolnshire) but his passion for the sporting estate ("Dear Old Sandringham, the place I love better than anywhere else in the world") blinded him to its costs.[5] By 1913 the estate was losing £50,000 a year forcing him to charge to the Civil List £5,294 for "game" costs which previously had been paid from his own pocket.

After the war, with game expenses still surpassing £2,000 a year, he introduced the growing of flax to balance the budget and made half-hearted attempts to control the wage bill, but in truth he had no idea of how to run a farm. Despite the depression, costs spiralled in the thirties: the estate lost £8,637 in 1933, £6,466 in 1934 and £8,561 in 1935.[6]

After watching how his father's extravagance had turned Sandringham into "a voracious white elephant" Edward VIII on acceding the throne decided that something must be done. He instructed the Duke of York, the future George VI, to draw up a cost-cutting plan and within a few months the adjoining farms of Anmer and Flitcham had been put up for sale and redundancies of 100 of the 400-strong workforce carried out. By the end of the year the wage bill had fallen by £6,150.

On simple cost grounds, Edward VIII was probably justified in taking the axe to Sandringham but his motives were far from pure. Despite promising his dying father that he would not sell the family home, he did not intend to keep it. As king, he only overnighted there once since he had no use for a rural retreat in Norfolk. A smart-set city-slicker, he had his own bolthole at Fort Belvedere, Windsor, which was within a short drive of the West End fleshpots. But in the later abdication settlement, the lack of any emotional attachment to Sandringham didn't stop him from threatening to hang on to the property if his brother did not offer him adequate compensation. In the end, after a heated dispute over the value of the estate (the farms alone were valued at around £100,000 but no one could agree on how long their leases were) George VI had to pay in the region of £150,000 to gain title to it. The Queen Mother later admitted to her friend Woodrow Wyatt that when they bought Sandringham they had to borrow money to afford it.[7]

Under the diffident new king, Sandringham was run in a modest manner. The radical sale of large chunks of the estate was halted and economies were sought in less draconian ways. In 1936-37 he added apple orchards to the estate and during the war, the lawns were turned into arable land and the Big House mothballed; when the family came to stay, they used a smaller property at Appleton. But the high overheads would not go away and when in February 1952 George VI died at Sandringham of a blood clot, the estate was still haemorrhaging money.

So, if Edward VII, George V, Edward VIII and George VI all failed to stop the loss-making how did Elizabeth II succeed? Was it down to less extravagance, better management or some other X-factor?

When she acceded to the throne, the young Queen acknowledged that savings could be made from Sandringham. According to newly-discovered documents from the 1952 Civil List review, "Her Majesty the Queen has voluntarily offered to abate the allotment to the Privy Purse by a sum of £17,000, to be provided by savings on the private estates."[8] Interestingly for a monarch who was then personally exempted from income tax, the Treasury documents pointed out that any revenue from Sandringham and Balmoral would be liable to "income tax and surtax" – although their high overheads probably meant that there was then nothing to pay.[9]

At the time – as the papers reveal – the sovereign was overloaded with work: "In spite of the existence of a devoted staff and notwithstanding constant attempts to lighten the work of the sovereign, the burden of Her Majesty's duties is still formidable and likely to remain so."[10]

Therefore, if Sandringham required better supervision and she was too busy to do it, the only answer was to delegate. In normal circumstances such work could have been handled by the land agent but since her own consort was at a loose end having been forced to give up his naval command and his surname Mountbatten in favour of Windsor on her accession to the throne ("I am just a bloody amoeba. I am the only man in the country not allowed to give his name to his children") Prince Philip proved the perfect fit.

His management brief applied to Balmoral Castle and the Buckingham Palace as well as Sandringham. But he soon found that the Aberdeenshire estate was too far away for proper hands-on control and the London palace was monopolised by the old guard. Indeed, his first attempts to modernise traditional practices horrified some of the crustier courtiers. Lord Tryon, the Queen's Treasurer, complained in confidence to Treasury officials about Philip's dangerous ideas: "while small economies could be made... there was not... any radical economy that could be made without making substantial alterations to the way in which the appearance of the monarchy presented itself."[11] The Treasury generally sided with the palace over Philip ("I told Lord Tyron that it was difficult for us to disagree with his analysis" noted E.S. Shill) but as the department responsible for ensuring that public money was properly spent, they could not be *seen* to oppose him ("I am sure that it would be a mistake for us to appear to be discouraging of any desire Prince Philip may have to look for economies," responded the Treasury permanent secretary Norman Brook).[12] Eventually Philip got the message ("I was told to keep out and I did") and refocused his sights from the official residence to the private one.[13]

The number of staff remained Sandringham's heaviest burden. In 1952 the Big House employed 5 housekeepers/linen maids on £793 a year and a tappisier/upholsterer on £368. Also in service were an army of gardeners, many of whom had been there for decades.[14] When Philip questioned one about the peculiar flower arrangements in the bedrooms, he was told that it was done that way because that was how Queen Mary wanted it.

With 360 rooms, the house was clearly too big for its limited occupancy. Various plans – including one in the sixties to demolish it entirely – came and went before in 1974 it was decided to pull down the staff wing. The project which was finished in November 1976 cost an estimated £400,000 but it made economic sense as the leaking three-storey block with its warren of 100 under-used rooms ate up a small fortune in maintenance and would have needed renovation had it not gone.

But in the seventies the estate was still struggling to break even. In 1971 Lord Cobbold, the Lord Chamberlain and head of the royal household, admitted in private to the Chancellor of the Exchequer and a few select members of a parliamentary committee on the Civil List that "Some information could be provided and this would certainly show that they [Sandringham and Balmoral] were not income earning assets."[15] That information when the Select Committee report came out in 1972 showed that money from the Duchy of Lancaster was keeping Sandringham afloat.[16]

To commemorate the Queen's Silver Jubilee in 1977 the Big House was opened to the paying public but what was needed was aggressive commercialism in agriculture rather than admissions. Here Ribena proved a tonic. 110 acres of blackcurrant bushes were set aside for harvesting by a mechanical picker every July. After being checked for quality control in the fruit store, the produce was transported by lorry to the Ribena plant in Somerset where they were pressed into the purple nectar.

It was not quite enough, though, to push Sandringham into the black. The real money-spinner lay in agricultural rentals. At the time about 12,000 of the 20,350 acres were allocated to tenant farmers, while the Queen retained 3,000 acres to grow wheat, barley and other cash crops and a further 2,000 acres were left for forestry.[17]

What had reduced profitability was fragmentation: there were simply too many small farms with too many workers producing too few profits. Mega farms were created by amalgamating the smaller units and as a result, the number of tenant farms fell from thirty to around twelve and the workforce shrunk to a tenth of its pre-war size. Today, the land is rented to just half a dozen tenant farms.

Prince Philip deserves some credit for overseeing this turn-round since the early seventies, but the move into profitability coincided with a welcome handout from Brussels. After the United Kingdom entered the EEC in 1973, Sandringham as one of the largest farms in Norfolk became eligible for a large slice of the Common Agricultural Policy's farming subsidy budget. In the first decade of the new millennium the Queen received £7m in farming subsidies, according to a BBC *Panorama* investigation, with the annual payments rising to £224,000 in 2010. It took a Freedom of Information request to unearth this data but today the exact figures are available on the agricultural department's website: Sandringham received £553,051 in 2015,

£524,466 in 2016, £695,001 in 2017, £604,844 in 2018 and a massive £935,908 (boosted by £313,510 in rural development aid) in 2019.[18]

The agricultural support was based on acreage alone and took no account of the wealth of the landowner. When the size of the payments was revealed, there was an uproar about "handouts for the rich" and calls to "Give it back, Ma'am." "It's completely indefensible," howled Labour MP Chris Bryant about the CAP system, while visitors to Sandringham complained that "money always goes to money – it will never change" and "it's the old boys' club – it is all the rich boys in the rich club looking after each other."[19] A Buckingham Palace spokesman responded that "subsidies are open to all farmers; and like others with agricultural interests, subsidies are received on the Queen's private estates."[20]

The true test of how important European Union support has been to the viability of Sandringham will come after the 2020 Brexit departure date when the CAP tap is turned off and the estate will have to make do with proposed replacement payments for "public goods," such as access to the countryside, planting meadows and restoring woodland.

Another reason why Sandringham is in the black is that Elizabeth and Philip are more frugal than Bertie and Alexandra or even George and Mary. When Mary's official biographer visited her granddaughter's private chambers in 1956 he found them distinctly unshowy: "It is now like the bedroom of an anonymous mouse."[21] Famously, when the young Prince Charles turned up in the Big House without the lead after walking the dog, the Queen sent him back out into the grounds with the admonition "Dog leads cost money!" Nowadays, Her Majesty travels to and from Sandringham not by helicopter or the royal train but by the standard rail service used by commuters between King's Lynn and King's Cross at £58 a ticket.

The royals still make use of the estate as a private shooting range (the Boxing Day shoot has become a fixture in the Windsors' calendar since the late eighties) but do so with less extravagance than their predecessors (in 2017 Prince Harry, hitherto a keen blood sportsman, decided not to partake in the Christmas tradition in deference to the anti-hunting views of his then fiancée Meghan Markle and in 2019 the now married couple preferred to spend their Christmas in Canada).

Sandringham has also become noticeably greener in recent years. Prince Philip can be justifiably proud of his record in planting new hedgerows and trees and increasing public access to woodland. A marsh sanctuary has been set up and extra coverts offer game birds better protection. Wood chopped locally helps to heat Sandringham House which uses bio-ethanol fuel. In a nod to waste recycling, an accelerated composter has been installed near the restaurant so that all the leftover food can be ploughed back into the land.

The Sandringham kitchens can also benefit from the produce of an organic black truffle plantation that has recently been given the seal of approval. This contrasts with the loss of the royal warrant in January 2018 for the German multinational Bayer Crop Science which for many years supplied pesticides to the estate. "It's no secret that the royal family farms at Sandringham and Windsor are converting to organic farming," confirmed a company spokesman, "so obviously our products wouldn't be appropriate."[22]

Some of these changes bear the imprint of Prince Charles's green Wellies. In recent years Philip ran the estate in tandem with his son, like one of his two-man horse and carriages, until 2017 when he handed the complete set of reins to Charles after announcing that he was stepping down from all public duties at the age of 95. With the exception of his 2020 coronavirus lockdown at Windsor Castle, he now prefers to spend his time in his Sandringham bolthole, not the Big House but the more modestly furnished Wood Farm where he installed a small kitchen as part of his gradual renovation of the property over the last years. There in his royal retirement home he can read, write letters, paint watercolours and invite guests to stay. One visitor observed: "He's enjoying reading things he's always wanted to read and gets up to what he wants without an equerry telling him he has to be elsewhere, or a camera following him."[23] Another royal consort, Queen Alexandra, found Sandringham the ideal place to spend her final days and both George V and George VI died there.

When Charles inherits the estate on the death of the Queen, he might splash the cash on it in much the same way as he did on his private country home Highgrove House – or so suggest some palace whispers. But that might depend on how long Her Majesty lives and how much it costs to run after it loses its generous subsidy from the EU. It is also far from clear how much the property is actually worth. In 2001 the *Mail on Sunday's Royal Rich Report* valued it at £30-40 million, whereas sixteen years later in 2017 *Fortune* Magazine put a price tag on it of only £40-45m.

These figures are estimates based on its fundamental cadastral value which significantly do not take into full account the extra value attached to the royal name. If that is factored in, then – as we have seen from inflated prices paid at auction for other royal property – Sandringham might easily be worth £60-£80m on the open market.

Chapter 5:

The High Cost of a Highland Home

As a piece of real estate, Balmoral may not be as valuable as Sandringham but as a place of sanctuary, it holds a special value for the Queen. "It has an atmosphere of its own and you just hibernate," is how she regards her spiritual home. Nestling in the hills of Aberdeenshire 600 miles from her official London residence, her private estate offers an escape from the gilded cage of Buckingham Palace life.

She squirrels herself away in the hideout for two months every summer, normally arriving late July and departing late September, and since this has been the routine for a large part of her 58 years on the throne, she must now have spent close to a decade of her reign in the Highlands. She was there in August 1997 when she had to shield William and Harry from the media explosion of Princess Diana's death and in December 1992 when Princess Anne discreetly wed Timothy Laurence in the nearby Crathie church – not forgetting her own secluded honeymoon in November 1947 on the estate where Philip had proposed to her the year before.

With its 50,000 acres of Scot's Pine forests and heather-strewn hills in the shadow of the 3,786-foot Lochnagar mountain, the estate's main attraction lies in outdoor activities. Close to the castle is a 9-hole golf course where Prince Andrew liked to practice his swing, a cricket pitch which is probably more popular with the staff than the sovereign and just beyond the magnificent lawn and fine rose garden a welter of beauty spots for family picnics where famously Prince Philip barbecued the steaks and sausages, leaving his wife to do the dishes.

Further afield is the rugged hill country on the edge of the Cairngorms where she can walk her gun dogs and enjoy the wildlife. At her age she of course no longer stalks deer although she has always been a good shot. She killed her first stag at the age of 16 and has never been one to show sentimentality about dispatching any of the 4,500 red deer, either to keep numbers down or for the sheer pleasure of the sport for guests and her family. Charles was encouraged to shoot there when young and more recently Kate before her marriage to William learned how to fire a hunting rifle – although only at a mock stag target. It is unlikely, though, that when the anti-blood sports Meghan made a visit there with Harry in August 2018 she was invited to join in the shooting.

Since the fertile waters of the river Dee cut through a large swathe of the estate, fishing is the other main sporting attraction. Although the Queen was never a keen angler, her mother was hooked early and was still casting a reel well into her seventies. Fortuitously her summer house Birkhall was located on the banks of the river Muick which in April teemed with spawning salmon night and day. Late one evening when she failed to show up for dinner her house guests grew worried until a figure appeared out of the dark clasping something. "This is what kept me" the Queen Mother declared, proudly displaying her twenty-pound salmon.[1]

On the basis that "where there's Muick there's brass" and that Balmoral is blessed with some of the best fishing in Scotland, the paying public are now being reeled in too. In November 2016 its salmon fishing rights began to be registered with the Scottish land registry office under the company name of Canup Ltd. The application records that the sporting and other property rights in the Forest of White Mounth and its surrounding waters were originally purchased in July 1950 for £6,500 by trustees acting on behalf of George VI. In Scotland fishing rights are regularly owned separately from land rights and the commercial company in action here was named after a rocky hill on the estate called Canup which supplied the granite that built Balmoral Castle.

Companies House lists Canup's secretary as Richard Gledson (the factor of Balmoral estate who replaced the previous land agent Peter Orde in

2009) and the other directors as the Earl of Airlie ("a retired banker" and former Lord Chamberlain), the Earl of Dalhousie ("landowner" and Lord Steward of the Queen's Household), Sir Michael Stevens ("Keeper of the Privy Purse") and Sir Alan Reid (the former "Keeper of the Privy Purse").

But why would such august personages as the Lord Steward of Her Majesty's Household busy themselves with something as mundane as fishing permits? Sink your line deeper and you discover that Canup is much more significant to Balmoral than just sporting rights. The company which was first set up in 2005 to act as a trustee, custodian or nominee for a trust or any named body owns almost the entire estate under a separate title. According to the Scottish land registry office, the Registers of Scotland, Canup Ltd is the owner of the property at "Balmoral, Crathie, Ballater... value over £5,000,000."[2] This voluntary registration was applied for in November 2016 and by February 2018 the process of mapping all its 18,590 hectares of lochs and mountains and identifying the 19 covenants restricting land access had been completed and the new title of ABN130387 was issued along with a separate title of ABN130388 for the fishing rights.[3]

It is not clear what triggered this application for a new deed in 2016 as the palace declined to comment on the matter since Balmoral is a "private estate," but given that the Queen had just turned 90, one consideration may have been the need to tidy up any ownership issues ahead of the succession. As an official for Registers of Scotland explained, "there is no statutory requirement for any person to register their land or property but it is always in their interests to do so to affirm good title."[4]

The registry went on to confirm that "the previous title holders were named as the Trustees of HM Queen Elizabeth II, the last name attached to the trusteeship was David Ogilvy (The Earl of Airlie)." Ogilvy had been a trustee at least since 1997 when the other title-owners included his son-in-law, the prominent Scottish businessman Sir Iain Tennant, and the then Keeper of the Privy Purse, Sir Michael Peat.[5] The registry added that "the trustees changed between 2007 and 2016 but there [was] no deed transferring title from A to B recorded" which suggests that the most recent registration process was driven by desire to ensure that the name of the new trustees was also on the land deeds.

These formal transactions confirmed that at least since the late nineties Balmoral was controlled by trustees with close ties to the crown. But why put it in a trust in the first place? Traditionally trusts have been used by the royal family as a conduit to transfer their property from one generation to the next. Sometimes it may be for reasons of taxation (particularly for junior royals who have fewer tax privileges than the monarch and heir) and sometimes for considerations of privacy (unlike a will, the contents and value of a trust do not have to be disclosed). Almost all royal wills are closed to the public by statute or legal precedent but two were published. We know from the unsealed will of Queen Victoria's granddaughter Princess Helena Victoria that most of her moveable property was placed in a trust for her close relatives. Even more revealing is the published will of Princess Alice, the dowager Duchess of Gloucester, who put the bulk of her £570,000 estate in several trusts. A palace spokesman later confirmed that the Gloucesters' multi-million pound country pile Barnwell Manor had been placed in a separate family trust.[6]

So, if the private royal estates of Barnwell and Balmoral both reside in a trust, then shouldn't Sandringham be in one too? Again the palace was tight-lipped but there are a number of clues pointing to two possible candidates as its trust holding company. Both bear the name of Flitcham, the village in Norfolk nearest the estate. In 2000 it was reported that Sandringham's home-grown apple juice had been registered as a trademark with a company called Flitcham Ltd.[7] Its secretary was the Queen's private solicitor Sir Mark Bridges and its directors included her former solicitor, Sir Marshom Boyd-Carpenter, her former Treasurer Sir Alan Reid and the head of the royal household, the Earl Peel. All the records said about the nature of its business was that it was "a non-trading company."

It was also reported that in 1987 a second company called Flitcham Nominees purchased on behalf of the Queen the 125-year lease of Sunninghill Park as the country home of the newly married Prince Andrew and Sarah Ferguson.[8] Its company secretary and directors were almost the same as for Flitcham Ltd but this time the nature of its business in land ownership was made clearer. Its 1987 revised articles of association stated that its role was "to acquire and deal with any estate or interest in any freehold or leasehold land… to act as an agent, nominee or trustee for any person, corporation, government, sovereign ruler… to acquire, hold and deal with property of every description… to undertake and execute trusts of every description."[9] Since it acquired the lease for the country estate of the Queen's second son, it is perfectly possible that it, or a related holding company, did something similar for parcels of land within the Queen's own estate.

What we do know for certain is that the Queen owns *parts* of the estate in a personal capacity. According to a recent search of Land Registry records, the proprietor of the area around the estate office at West Newton and the land near the Sandringham fruit farm at Flitcham is "Her Most Gracious Majesty Queen Elizabeth the Second" but it is unclear whether other parcels of the land – including the other Sandringham farms or associated businesses – are owned by a trust or shell trading company. The most likely state of affairs is that much of the land is privately owned but some of the commercial activities take place within the shell of a trust-like limited company.[10] The palace declined to comment one way or another on the issue since Sandringham as well as Balmoral "are private estates owned by the Queen… run and funded privately."

For the Balmoral estate, the mystery is not so much *if* it was put in a trust as *when*. Was the transfer made during the Queen's reign or earlier? Some historians have stated that it was the abdication row between George VI and the Duke of Windsor over ownership of the private estates that triggered the change of status,[11] while others have suggested that Balmoral may have been put in a trust as far back as the mid-19th century.[12]

In order to get a clearer picture of the various claims to title, we need to unwind the estate's chain of ownership to the reign of Queen Victoria. When she and Prince Albert initially moved to Deeside in September 1848, they did not own the house but rented it. That 27-year lease to the Balmoral estate was held by the family of her Foreign Secretary Lord Aberdeen who had recommended that the illness-prone royal couple might benefit from its healthy Highland air and its relatively low rainfall. Victoria and Albert were soon smitten. The Queen later wrote in her diary that the peaceful-ness and freedom of the place allowed her to forget the sad turmoils of the world, while the primitive and romantic mountain life reminded her

German consort of his childhood at Schloss Rosenau in the Thuringian forests.[13] What she failed to appreciate was that this all coincided with the height of the second wave of Highland clearances when both crofters and landlords were feeling the full brunt of Scotland's economic recession and being forced off their property.[14]

The estate was purchased on 17th June 1852 from the family of the Earl of Fife, not by Victoria but Albert. He was a skilled negotiator and was able to knock down the price to a mere £31,500 by playing on the kudos of the royal name and the fact that they were already well-entrenched sitting tenants. Nothing would stand in his way: when the sale was threatened by the fact that the property was owned by family trustees rather than the earl himself the legal difficulties were ironed out by a special private members' bill – the Balmoral Private Estates Act – being rushed through parliament in June 1862.[15] Such was the complexity of Scotland's trust laws that when the title deed was registered in the Scottish land registry in December that year the document ran to 37 pages.

The reason why Albert bought it instead of the Queen was to ensure that it was not taken by the Crown. Although the Crown Private Estates Act had been passed in 1800 to allow the sovereign to own private property for the first time, due to a drafting error it did not apply to Scotland and as a result, if Victoria had bought Balmoral it would have belonged effectively to the state, not her.[16]

But possession of a clear title was put in doubt again by Albert's sudden death in December 1861. Although his will incontestably bequeathed Balmoral to Victoria, another special bill had to be pushed through parliament to guarantee that it did not become Crown property. According to the 1862 Crown Private Estates Act, any private royal estate "shall be vested in some trustee or trustees for Her Majesty, her heirs and successors." It is significant that nowhere in the act was there provision for the sovereign to acquire the property in a purely private capacity which some have interpreted to mean that Queen Victoria had no choice but to put Balmoral in a trust since she could not own it personally. The fact that the half-way house of a trustee was employed suggests that the framers of the legislation were still worried that if Balmoral were transferred directly to the sovereign then the Crown might retain a claim to it – particularly if it was in Scotland which inadvertently had been left out of previous legislation. Also worthy of note is that the bill differentiated between Scottish and non-Scottish estates and provided for the heir to the throne to vest his property with trustees just like the sovereign. This opened the possibility for the decidedly non-Scottish Sandringham – which was then owned by the Prince of Wales – to be put in a trust.

So, does the timing of the act mean that Balmoral was transferred to trustees in 1862 soon after Albert's death? This seems perfectly plausible but there is no firm evidence for it. An alternative possibility is that it was done sometime in the late 1870s after yet another piece of legislation – the 1873 Bill to Amend the Crown Private Estates Act 1862 – altered the earlier act by clarifying that on the death of the sovereign the property would pass to her heir and not the Crown. It may be a coincidence but the first recorded reference to any Balmoral trustees in the Scottish registry lies in documentation about a property owned by her heir Prince Albert Edward ("Bertie"). The deeds for the Birkhall estate records that on 5th May 1885 the owner made a property transfer to the "trustees for behoof of Her Majesty Queen Victoria and her royal successors, proprietors of the estate of Balmoral... nominated and appointed, dated 20th and 28th October 1879."[17] Many contemporaneous documents link the trustees to the latest will of the Queen dated 18th September 1875 – which again would point to the Balmoral trust being set up in the late 1870s.

By that time the estate had undergone a complete transformation. When Victoria and Albert first set up home on Deeside they found the place too cramped for the needs of a growing family of 5 and a royal entourage of over 50. With the help of local architect William Smith, they demolished the old castle and built a new one 300 yards away, complete with an 80-foot central tower, Gothic turrets, two courtyards and a ballroom. The engineer Isambard Kingdom Brunel was enlisted to construct a bridge across the river Dee as part of a major reshaping of the gardens and surrounding grounds. The neighbouring 6,000-acre Birkhall estate was also bought in 1849 as a retreat for the Prince of Wales.

But how could Victoria, who famously came to the throne "almost penniless," afford it all? The purchase of the Balmoral estate set her back £31,500 (£2.5m at today's prices) and on top of that there were the hefty rebuilding costs and the sizable down-payment on Birkhall.

One recent royal chronicler has repeated the misconception that it was financed by the "timely bequest" from the eccentric bachelor John Camden Neild who left her £250,000 in his will.[18] But this would have been impossible since he died on 30th August 1852 and Balmoral was bought in early June 1852.[19] The funds may have helped pay some of the later rebuilding bills but the serious money came from two key income streams.

Between her accession to the throne in 1837 and the purchase of Balmoral in 1852, the Queen saved £61,000 from her taxpayer-funded Civil List.[20] She did this by transferring into her (private) Privy Purse the shortfall in other categories of royal household expenditure such as staff wages or palace maintenance. In 1889 her Private Secretary and Keeper of the Privy Purse admitted to a senior Treasury official that around £400,000 of the Civil List savings had been spent on the purchase, rebuilding and expansion of the Balmoral and Osborne estates.[21]

An arguably more important source of funding was the mushrooming income from her private Duchy of Lancaster estate. In recent years net revenues to the Queen had more than doubled, rising from £12,000 in 1840 to £25,000 in 1860. Without such extra funds it would have been impossible to buy and run the estates of Balmoral and Birkhall – not to mention Osborne on the Isle of Wight which she bought in 1845 for £45,000.

The fact that these Duchy profits were free of tax in addition to the taxpayer subsidy which came from the Civil List savings has led some royal commentators to question whether Balmoral should be seen as a private estate? After highlighting that the estate was also immune from death duties, Robert Lacey in his biography of the Queen asked: "How far could such massive assets [Balmoral and Sandringham]… truly be considered "private" property? What public good was served by granting them tax exemptions granted to no other public servant?… Why should the properties not be considered as vested essentially in the state like the other residences."[22]

In fact, Queen Victoria wanted Balmoral to be reclassified as an official residence – in order to qualify for even more public money. Now that she had established her court there for several months of the year, cabinet ministers who previously had had little direct contact with Caledonian matters were forced to travel north of the border for Privy Council meetings and to conduct the general affairs of state. Many chaffed at the inconvenience of it all with Disraeli expressing a common if unsaid sentiment when he wrote that "carrying on the Government of a country six hundred miles from the Metropolis doubles the labour."[23] One of the ironies of staying in such a secluded retreat was that the Queen now found herself in closer interaction with ministers than at any of her other residences.

The Queen was also making a political statement by being based in a nation which only a century before had been torn apart and split from the Union by a revolt of supporters of Bonnie Prince Charlie's claim to the throne. Indeed, had it not been for the 1745 Jacobite rebellion then the Balmoral estate would never have been forfeited by the Farquharson clan to the loyalist Duff family whose Earl of Fife sold it to Prince Albert. In a politically savvy pivot, the Queen lost no time in upholstering every corner of her Highland home with tartan (including the Stewart-embossed curtains on the ground floor) and declaring "you know, I am a Jacobite myself."

It was its political connection to Scotland that may well have been the decisive factor in persuading Edward VII to keep Balmoral after the death of his mother in 1901. On coming to the throne, he was faced with an immediate cash crisis caused by the cost of running not one but three private estates. With Balmoral haemorrhaging £20,000 a year, Sandringham £40,000 and Osborne £17,000, something had to go.[24] He tried to ensure that Balmoral and Osborne were designated official rather than private residences but when that and a claim for a higher Civil List were refused, he decided to offload the Isle of Wight estate. The fact that the new king had no qualms about disposing of his predecessor's private residence to maintain another – just as before him Victoria had readily sold off George IV's Brighton Pavilion to purchase Osborne – gives the lie to the current assumption that King Charles could never sell the Queen's Balmoral estate in order to keep Sandringham.

In a politically astute nod to Scottish traditions, Bertie always wore a kilt in his Deeside lair – switching between Hunting Stuart or Balmoral tartan during the day and Royal Stuart in the evening when as a thunderous appetiser to the main course a Highland bagpiper would march three times round the dinner table.[25] But overall he spent much less time there than the old Queen, rarely staying more than a month each autumn, and making a conscious effort to rein in the extravagance of his mother. Her spirit of Balmorality – which outdoors turned a blind eye to the heavy consumption of alcohol by ghillies while indoors insisting on strict social etiquette – was replaced by a less potent brew. He outlawed drunkenness on the estate by reducing the stalkers' whisky and at the same time allowed greater informality over how guests were expected to behave.[26]

When George V inherited the property in 1910, one of his first acts was to move the statue of Queen Victoria's often drunken ghillie John Brown from outside the castle to a less prominent spot in the outer grounds. More austerity followed as both cocktails and card-games were banned and the main entertainment was confined to shooting and fishing. Despite these economies and the opening of the gardens and the new golf course to the paying public in 1931, Balmoral remained a constant drain on the royal coffers, losing £1,330 in 1933, £2,885 in 1934 and £2,167 in 1935.[27]

Edward VIII who preferred to holiday in the warmth of the Mediterranean rather than the chilly wastes of Aberdeenshire was more ruthless in taking the wrecking ball to the castle. In less than a year he cut £6,150 from the running costs – mainly by laying off staff.[28] Traditionalists among the family bridled at the heartlessness of the sackings and the general lack of consultation, with the normally restrained Queen Mary writing: "What a pity David went abroad when there is so much for him to do here & at Balmoral" and the Duke of York later replying "David only told me what he had done after it was over, which I might say made me very sad."[29]

An altogether different regime was installed after the Duke of York became monarch in December 1936. Arriving at Balmoral for the first time since the coronation, the new king and queen switched their car for a carriage which was then pulled not by the customary Windsor Grey or Cleveland Bay but by a detachment of estate workers headed by a piper in full Highland regalia. Staff relations instantly became more cordial and it was not unusual for servants and groundsmen to join the royal couple after dinner to watch a film in the big house.[30]

Although aware of the need to keep costs down, George VI eventually ended up making the estate larger. In 1947 he bought two wooded plots close to the Angus glens – half of the deer forest at Bachnagairn and all of Whitemonth forest which as we know from Canup's sporting rights application was bounded by valuable waterways stocked with salmon.

When his daughter Elizabeth became Queen in 1952 there was press speculation that she might downsize the estate but she too went the other way. In the mid-fifties she paid for a major extension to Birkhall castle which added a new drawing room and bedroom wing so that the Queen Mother could have a more comfortable retreat in her widowhood.[31] In 1978 she also bought 6,700 acres of the nearby Delnadamph grouse moor for £750,000[32] and in 1997 the other half of the Bachnagairn forest for £600,000.[33]

Like her father she showed loyalty to "her staff" (she refused to call them servants) despite their cost. At the time of her accession, there were 6 Balmoral-based housekeepers/maids each on a salary of £1,108 paid for by the Civil List and many more estate workers funded from her own pocket.[34] During her summer residence there were the extra staff who came with her from London or were recruited locally. Nowadays Balmoral in season employs around 120 workers, about 50 on a permanent basis, and the rest brought in from the south with the Queen's private secretary being relocated from his St James's Palace grace and favour apartment to the stone-built Craigowan House.[35]

The annual summer migration has been a costly military-like operation involving the transportation of not just men and women but much material too. Until recently, mattresses, kitchen equipment, reading matter and dog baskets – not to mention the corgis, Labrador gun dogs and her favourite horses – all had to be shipped in a fleet of heavy-goods vehicles and horse boxes. It took a troop of soldiers several weeks in July to complete the manoeuvre, while a second costly detachment of the Queen's Guards was required to protect her while in residence.[36]

Cabinet ministers also have to be transported to the head of state's Scottish home. Famously, in August 2019 Jacob Rees-Mogg, the Leader of the House of Commons, Baroness Evans, the Leader of the House of Lords, and Mark Spencer, the Chief Whip, all had to travel up to Balmoral for a short Privy Council meeting where the Queen gave her approval for the controversial – and as it turned out – unlawful prorogation of parliament in the run-up to the October 31st Brexit deadline to leave the European Union.

But some government ministers make the long journey more reluctantly than others due to the perceived loss of time and by extension money. Richard Crossman, the anti-monarchist Lord President of the Council in Harold Wilson's first government, found it absurd that the Privy Council had to decamp to Deeside to carry out its constitutional duties. "It's interesting to reflect that four Ministers, busy men, all had to take a night and a day off and go up there [Balmoral] with Godfrey Agnew [the Clerk of the Council] to stand for two and a half minutes while the list of Titles [of Orders in Council] was read out," he railed in his diary after one wasteful journey in September 1966. "It would be far simpler for the Queen to come to Buckingham Palace but it's lèse–majesté to suggest it."[37] He wasn't much taken by the castle either describing it as "a typical Scottish baronial house, looking as though it had been built yesterday, with a nice conventional rose garden and by the little church, a golf course which nobody plays on except the staff."[38]

Even though he too regarded Balmoral as in "a time warp," Harold Wilson had no qualms about making the long trek for the Prime Minister's traditional autumn audience since he was, in Crossman's words, "devoted to the Queen and is very proud that she likes his visits to her."[39] It was at Balmoral in September 1975 that he told her that he needed to pass on some highly confidential information. After leaving their private detectives behind in the castle, he and his wife Mary were driven by the Queen to an isolated cottage a mile away on the other side of the estate. There over afternoon tea the Prime Minister informed the sovereign of his decision to retire the following March. He did this not just out of constitutional rectitude but to put on the historical record that he left of his own volition and had not been pushed out. Afterwards Her Majesty put on an apron, handed another to Mary and set about washing the dishes together.[40]

By contrast Margaret Thatcher was never terribly comfortable at Balmoral – almost literally since on her first visit there as Secretary of

State for Education she arrived for the mandatory walk round the grounds without any country shoes and was forced to borrow an ill-fitting pair of hush puppies padded by layers of thick socks from a lady-in-waiting.[41] Later when Prime Minster she was persuaded to don green Wellington boots but eventually she recognised that hill walking was not her bag – or as the Queen wryly observed when organising a hike "I think you will find that Mrs Thatcher only walks on the road."[42] In truth, the outdoor pursuits of Balmoral held little appeal to a grocer's daughter steeped in the middle-class work ethic and suburban values. So keen was Mrs Finchley to get back to London that courtiers could not fail to notice that her suitcases were always packed well ahead of the scheduled departure time.

Unlike Margaret Thatcher, David Cameron "lapped up" the country pursuits on offer at Balmoral with all the enthusiasm you would expect from a scion of a grand upper-class family raised in Berkshire. When invited to Balmoral for the weekend, he was told that he could choose from salmon fishing, grouse shooting, riding the Queen's Highland ponies or stalking red-deer – but the main appeal lay in doing it all in privacy away from the cameras. In his memoirs, he admitted to having to give up shooting when he became leader because it projected the wrong image: "I had enough problems with the 'posh accusation' without being photographed with a gun in one hand and a dead bird in the other. Still, I managed all the sports at Balmoral except deer stalking."[43] On another now famous visit in September 2014 he urged the Queen to support him with "a raised eyebrow" in his Scottish referendum campaign – an indiscreet disclosure about a possible political intervention which caused "an amount of displeasure" at Buckingham Palace according to an official source.[44]

Like Margaret Thatcher, Tony Blair was also eager to slip off early. Instead of the traditional long weekend sojourn of Friday-Monday, he would often arrive on the Saturday and depart the next day.[45] In his memoirs he is frank about the essential weirdness of the place recalling "a vivid combination of the intriguing, the surreal, and the utterly freaky. The whole culture was alien." The lifestyle on offer was one of considerable extravagance: "there are footmen… [and] the valet – yes you got your own valet – asked me if he could fold my clothes and generally iron the underpants… Breakfast was huge. Lunch was huge. Dinner was huge. If you indulged you could put on a stone in the weekend."[46] His wife Cherie later revealed that she was so embarrassed about staff unpacking the toilet case in her luggage that in 1999 she left behind her contraception kit and as a result her son Leo was conceived in Balmoral.

If its topsoil were as fertile as its top sheets then the estate might be a going concern. Unfortunately making money from agriculture is literally an uphill struggle thanks to the flinty mountainous terrain. Less than 5,000 of its 50,000 acres is arable (although some pastureland does support the Highland cattle which along with Highland ponies are bred commercially) and the rest is moorland and forest. In 2017 it qualified for £14,202 in CAP support payments on the basis that it faced "natural and other specific constraints" but by 2018 the total figure had shot up to £106,716 on account of the £100,000 specially allocated for "investment in forest area development and improvement of the viability of forests." In 2019 the funding fell back to £7,512.

The Balmoral website no longer specifies how much the estate costs to run but a decade ago it gave a figure of £3m which is unlikely to have changed much over the years due to its fixed labour costs. As we saw earlier, back in 1971 Lord Cobbold, the head of the royal household, admitted to the Civil List Select Committee that Balmoral was loss-making and had to be subsidised by money from the Duchy of Lancaster.[47]

An estimated half of the £3m running costs are clawed back through the estate's many commercial ventures.[48] For £60 you can now go on a 3-hour Spring Safari Tour and shoot red deer and black grouse through your camera lens – or if you prefer to go alone as Land Rover Self Drive Treks are available for £120 per vehicle. For those wanting an extended stay, five holiday lodges can be rented for around £500 a week.

With the business community clearly in the crosshairs, the estate recently introduced a golf course corporate day with prices starting at £85 person. But when numbers fell due to the 2017 slump in the North Sea oil industry in nearby Aberdeen, the general public was admitted at £50 a head.

But probably the most profitable venture is salmon fishing. Despite the recent depletion in wild Atlantic stocks, three beats are available with the prime spot being Birkhall where for around £100 a day you can fish where the Queen Mother cast her evening rod. Back in 2001 Balmoral's salmon fishing rights were valued at £5,000 a fish based on the average five year catch but now that the average for a Scottish river has shot up to £7,000 a fish it is no wonder that Canup Ltd lost no time in registering the fishing rights.

Today it is not unusual for a property backing onto a prime salmon river to come with a premium of 10-20%. So, what would the addition of fishing rights make Balmoral worth? The most recent valuation in November 2017 by *Fortune* Magazine gave an astonishing figure of £107m which if accurate would make it more valuable than Sandringham. But the most detailed valuation was undertaken by the *Mail on Sunday* in 2001 when Peter Prag, a leading authority on rural property, put a price tag of £2.15m on the house and £14m for the entire estate. This figure included the sporting rights but not the additional premium that came with the royal name which can more than double its standard value. When that and the recent rise in land values are taken into account, Balmoral could easily be worth £40-£50m.

Chapter 6:

The Shape Shifting Estate

Queen Victoria would never have been able to buy Balmoral or Queen Elizabeth run it without money from the Duchy of Lancaster. Like Balmoral it is officially described as a private estate but, as with Balmoral, its status has been called into question. If it's effectively controlled by a trust rather than the Queen, then shouldn't it be classified public rather than private?

Who actually owns the Duchy was the question on many members' lips when its chief executive, Paul Clarke, appeared before the Public Accounts Committee in February 2005. When asked by one MP whether its income could be regarded as "public money" he argued that it was totally separate from the Crown and that it was like Sandringham "private property." But when pressed whether its capital could be accessed in the same way as if it were private property he replied that "no, the capital cannot be accessed but it is like a statutory perpetual trust."[1]

If the Duchy is a *de facto* trust, then its chief executive is *ex-officio* one of its trustees. By virtue of his office he chairs the Council of the Duchy of Lancaster, whose eight members are vested with the authority to run the estate. They determine the overall management strategy, while the day-to-day running is handled by a team of eighteen full-time employees, consisting mainly of estate managers, chartered surveyors and accountants. They oversee a rural estate of 18,450 hectares, spread over Cheshire, Staffordshire, Lancashire, Yorkshire and parts of the East Midlands and South Wales. The lands include everything from an 18-hole golf course at Rushden and a grouse moor in Yorkshire to a private airfield and the picturesque village station of Goathland filmed in the Harry Potter franchise. There are ten castles (the grandest being Lancaster's very own), sixteen luxury holiday cottages, half the bed of the river Mersey and almost all of the Lancashire foreshore.

Much smaller but more valuable is the urban estate which generates two thirds of all profits.[2] It consists of commercial property in Birmingham, Bradford, Leeds and Manchester as well as some prime real estate in Harrogate, including a hotel, an apartment complex and a converted 18th century villa. But the jewel in the crown is the Savoy Estate in London which runs over two acres from the Savoy Hotel on the Strand down to the Embankment and along to Waterloo Bridge where the Duchy's own offices are located. A change to the law in 1988 allowed its managers to develop the site commercially and today it brings in a king's ransom in office rents. The latest multi-million pound development is to refurbish the 1920s Norman House at 105-9 Strand into lucrative office, retail and restaurant space in the heart of the city.

The Savoy land has been part of the Duchy since the end of the 13th century but you have to go back further still to find out how the estate as a whole ended up being owned by the monarch. One of the great ironies of the claim that the Duchy is the private property of the sovereign is that it only came into the monarch's possession as a result of an attempt to overthrow the monarchy and replace it with a parliament with greater public legitimacy. In 1263 Simon de Montfort led a revolt of fellow barons against Henry III which produced England's first broadly representative parliament with delegates from both shires and towns. But when de Montfort was deposed after governing like a king in all but name his estate was handed over to Henry's son Edmund who expanded it with land seized from other rebel barons. By the end of the 14th century it had grown into the second biggest estate in England.

No wonder that in 1399 when its owner John of Gaunt died, Richard II made a land grab by confiscating the estate and banishing its rightful inheritor Henry Bolingbroke to France. But the son and heir soon returned to England with an army and seized the crown to become Henry IV. With the Duchy now directly tied to the monarch for the first time, the new king immediately safeguarded his estate against future usurpations through a charter in 1399 stating that it was the private property of the sovereign. A second charter by Henry VII in 1485 reasserted that the Lancaster inheritance should be held separately from all other Crown possessions and should be passed down as a private estate.

These charters today form the legal justification for the Queen to claim the land as her personal property. The details are clearly spelt out in the opening pages of every recent annual report from the Duchy. But English common law is based on precedent as much as statute. So how has the inheritance worked in practice down the centuries?

The first big test came in 1649 when the monarchy was eventually replaced by a Commonwealth after the trial and execution of Charles I. Under the letter of the law, the Duchy should have passed to the king's heir since the change of regime was in theory irrelevant to the inheritance. In the event, Cromwell's men simply took control of his landed estate in much the same way as they had seized his art collection. This was legitimized just six weeks after his death when parliament passed an act banning his heirs from holding the Crown or its property, specifically naming the Duchy of Lancaster as one such possession. The reason for the rush was to raise quick money to pay for the heavy costs of the war.

Duchy and Crown lands were lumped together and put on offer in a single fire sale. Lancaster farms with valuable leases were soon snapped up by disbanded soldiers with a close ear to the ground. Also placed on the market were five forests (Needwood was valued at £7,525 and Enfield at £3,000) and three prime historic sites (Tutbury fetched £3,245 Knaresborough £4,669 and Pickering £6,750). By 1654 – when the sale of Duchy and Crown lands ended – the total proceeds reached a massive £2m.[3]

"So far as the Duchy was a landed estate it had ceased to exist" lamented the Duchy's official historian.[4] Royalists had good reason to be sorrowful since the Commonwealth transfer undermined their twin arguments that the estate was totally separate from the Crown and that it could not be surrendered even if the sovereign lost his throne.

By mixing Crown and Duchy lands together the fire sale showed that *in extremis* the state could treat them as one and the same. But more importantly, by decoupling a dead king from his estate it suggested that without a monarchy a Duke had no claim to the Duchy. In other words, if, say, a Corbynite Britain followed the example of the Cromwellian Commonwealth and became a republic again, the monarch could lose his or her estate.

But in the event rule by a Lord Protector proved a historical blip. Once Cromwell died in 1658 the Commonwealth soon collapsed and the old order was restored under Charles II in 1660. The sale of Duchy lands was declared void and the forests and historic castles were returned to the new king as if nothing had happened – although it would take several decades before all the rental property was recovered. By that time, the estate faced a second key test to its legal status.

In 1688 when Charles II's successor James II was deposed by William and Mary in the Glorious Revolution, he lost not only his throne but the Duchy too. The ancient charter should have protected his right to his private estate which nominally was separate from the Crown, but in practice this cut no ice with the new constitutional monarchy. James was forced into exile in France and deprived of any benefit from his landholding. The letter of the law had been trumped by the force of political reality and even the Duchy's official historian had to acknowledge that "the succession to the Duchy... was [by the early eighteenth century] governed less by the early charters than custom and usage, which had established that the Duchy followed the Crown."[5]

The next major challenge to its status came in 1760 when parliament demanded that George III surrender to the state the income from his hereditary lands in return for granting him more money to fill the black hole in his finances. Under the new financial settlement the king got a guaranteed sum every year provided he handed over all of the Crown lands. But what was missing from the deal was any mention of his other hereditary estate, the Duchy of Lancaster. So why was it left out?

Duchy supporters fall back on the old argument that it was separate from the Crown. When the Clerk of the Duchy, Ernest Wheeler, was challenged on this point by a parliamentary Select Committee in 1971, he replied: "the Duchy was already a separate and recognisable organisation and I suspect that its profit was earmarked already for the personal enjoyment of the Sovereign of the day. One would not have expected in those circumstances that it would form part of the deal… But it is difficult to find out; I think there must be a good reason."[6]

A better reason may be that at the time its revenues were too small to be worth including. A Treasury document from the same Select Committee inquiry revealed that it "only produced the derisory sum £16 18s and 4p in that year [1760]."[7] But its poor profitability was no accident. Successive monarchs had emptied the coffers by buying off parliamentary opponents with the offer of land or rewarding favourites with lucrative leases. This brazen use of Duchy assets for political purposes further undermines the argument that the estate was a purely private concern.

It was not until 1830 and the arrival of William IV that the House of Commons made a formal bid to appropriate the Duchy. By now the expiry of many long leases on low rents had returned the estate to profitability and many parliamentarians (including Sir Robert Peel and Lord Palmerston) thought the money would be better spent on the whole nation rather than a single monarch. When William announced in his first speech from the throne that he was surrendering the hereditary lands they took this to mean that the Duchy would go as well. But the free-spending king had no intention of giving up his cash cow and in the ensuing battle with ministers he only managed to survive by pleading poverty ("[it is] the only remaining pittance of an independent possession") and playing on their need for his support for more important constitutional reforms (1832 Reform Bill was then in discussion).[8]

But a minor breakthrough was achieved when Queen Victoria came to the throne in 1837. This time the big guns were rolled out in the shape of the Chancellor of the Exchequer who pounded the Duchy with calls for its profits to be handed over to the public purse. Despite the added pressure of a heated debate in the Commons, the estate's defences proved hard to breach until eventually a compromise was agreed. The Duchy would keep its money provided it submitted its annual accounts to both the Treasury and parliament. "A ridiculous mouse, indeed," according to its official historian "but fraught with trouble for the Duchy."[9]

This small victory had significant long-term consequences as the enshrinement of the financial agreement in law established a formal and lasting link between the private estate and the public purse. Without it the Public Accounts Committee would have had no authority in 2005 to call Paul Clarke, the Duchy's chief executive, to give evidence. The final report reminded its officers that "Under the Duchy of Cornwall and Duchy of Lancaster Act 1838 the accounts of both Duchies are required to be presented to Parliament and they are therefore available for scrutiny by the Committee of Public Accounts."[10]

The legal requirement also prompted Kenneth Clarke, the Chancellor of the Duchy of Lancaster, to express doubts about its true status, confessing in 1987 that "a private estate" which was regulated like a government department "puzzles me."[11] Today, critics of the Duchy regularly use this anomaly to argue that it is not as private as some would have us believe.

It is understandable why Queen Victoria was so reluctant to accept that the estate was public since it was soon the wellspring of her personal wealth. During her reign its profits turned from a trickle to a flood. On her accession in 1837 they stood at £5,000; on her death in 1901 they had soared to £60,000. So, how did she bring about this remarkable transformation?

Prince Albert deserves much of the credit since the key changes took place on his watch. Rather like Prince Philip a century later, the consort was charged by a young Queen to modernise the administration of her private estates and the royal household. But in sharp contrast to his modern counterpart he was granted real power (the Foreign Secretary Lord Clarendon called him "king in all but name") and was able to bring to the task his own considerable powers as a polymath (another chronicler described him as "one of the most intelligent and industrious of consorts").[12] He cut waste in the household by doing away with many archaic privileges such as the weekly grant of 35 shillings for "red room wine" to officers supervising the Queen's guard – from a room (rather than a wine) of that colour. He also tackled the problem of the lack of coordination between courtiers which meant in the most notorious case that it was the duty of the Lord Chamberlain to lay the fire but not light it – a task that could only be performed by the Lord Steward. As a result of the new efficiency drive, it is estimated that between 1842-53 the household saved over £55,000 (about £4.5m at today's prices).

When it came to modernising the estate, he was able under the new 1855 Duchy of Lancaster Lands Act to buy and sell property more freely and he worked with Duchy officials to boost profits in city areas rather than the traditional rural estate. As a result, acreage on the outskirts of London which had been used as cheap pasture land was turned into valuable urban real estate and the sleepy town of Harrogate was developed into a thriving spa with the rateable value of its property shooting up from almost nothing at the start of the reign to £30,000 in 1861.[13]

Following Albert's death in 1861, Duchy profits began to plateau and more worryingly the government made another attempt to seize the estate. Backed by the Prime Minister Earl Russell and the Chancellor of Exchequer William Gladstone, in December 1865 a parliamentary committee examined the books of the Duchy to assess whether the profits were excessive and if they were, how they might be surrendered to the public purse. But when the Queen made clear her opposition and the committee apparently found little evidence for abolition, no further action was taken,[14] although a later study revealed that she had saved in total £500,000 from Duchy receipts.[15]

The public had to wait until after Victoria's death to learn that her estate was not as private as she claimed. In March 1901 George Percival Best, the civil servant responsible for running the Crown Estates and an expert in hereditary estates in general, published pseudonymously an explosive article in the *Fortnightly Review* disclosing how the Lancaster lands could only be deemed "private property... in a very limited sense."[16] Through detailed historical evidence he showed how over the centuries the estate had always been considered part of the hereditary revenues of the Crown and that William IV (and by extension Victoria) had been wrong to claim it as private property, separate from the office of sovereign. He concluded that the transfer of this land to the public should now be "fully considered by parliament."

The revelations fed into the debate over how much the new king Edward VII should get from the Civil List. "Its amalgamation with the Crown lands was seriously considered," acknowledges the Duchy's official historian but once again the monarch pleaded poverty and got off the hook.[17] This was repeated in 1910 with George V who later successfully lobbied the Treasury to have the tax waived on his £60,000 per year Duchy receipts, a saving of £20,000 a year.[18]

Surrender was back on the agenda when Edward VIII acceded in 1936 but this time the assault was led by a politician rather than a mandarin with inside knowledge. When Clement Attlee stood up in the House of Commons on May 7th to deliver the Opposition's response to the Civil List Bill, he was speaking with the authority of not just being the Leader of the Labour Party but of having served as Chancellor of the Duchy of Lancaster from 1930-31. With icy politeness he argued that both the Duchies of Lancaster and Cornwall "cannot be considered in any way to be private estates... Whatever may have happened in the past, they had now descended with the Crown and have in fact become attached to the positions of the King and Prince of Wales. Therefore, we think they should be assimilated to the position of the other Crown lands."[19] His amendment to have the revenues surrendered in return for a fixed sum set by parliament might have been carried had MPs known that the king was – as noted earlier – then raiding the capital reserves of the Duchy.

If George VI was unique among recent monarchs in escaping an attempt to surrender the Duchy it is probably because MPs felt sorry for him after his financially crippling abdication settlement. We now know from previously unreleased papers that in 1937 £17,000 of his £80,000 Duchy revenues had to go to "the executors of HM King George V" with another £8,000 being deducted for the same purpose in 1938.[20] By 1940 all the debts had been cleared but it wasn't until after the war that revenues began to show any growth, inching up from £90,000 in 1945 to £100,000 in 1952, the year of his death.

When preparations began in May 1952 for the new Queen's Civil List, there was widespread concern that Clement Attlee and other Labour members on the Select Committee might try to reclaim the Duchy. Its chairman, the Conservative Chancellor of the Exchequer Rab Butler, had already decided "we cannot and should not interfere with the Duchies of Cornwall or Lancaster"[21] and his officials liaised with the Queen's Treasurer,

Sir Ulrick Alexander, on the tricky issue of whether Duchy revenues should be mentioned in the memorandum on which the report was based. Both were reluctant to flag up money they regarded as private but in a move straight out of a *Yes Minister* storyline, a Treasury mandarin proposed that the wind might be taken out of Labour sails if the matter *was* mentioned provided it was finessed in the right way: "the Chancellor may judge it tactically wiser to meet Mr Attlee to the extent of including a reference to the Duchy of Lancaster in the memorandum rather than compelling him to raise the question if he so wishes to in committee. Sir Ulrick Alexander is content so far as the palace is concerned to leave the choice to the Chancellor."[22]

The very next day, May 14th, the Chancellor wrote an emollient letter to the Labour leader thanking him for his helpful suggestions about amending the memo and agreeing "to make suitable references to the questions of tax liability and the Duchy of Lancaster."[23] When a week later the Committee met to the discuss the memo, no amendments on the Duchy were requested by Attlee or any other Labour member and the final report proposed no changes to the Duchy – although a record of its payments to the Queen was tucked away in Statement VI of the appendix.

The table highlights another likely reason why the Duchy's status went unchallenged: its profits were relatively poor. The 1952 income account shows that from a gross revenue of £319,000, just £100,000 was left for the Queen's Privy Purse, while on the capital account, its £323,198 holding of stocks brought in a mere £11,822. By comparison, in 2018-19 its £27.1m revenues yielded a net income of £21.7m and its £61.6m investment portfolio returned £2.6m in finance income.

In 1958 with its annual payments to the Privy Purse still stuck on £105,000 the Duchy set up a committee to investigate whether its "resources were properly exploited" and found that "too great a proportion of the assets were in agricultural land."[24] After it sold some farmland and developed urban sites, in 1961 its capital had risen to £450,000 and the annual payment to the Queen to £140,000. By the mid-sixties the yearly Privy Purse income was regularly hitting the £200,000 mark.

This boost in profitability coincided with the Treasury taking a renewed interest in Duchy affairs. In a revealing internal Treasury memo dated 19th

November 1964, the Assistant Secretary asked a junior colleague whether the Queen was entitled to all of the Privy Purse money "and if so, is there any understanding formal or otherwise about the amount that should be paid annually to the Privy Purse… [and] if, for any reason, the Government wished to intervene in the way the Duchy of Lancaster was managed, what formal power, if any, would they have to do so?" adding as an after-thought "If you can't answer the questions without talking to the Duchy please let me know. I don't want anyone to think there is some exercise afoot."[25]

One reason why things were afoot was that the Treasury was apparently exploring the possibility of using more Duchy money to top up the Civil List funding which had been gradually eroded by inflation in the mid-sixties. The status of the estate came up again when another Treasury official, K. Whalley, unearthed the 1901 article by the Crown Estates administrator which discussed the possible surrender of the Duchies of Lancaster and Cornwall suggesting that the "Duchies should be brought under public control and their ornamental offices should be abolished."[26] When Miss Whalley rather cheekily sent the Clerk of the Duchy of Lancaster a copy, Robert Somerville responded immediately with a formal rejection of the argument: "the reasons why the revenues of the Duchy have never been surrendered is that they have never been considered to be part of the hereditary revenues." The suitably chastised mandarin then scribbled on the letter a note to her boss R.T. Armstrong: "You will wish to be aware that the Lancaster defences are in good order!" to which he added "I have been warned! 'Ware the winds of change."[27] The Treasury's legal advisor, Sir John Fiennes, later spelt out the Duchy's position: "On all previous occasions one of the things which the palace has insisted on is that there should be no surrender of Duchy Revenues comparable to the surrender of the hereditary revenues of the Crown."[28]

The game of cat and mouse between the Treasury and the Duchy continued during the 1970-71 review of the royal finances by the Select Committee on the Civil List which had been prompted by a budget crisis caused by a new burst of inflation in the late sixties. One key issue which needed resolving was the involvement of the Duchy of Lancaster. Should the retention of its profits by the Queen be considered or should they accept the argument of the Duchy that it was a private estate?[29] And if so, shouldn't it by logic lie outside the realm of a parliamentary inquiry into the public funding of the monarchy?

But the Treasury took a contrary view – at least in private. In November 1964, an internal memo recorded that "at the beginning of each reign these revenues [the Duchy profits] are taken into consideration when the Civil List is settled."[30] In other words, they should always be part of the mix when the amount of funding was being calculated or recalculated. Indeed, as inflation began to bite, the Civil List shortfall had to be plugged by Duchy profits – to the tune of £60,000 in 1970 and £41,000 in 1971.[31] This was only possible because by now Duchy profits had mushroomed to £300,000 a year. But the new profitability created a dilemma for the palace. If the surpluses were needed to keep the Civil List in the black, then how could they be justified once the Select Committee agreed to grant more public money to plug the shortfall? As another Treasury memo put it, "it may not be easy to offer a convincing defence for the retention of so large a sum were it not for the fact that the Privy Purse is meeting the deficit on the Civil List in 1970 and 1971," with another memo adding "at some stage we should invite the Chancellor and perhaps the cabinet to confirm that they accept the palace view that these revenues are inviolate and defend [to parliament] …the retention by the Queen of an annual income of this order of magnitude."[32]

But the government of Edward Heath which was already under fire for its poor stewardship of the "boom and bust" economy did not want a public row with parliament and so decided to keep everything under wraps. Even before the Select Committee had made its final recommendations in October 1971 – let alone heard evidence from the palace in July of that year – a Treasury memo in March showed how the government had already decided that the Duchy would be left untouched: "the Chancellor's proposals do not envisage any interference in the traditional arrangements which were confirmed on the accession of the present Queen, namely that the Duchy of Lancaster and the private fortune should continue to be disregarded in any arrangements between parliament and the Queen."[33] The status quo would reign.

When John Boyd-Carpenter, a Conservative and pro-monarchy committee member, proposed a new financing mechanism that inadvertently altered the status of the Duchy and made it more liable to being surrendered to parliament, the plan was discreetly shelved by the chairman before it could do any lasting damage.[34]

But not all members of the committee were content to see Duchy affairs buried so readily. Willie Hamilton, who viewed the estate from the diametrically opposite perspective of a committed anti-monarchist, was determined to put on record his unhappiness with the way it was treated with kid gloves. Dismissing the committee's recommendations as a "whitewash" he issued his own minority report which highlighted among other issues how the Duchy had given no satisfactory reason why the estate was not surrendered in 1760 with the other hereditary lands. "This is a public estate," he argued in the parliamentary debate in December 1971, "and should be recognised as such."[35] Two months later he introduced his own private members' bill to nationalise the Duchy of Lancaster along with the Duchy of Cornwall and the Crown Lands. This provoked another heated debate in the Commons and although the bill did not pass, as many as 104 MPs voted for it.

Parliament had to wait until 2005 for its next chance to challenge the status of the Duchy when, as seen earlier, its chief executive, Paul Clarke raised eyebrows among members of the Public Accounts Committee by suggesting that its capital was less private than its income. By then its profits had shot up to over £8m a year and MPs were keen to find out why. Part of the reason, it emerged, was the shift in the property portfolio from rural to urban land which coincided with the end of some long leases and the start in the boom in city rents. The Duchy also cut costs trimming its staff from 40 to 16 which allowed it to vacate highly valuable commercial space for rental at its Brettenham House head office on the Strand.

But the parliamentary committee also highlighted how the Duchy benefited from many commercial privileges. It did not have to pay corporation or capital gains tax and more significantly, when it came to the recent record profits there was no outside assessment of how well the surplus corresponded to the needs of the royal household. Put bluntly, no one dared ask whether the Queen was receiving far more than she required.

What the Public Accounts Committee was now observing was what a few prescient members of the Select Committee on the Civil List (and one or two Treasury officials as well) had earlier warned about. Back in July 1971, the Labour MP Joel Barnett, a trained accountant with a wealth of experience in government finance, had put his finger on the problem of what might happen to Duchy profits if they did not have to go to pay for the Civil List deficit – "once that is no longer necessary, if we decide on certain figures, then there is going to be substantial surpluses."[36]

The scale of the profit growth was brought home in another parliamentary study in August 2017 – but this time it came not from MPs but a researcher in a House of Commons Library Briefing Paper. By charting the rise in payments to the Privy Purse from 1952-2016 and then the adjusting the figures for inflation, Cassie Barton revealed a killer fact: the Queen's income from her estate had gone up by more than £16m in real terms since the start of her reign.[37] The serious growth only occurred after 1971 since between 1952-71 it was below £1m, rising by £3m from 1972-91 before leaping by £8m between 1992 and 2011. With it shooting up by a further £5m between 2012 and 2017, the Queen had clearly hit the jackpot in the last two thirds of her reign.

Today, this rise in profits has led to renewed calls for the Duchy to change its status. On one extreme, the anti-monarchist campaign group Republic argue that in terms of ownership the Duchy should be treated in the same way as the Crown Lands. In other words, it should be surrendered to the state. "I don't think the Queen has any legitimate right to the revenue," says its chief executive Graham Smith. "Ultimately it's either hers or ours, if hers then so be it, she should keep it and be taxed as everyone else is. But I don't think she has a credible claim, so 100% needs to go to the Treasury."[38]

The royal correspondent Richard Palmer who describes the Duchy as "semi-public" has some sympathy with this argument but thinks that the estate would reveal its true colours only after a major constitutional upheaval: "My view is if you did not have a monarchy the Duchy of Lancaster… would be sending its money to the Chancellor of the Exchequer and in that sense the pressure group Republic are right."[39] Since that this is exactly what happened to its cash when you did not have a monarch during Cromwell's Commonwealth, then Palmer may have a point.

"To allege that it is a private estate is, I'm afraid, a little bit disingenuous," argues Dame Margaret Hodge MP who can't understand why if no public funds were involved the Public Affairs Committee which she chaired (and to a lesser extent the National Audit Office) had legal authority to scrutinise Duchy affairs. To deny its public side smacks of "deliberate ambiguity."[40]

Her Labour colleague Chris Bryant MP feels that any change will only happen after the Queen dies "because the general view is that she has done a pretty good job for longer than anyone else has had to do the job, but there is a bit more worry about her successor who might be a bit more interfering... One of the *quid pro quos* at the moment is that nobody is rattling this cage very much whilst the monarchy more or less behaves and steers clear of politics but the moment that changes everyone will want to rattle that cage."[41]

When Paul Clarke was asked by the 2005 Public Accounts Committee how parliament could gain more control over the capital of the Duchy, he admitted that the original 14th and 15th century charters could be amended by an act of parliament. MPs today would have good grounds to do so since the evidence is overwhelming that for much of its 600-year history the Duchy has not been a purely private estate.

Chapter 7:

Geeks and Greeks Bearing Gifts

If the line between private and public assets is blurred with the Duchy of Lancaster, then it is even more indistinct when it comes to another source of royal wealth – gifts. This appears odd in many ways: not just because it looks incongruous that one of the richest women in Britain would rely on the largesse of others to bump up her wealth but because nowadays the gift-gifting is mostly undertaken in full public view and governed by a clear set of guidelines.

In what is now a regular media event, the palace releases in the spring the list of all official gifts received by the royal family. When this was first introduced it looked like a welcome act of transparency, but to the royal correspondent Richard Palmer it allows the palace to escape criticism for most of the year by taking a single hit early on: "that was the one chance when you can ask about royal gifts… It is quite a good tactic: we will tell you once a year in a very controlled way [but] you cannot actually see a picture of this gift… and you cannot go down to the place where it is stored and look at it as a taxpayer."[1]

In 2018 the Queen was presented with a mixture of the expensive and the extraordinary – everything from a pewter horse statuette and a Newfoundland tartan Scottish Highland rug to a Lego post box and a framed picture of a Jersey cow. The more valuable gifts tended to take the form of jewellery: the prime minister of Singapore presented her with a pair of drop gold earrings with garnets, the president of South Africa gave her a Zulu beaded necklace, and she also received a delicate brooch encrusted with rubies. A year later when President Donald Trump made a state visit in June 2019, his and Melania's gift was a silver and silk poppy brooch from Tiffany's.

Presents such as these which she receives on an official engagement or in connection with official duties are not her private property. She can't sell or exchange them as they automatically become part of the Royal Collection. But if the gift comes from a personal friend unconnected with an official engagement then she could dispose of it as she so wished.

These are the guidelines that were drawn up in 2003 after the collapse of the Paul Burrell court case. When Princess Diana's butler was wrongly accused of selling off gifts given to her and Prince Charles, an internal investigation was launched to see whether there had been any improper behaviour in the royal household. Although the final report exonerated Charles from any blame (the Queen was surprisingly not required to be interviewed), it discovered that a number of official gifts had been sold or exchanged and that palace procedures over the receipt of gifts were "deficient." Its main recommendations were for tougher guidelines and a clearer definition of "official gifts."[2]

The code received its most recent test in May 2018 with the marriage of Prince Harry and Meghan Markle. In an attempt to avoid any controversy about inappropriate gifts, the couple requested that in place of a wedding present a donation be made to one of their favourite charities. The Australian and Canadian prime ministers duly made five figure contributions, but £7m of unsolicited presents from well-wishers and commercial firms promoting their wares had to be returned as they broke the official rules.

The code faced a stiffer test in June 2006 when the then Lord Linley (now second Earl of Snowdon) got into hot water for auctioning at Christie's some of the "personal possessions" of his late mother, Princess Margaret. When it was discovered that they included a number of official gifts – such as a pair of silver model kiwis given by the New Zealand government as a wedding present – the Queen soon made her displeasure known and her nephew duly donated the revenue from the sale of 47 lots to charity.

So, if it was possible for public gifts for Margaret's marriage to slip through the net and become private property, then could the same thing have happened with her sister's wedding? In theory, it should have been easier since back in November 1947 when Princess Elizabeth tied the knot there were no written guidelines.

The wedding presents came from a variety of sources – some wealthy, some less so. Unable to afford an engagement ring fit for a princess, the impecunious Prince Philip had to recycle the diamonds on his mother's tiara into a wedding piece. Four small stones were reset around a square three-carat diamond. Unfortunately the jewellers had to work at such speed and secrecy that there was no time for a proper fitting and when the bride appeared in public for the first time after the announcement the ring hung loosely round her finger. Although much plainer than traditional royal gems, a jeweller recently valued the item as "approaching six figures if not more."[3]

The tiara in question was originally his Greek mother's wedding present – one of 2,600 gifts that arrived from all round the world. So great was the public's generosity that Grenadier Guards had to be dispatched to transfer 1,500 of them from Buckingham Palace to St James's Palace where they were put on display. Even at an entrance fee of 5 shillings for the first day and 1 shilling later, the exhibition proved a big hit with the 200,000 visitors as queues snaked around St James's for almost a mile. When the royal party took their own tour of the gallery, Queen Mary came to a sudden halt before a piece of white yarn sent by Gandhi which looked suspiciously like his loincloth. "Such an indelicate gift! What a horrible thing?" Prince Philip heard her mutter in her best Downton Abbey dowager voice. "I don't think it horrible. I think he is a wonderful man," he courageously butted in explaining that it was just a piece of linen that the Mahatma had woven himself. His future grandmother-in-law was not convinced and moved on in a huff.

Many of the presents were indeed prosaic. A woman who would soon be rich beyond most people's dreams was sent 148 pairs of nylon stockings (for many housewives struggling to keep up appearances under rationing they were a prized possession) as well as a hand-knitted jumper, a rabbit tea cosy, a Siamese kitten and a turkey (from an American lady because "there was nothing to eat in England").

All were primly catalogued in the 264-page official handbook with the entry details giving few clues to the possible riches on offer. "A cheque (sum unspecified)" was the gift number 1334 from Mrs Kate Grouse – the same present as the one given by Mrs H.A. Pullen, Alexander Brown and naval officers on HMSAS *Protea* – while number 2126 was listed simply as "Dr J.T. Williamson a large uncut diamond".[4] A little drilling down reveals John Thorburn Williamson to be an eccentric Canadian geologist who in 1940 struck lucky by finding a diamond pipe at a site in Mwadui, Tanganyika. It turned out to be the richest diamond mine ever discovered and over the next decade it would make him one of the richest men in the world. When he eventually sold out, the millionaire bachelor, now an almost total recluse, found that his only pleasure in life was giving generously to royalty.

The "uncut diamond" cited above was described by one jewellery expert as "the most perfect pink diamond in the world" by virtue of its 54.5 carat size. In 1953 it was refashioned by Cartier into the centrepiece of a stunning flower brooch which was presented to the Queen for her coronation. Its value today would be in the hundreds of thousands of pounds.

Reclusive millionaires handing over their fortunes to queens who may be equally rich is an interesting psychological phenomenon which might be linked to finding surrogate children for the offspring they never had. Whatever its precise motivation, it certainly proved a lucrative income stream for Princess Elizabeth's sister, mother and great-great-grandmother. In 1852 another eccentric bachelor, the property developer John Camden Neild, left the bulk of his landed property to Queen Victoria. On being told that she had inherited £250,000 from a miser, her retort was "how very odd" but, as noted earlier, that did not stop her using the money to refurbish Balmoral.

Dame Margaret Greville, the heiress to the McEwan brewing empire who had no near relations, tried to go one better by leaving her entire country mansion Polesden Lacey to the future George VI and Queen Elizabeth. But when such largesse was deemed inappropriate after they acquired their own private estate following the coronation, she left the house to the National Trust. Nevertheless on her death in 1942 she bequeathed £200,000 in cash to Princess Margaret and her priceless jewellery collection to the then

Queen which included Marie Antoinette's diamond necklace, Catherine the Great's diamond ring and some very precious ivy-leaf clips.

On her wedding five years later Princess Elizabeth also received a cascade of expensive jewellery. No doubt keen to curry favour with the mother country just a couple of months after it granted India independence, the Nizam of Hyderabad gave her a fabulous floral diamond tiara with a matching English rose necklace designed by Cartier of Paris. Equally valuable was a diamond-encrusted Fabergé cigarette case from Prince Louis of Hesse which had once been owned by his aunt Alexandra, the last Romanov Empress.

Louis's grandfather – another Prince Louis – had himself hit the jackpot when he married into the British royal family. After tying the knot with Princess Alice, Queen Victoria's third child, at a private ceremony at Osborne House in July 1862, he was given a dowry of £30,000 (worth £2.5m today) and a treasure chest of priceless family heirlooms including a diamond tiara from the Queen, two opal and diamond brooches from Prince Albert, a set of sapphire and diamond earrings, necklace and bracelet from the Prince of Wales and three diamond, ruby and emerald keep-rings from Princes Alfred, Arthur and Leopold.[5] When the happy couple sailed away from the Isle of Wight, the royal yacht *Victoria and Albert* was so packed to the gunnels with an array of gold and silver objects that many feared that it might sink under the weight.

To put it crudely, the British monarchy was using the occasion of marriage and other rites of passage or significant anniversaries to transfer obscene amounts of wealth. As one royal historian observed, "in one day more capital gain could be accrued than many worthy citizens accumulated in a lifetime."[6] It was a practice often employed by their Romanov cousins who were by far the richest royals in Europe. When Queen Victoria's granddaughter, Princess Ella of Hesse, wed the son of Tsar Alexander II, Prince Sergei, she received a dowry of Fabergé gems and other valuables worth a staggering £700m today.

Sometimes the cascade of jewels started with a trickle. Victoria began the practice of giving each of her five daughters two stunning pearls a year from birth, allowing them by adulthood to have sufficient gems for a full necklace. A stickler for tradition, Queen Mary was keen to follow in Queen Victoria's footsteps and pass the family wealth by stealth to Princess Elizabeth. After a lifetime of buying, browsing and a bit of bullying she had amassed one of the finest collections of jewellery of any British monarch and the wedding of her favourite granddaughter was the perfect excuse to effect the transfer. The official catalogue records that she gave a total of twenty-five gifts, almost all heavily sprinkled with diamonds: a pair of pearl earrings with diamonds on top, two bracelets with diamonds all around, a massive stomacher brooch with a diamond floral scroll, a bandeau with two bands of diamonds and a bracelet with a ruby and diamond centre.

Some of these presents came from her own wedding in 1893, others were specially fashioned for a future queen. The most valuable was the magnificent Granny's Tiara which had been assembled from De Beers diamonds given to Mary on a tour of South Africa and would in the future hold a special place in her granddaughter's heart as the princess's first tiara.

In keeping with their shared love of outdoor sports, her father gave her a pair of Purdey guns – as well as some of the most valuable family jewellery including a ruby and diamond necklace with matching earrings, a sapphire and diamond necklace, a pair of diamond drop earrings and two rows of pearls.

Not all these gifts were her personal possessions to be disposed of freely. Some might be classified "family heirlooms" which although private property would be expected to stay in the family and be passed on to the next generation. Others might be designated "Crown Jewellery" and as such would be treated as national property to be put on show like the treasures in the Royal Collection. It is possible, though, that a few of these items may have inadvertently been placed under the wrong classification. For instance, two pearl necklaces given as personal presents by George VI and Queen Elizabeth contained pearls that were technically Crown property since they had originally been owned by Queen Anne and Queen Caroline.[7]

When it came to public gifts, the palace generally took a relaxed position. In 1947, for the first time, the bride and groom did not have to return presents from people who were not personal friends or in any way associated with the royal family.[8] Many of these items, as we have seen, were of small monetary value and were probably passed on to charity, although it is worth noting that today's guidelines allow items from the public costing less than £150 to be accepted.

As for the more valuable gifts, several came from political leaders and thus would probably have been retained – particularly the hunting lodge in the Aberdares given by the government of Kenya. The French administration presented her with a Sevres dinner service and Taiwan's leader Chiang Kai-shek a 175-piece set of porcelain tableware. More than likely such presents ended up not in the auction room but the dining room or store room although that would not have been possible for the Aga Khan's gift, a chestnut filly called Astrakhan, which went on to earn her some prize money by winning one race.

Of course Elizabeth had received plenty of valuable gifts well before her marriage. When she was six months she was given her first necklace – a set of pink coral beads from her mother – but she had to wait until she was three before getting her first pearl necklace which came from her father who – just like Queen Victoria – added two pearls to the platinum chain on each birthday.[9] Respecting the tradition of passing on the family silver at significant anniversaries – or "giving by degrees" as Queen Mary described it on one of her many gift cards to Princess Margaret – Elizabeth would go on to receive a stash of Cartier jewels on each birthday: for her 16th birthday she was given a diamond and sapphire brooch, for her 18th a diamond and sapphire bracelet and for her 19th a gold spray brooch.[10]

The big bonanza came on her 21st when she was on an official tour of South Africa. Being away from home for four months did not stop Queen Mary from giving her a pair of Victoria's pearl and diamond earrings or her parents presenting her with a pair of Cartier diamond brooches, ivy leaf clips from the Greville bequest and later her own car with the number plate HR H1. But the greatest riches came from outside the family: the South African government gave a necklace of 21 large diamonds which today are regarded as her "best" diamonds and the De Beers company on a visit to their Kimberly mines handed her a fabulous six carat blue white diamond. The South Africa diamonds are thought to be worth £2m-3m.[11]

When she became Queen, the flow of valuable gifts went up a level.

For her coronation in 1953 the Brazilian president presented her with a magnificent aquamarine and diamond necklace, and the Pakistan president Mohammad Ayub Khan gave her a glittering turquoise and pearl necklace on a state visit to Britain in 1966. A year later, King Faisal of Saudi Arabia went one better and handed her a magnificent fringe necklace made from 300 diamonds with a combined weight of 84 carats. In 1979 his successor King Khalid gave her another stunning Harry Winston-designed diamond necklace on an official visit to Saudi Arabia.[12] Under today's gift code, such presents would probably not be deemed her personal property.

In its official statements Buckingham Palace has always tried to play down the personal benefits of such gifted jewellery. Speaking before the 1971 Select Committee, the Lord Chamberlain, Lord Cobbold maintained that "in no practical sense does the Queen regard any of the items [of heirloom jewellery] as being at her free personal disposal."[13] Early on in the reign, the palace made it clear that she would only accept gifts in "very exceptional circumstances" unless they were from close friends.[14] Sometimes this was easier said than done. In 1965 two spinster sisters Eva and Catherine Godman presented her with a diamond and emerald necklace which their late father, the naturalist Frederick Godman had bought in Bavaria in the 1890s and which was supposedly first owned by Napoleon's wife Empress Josephine who left it to her son Eugene who married Princess Augusta of Bavaria. A subsequent inspection by the Surveyor of the Queen's Works of Art could not confirm its royal provenance but Her Majesty liked the glittering piece with its seven pendants so much that she decided to accept the offer. She invited the two sisters to a private audience and agreed to their one request to wear it occasionally.[15]

The fact that people often fall over themselves to hand her things can blur the dividing line between a public and a private present. The gift-giving of one artist to her mother and her husband illustrates the grey area. The Norfolk painter Edward Seago became friendly with Queen Elizabeth during her frequent stays at Sandringham – so much so that on the night before George VI died on February 5th, 1952, she showed the king some of his watercolours after spending the day at his house at nearby Ludham. She later told him that her husband was "enchanted with them all."[16]

Over the next 20 years, Seago regularly gave her paintings at Christmas or on her birthday and she displayed them prominently in her Clarence House and Birkhall homes, so raising the profile of a once unfashionable landscapist and portraitist.

Princess Anne sat for a portrait and partly as a result Prince Philip also became close. In 1956, after opening the Melbourne Olympic Games, he invited the artist to join him on the return voyage of *Britannia* from Australia via Antarctica to Gibraltar. They got on famously during the two-month trip, with amateur and professional artist sitting side by side on deck with paintbrushes in hand trying to capture the spectacular South Atlantic seascapes. Seago painted 60 paintings and gave them all to the prince. They are now a highlight of his private art collection and are sometimes loaned from the walls of Balmoral and other residences to public exhibitions such as the one at Bonham's in Bond Street in May 2007. Today with this newfound-fame Seago's paintings regularly command five and six figure sums. While it is clear that Philip in no way solicited these gifts nor breached any code, they did come into his possession as a result of an official engagement (the Olympic opening) and on publicly-funded transportation (the Royal Yacht). *Cui bono?* Both painter and prince – and perhaps the Queen too if Philip bequeaths her his artworks.

The grey area between the public and the private makes it impossible to put an exact figure on the value of her gifts. Today's *Sunday Times Rich List* does not even hazard a guess, but back in 2001 the *Mail on Sunday's Royal Rich Report* estimated that the wedding gifts were worth £2m in 1947 (£47m at modern prices) and that when you added on another £2m for the South Africa diamonds in 1947 and included the other riches she later received, the total sum would surpass £50m. But under the 2003 revised code some of the wedding presents (particularly those from national governments) would now be deemed public gifts. But against this the Queen has had another two decades since 2001 to acquire gifts boosted by the celebrations for her Jubilee year and 90th birthday. So, the *Mail on Sunday's* £50m figure might in a roundabout way be on the money.

Chapter 8:

Savings from State Subvention

Princess Elizabeth's wedding in November 1947 triggered a government review of her marriage allowance which highlighted another source of royal wealth – savings from the publicly-funded Civil List. This dubious practice employed by her father had been going on since Victoria's day but what made the revelation particularly sensitive was the timing: at the moment when the glamorous young princess was getting richer, the war-damaged country was feeling poorer.

"A flash of colour on the hard road we have to travel" was how Sir Winston Churchill greeted the wedding announcement in July 1947 and the response of the press was similarly upbeat. The *Daily Express* rejoiced that "today the British people, turning aside from the anxieties of a time of troubles, find hope as well as joy in the royal romance," while the *Guardian* welcomed what "is clearly a marriage of choice, not arrangement." The only sour note came when several newspapers warned against mounting an over-lavish ceremony in a period of national austerity.

In the summer of 1947 Britain was facing economic meltdown. A few weeks after the announcement of the marriage, Harry Truman's administration suddenly cut the US credit that financed consumer spending in the immediate post-war period, and on August 20th Clement Attlee's Labour government was forced to suspend sterling's convertibility to the dollar after a run on the pound. Controls of the imports of tobacco and paper were also imposed and food rationing was tightened. The British diet, observed one commentator, "remained on a thin line that divided discomfort from malnutrition." Food was now in shorter supply than during wartime.

The summer slowdown came in the aftermath of one the coldest winters in decades which had witnessed the Thames freeze over at Windsor. It had also produced a severe fuel shortage. Coal stocks were low, petrol imports had to be limited and a miners' strike in Yorkshire had forced industrial plants to close. With unemployment rising and production falling, the nation was on its knees.

Against this backdrop of economic woe, the Labour government had to decide what level of marriage allowance to give the princess – and more urgently what sort of wedding it could afford. A private ceremony at Windsor – in the tradition of the future Edward VII's marriage to Princess Alexandra in 1863 – would certainly be much cheaper, but would it disappoint the mass of the people hungry for a day out full of pomp and circumstance? In the end, ministers ruled out declaring a national holiday on the grounds that the loss of working hours would be too costly but agreed to hold the ceremony in Westminster Abbey, ensuring that it would be a public event with crowds able to view the pageantry from the pavement. The prime minister also hoped that with so many visiting heads of state in attendance under the glare of the international press the gala would send a positive message to the world about the stability of Britain's constitutional monarchy.

Prince Philip privately would have preferred a more modest affair. Undemonstrative by nature and perhaps unnerved by the prospect of marrying into the heart of the House of Windsor, he admitted to his uncle Lord Mountbatten that he was "entirely on the side of cutting down on the display of the royal wedding."[1] After the breakdown of his parents' marriage and the later wartime death of his father, he had led a peripatetic existence living off the hospitality of relatives, never having a home of his own or anything in the way of independent resources. On a naval salary of £350 a year he could afford only third class train travel and when after the engagement a valet was appointed to boot and suit the future consort, he found a wardrobe "scantier than that of many a bank clerk."[2]

After Philip's first public appearance since the announcement, Lady Airlie, Queen Mary's lady in waiting, noticed that he was wearing his "shabby" uniform with "the usual after-the-war look."[3] Lord Cobbold, the head of the Queen's household, later said: "I think it is not an unknown fact that he had no money of his own when he married."[4] Philip would soon clash with the tweedier courtiers since in some of these comments there was a suggestion that the impoverished Greek Prince – if not exactly a fortune hunter – might be on the financial make. In fairness to the genuinely love-lorn Philip, he did nothing to hide his impecunious status joking that he was just "dispossessed Balkan royalty."

So, on marriage, Elizabeth would not receive any additional wealth from her husband and her living conditions were far from luxurious either. The couple were forced to stay temporarily in the Clock House in Kensington Palace while their official London residence, the bomb-damaged Clarence House, was being renovated with the help of a £50,000 grant from parliament. But not all MPs were relaxed about allocating large amounts of public funds to the royal couple at a time of economic adversity and this rumbling discontent would soon spread to the cabinet. It would empower one of the monarchy's most effective political opponents and threaten to expose the inner working of the palace's finances to public scrutiny.

In the two months prior to the wedding, Clement Attlee's faction-riven government grappled with the tricky issue of how much public money the princess and her husband should get from the Civil List on marriage. The initial proposal from the king's treasurer Sir Ulrick Alexander was for the couple to receive £50,000 a year, which was £35,000 more than what the princess got when single.

On the weekend of 18-19th October – in order to work out a collective response to the offer and to discuss the more weighty matter of the contents of the emergency autumn budget – the self-styled "big five" (Clement Attlee, Ernest Bevin, Sir Stafford Cripps, Hugh Dalton and Herbert Morrison) decamped to the Prime Minister's Buckinghamshire retreat Chequers. Judging by the diary of Dalton, the Chancellor of the Exchequer, the fuel crisis was beginning to hit home ("Chequers is a very cold and uncomfortable house in winter") but the mini-summit was to prove "a very helpful weekend."[5]

After coming to an agreement on cuts to a new construction programme and to US food imports, they turned their attention to "the financial consequences of the marriage." The Chancellor made it clear that he was unhappy with the palace plan since "it would lead to a row in the house and in the country."[6] His four colleagues shared the misgivings and asked him to communicate this to the palace: "it is therefore left to the PM and I to see Lascelles [the king's private secretary] and speak to him very frankly on the subject and on the possible adverse effects on the whole status and repute of royalty in this country as well as on the possible influences in the Dominions as well as the USA."

What Dalton was referring to was the threat of a Labour backbench Commons revolt that might escalate into a full-scale public row. Several MPs had already made a formal complaint to the Chief Whip protesting against the extravagance of the wedding. The mood was best summed up by the member for Ilford North Mabel Ridealgh who on hearing that the government was giving the bride 100 extra clothing coupons for her dress wrote: "it is the general impression among the workers that it would not be proper to spend large sums of money on this wedding when we are asking the workers themselves to economise even in the necessities of life."[7]

Although the threat weakened the government's hand when it came to parliament, it could also be used as leverage over the palace – and few politicians were more adept at playing both ends than Hugh Dalton. On October 22nd the Chancellor and the Prime Minister met Sir Alan Lascelles and Sir Ulrick Alexander at 10 Downing Street. Lascelles, a wily palace operator who had lived through the abdication crisis, was "very sensible" about the merits of Dalton's proposal (as recorded in the latter's diary) "about a postponement of any new demand [for a Civil List increase] for the present" at least until the economy stabilised in a year or two and well aware of the "American difficulty" – presumably a reference to how it would look to the US administration if the British went to them with a begging bowl while simultaneously staging a luxurious wedding.[8] Alexander was less compliant trying unsuccessfully to get Dalton to state on the record that the amounts proposed by the palace were reasonable – although he did let slip that the king "had a nest egg from surpluses on Civil List during war years – due to small amount of ceremonial and entertaining."

Dalton then suggested that perhaps the money could be used to pay for Elizabeth and Philip and playing his trump card reminded the two courtiers that if that was unacceptable, the government might be forced to call a formal Select Committee into the Civil List where some of the royal family's dirty financial linen would be open to parliamentary scrutiny. Attlee then added that "it might even be impossible to prevent questions as to the extent of any private fortune belonging to the King and other members of the royal family."[9] Not unsurprisingly Lascelles thought the matter might be best resolved if Dalton met privately with the king.

What neither Alexander nor Lascelles fully realised was that the Chancellor disliked the monarch intensely – and the feeling was mutual. By breeding and education Dalton should have been a natural ally of the king. The son of John Dalton, Canon of the St George's Chapel, Windsor and tutor of George V, he had been educated at Eton and Cambridge before becoming a barrister and entering politics. On his mother's death he even inherited some heirlooms that had once been gifts to the royal family.

But when his father offered him the chance to be presented at court to George V, he surprisingly said no. He had come down from Cambridge with strong left-wing beliefs and a profound dislike of the rich and inherited wealth – symbolised by the royal family. As he became more prominent in left-wing circles he launched public attacks on the land-owning classes and the principle of inheritance. So when he himself inherited some royal heirlooms, it was hardly surprising that he wanted nothing to do with them giving away to some German friends a tea service presented to Queen Elizabeth.

There is some evidence that he may also have sold off some other royal gifts and that word may have got back to the palace of this unbecoming behaviour. There is no disputing, though, that George VI disliked him. In a remarkable diary entry by Dalton's successor as Chancellor Hugh Gaitskell, the animus was made crystal clear during an audience with George VI in May 1951: "[The king] spoke unusually frankly and said 'there is only one of your people I cannot abide… it is your predecessor but one' …I gathered that the King's dislike of him (I found this was shared by the Queen as well afterwards) really goes back to the Windsor days when Hugh Dalton's father was tutor to King George V and apparently very much like HD in having a loud voice and bullying manner."[10]

It appears that the king regarded Hugh Dalton ("your anarchist son") as a turn-coat – someone who committed an act of treachery by turning on his own landed class. This explains why in July 1945 when the king met with Clement Attlee to discuss the formation of the new Labour government he argued strongly against appointing Dalton Foreign Secretary. The job, in the end, went to Ernest Bevin although Attlee always denied he was swayed by palace pressure.

Before his meeting with the king on 27th October 1947, Dalton had a short discussion with Lascelles where he showed him the explosive letter to the Chief Whip from MPs hostile to a costly wedding and mentioned in a thinly veiled threat that it would certainly leak. In a similar vein he then warned the king that "the essential point was to prevent the development of an embarrassing debate." Outwardly, the audience progressed smoothly – at least in the eyes of Dalton who perhaps was not fully aware of the personal animus towards him "found the king in a very happy mood."[11] It ended in them agreeing to a slightly underhand strategy: nominally a Select Committee would be called but since the king would also announce that he would waive any request for public funds until the economic crisis was over, it would not have to investigate the royal finances.

In private, though, the king had made it clear that there was a limit to how long he could afford to fund the extra expenditure of the royal couple out of his own pocket. The negotiations stalled for ten days until Dalton came up with the bold idea of plugging the gap with the £200,000 that the king had saved from the Civil List during the war. Once surrendered to the Treasury, the sum could be used to give Elizabeth an extra £10,000 (on top her existing £15,000) and Philip £5,000.

The palace rejected the offer at a stroke, arguing that the proposed annuities were insultingly small and the surrendered sum far too large. When Dalton later admitted that this was not a serious offer but just a flyer without cabinet approval, Lascelles began to lose all faith in his interlocutor.[12] The impasse resumed for another fortnight – until the palace had a remarkable piece of luck.

Just a few minutes before he was due to deliver his budget speech to the

House of Commons on November 12th, Dalton inadvertently mentioned one of its key passages to the lobby correspondent of the London newspaper the *Star*. The journalist promptly filed the report and the story was on the newsstands before the Chancellor reached the part in question in his speech. Since it contained potentially market sensitive information, he felt duty bound the next day to offer his resignation which Attlee accepted.

His successor Sir Stafford Cripps was to prove far more palace friendly. Although also an upper-class left-winger with republican leanings, he had no stomach for a fight on this issue. In December he recommended to the cabinet a package that pushed the total provision up to £50,000 comprising of an extra £25,000 for the princess and £10,000 for her husband. But what must have sent the champagne corks popping at the palace was the news that the king needed to hand over only £100,000 of his £200,000 wartime savings from the Civil List.

His new package still had to be voted through. After cabinet members gave their unanimous approval on December 2nd, it was sent to the Select Committee where there was more serious dissent. Almost half the Labour MPs objected to the final report and it was only passed with the help of Conservative and Liberal votes.

Despite the cheering crowds who turned out in their hundreds of thousands to witness the wedding on a rainy winter day, the mood of the country seemed as conflicted as that of the Select Committee. "The Princess Elizabeth money debate has caused a lot of talk," wrote John Gordon of the *Daily Express* to his boss Lord Beaverbrook. "A large number of people think the king made a mistake in asking for so much at such a time. Many think that the royal family is well looked after and that they could afford to keep the heir out of the duchy funds… until she comes to the throne."[13]

In passing, it is worth pointing out that this is more evidence that the Duchy of Lancaster money was regarded by many outside the palace as an integral part of the Civil List settlement and not as courtiers claimed a purely private estate. When it came to setting the next Civil List for the now Queen Elizabeth in spring 1952, the Select Committee left the Duchy alone, but MPs did tackle another financial anomaly – the sovereign saving money from the Civil List. Strictly speaking there was nothing illegal about this longstanding practice although it did flout the spirit of the law and add to the overall cost to the taxpayer. The way it worked was for the monarch to switch money between the four different Classes of the household budget in the case of an underspend. For instance, if spending on Class II for staff wages or Class III for palace expenses did not reach its statutory limit, then the monarch was entitled to transfer the surplus into the Class I Privy Purse which was earmarked for personal use.

This is exactly what Queen Victoria did for most of her reign – thanks to the fall in household expenditure achieved by Prince Albert's efficiency drive and her own reduced spending in retirement after his death. On average she made £16,133 a year from the Civil List and by the end of her reign the total savings had come to an astonishing £800,000.[14] Despite being less frugal and having a shorter reign, Edward VII still managed to divert £32,700 a year of public money for himself, amassing a total of £261,592 in the first decade of the 20th century,[15] while in the course of his 25 year reign the abstemious George V pocketed £25,733 a year of a net total of £487,000 – and it would have been more had he not repaid the £100,000 saved during World War One.[16]

The government was well aware of this abuse and the 1936 Select Committee report on the Civil List went out of its way to draw MPs' attention to "these inquiries to show that the Civil List of the late reign was in excess of needs."[17] In other words, the fact that the king could save so much showed that the public grant had been set too high.

When the Select Committee of the Conservative Chancellor of the Exchequer Rab Butler met in May 1952 to decide how much Civil List money to give the new Queen, they had at their disposal all the figures for how much her father had saved. Although there had been no surpluses after World War Two, between 1937 and 1945 George V had saved from an underspend in classes II and III of the Civil List a gross sum of £391,950. In the Chancellor's official memo to committee members the savings were described as "modest" (and then "moderate" in a revised version) but even if you subtract the £100,000 repayment to the Treasury in 1948 for his reduced wartime spending, he still managed to save £232,845 between 1940-45 and another £59,105 before the war.[18] In fairness it should be noted that between 1946-51 he did transfer £190,000 from his Privy Purse to make up the deficit in the household budget – but even if you deduct that sum too he still saved a net total of £101,158 – which at £2.7m in today's money is hardly a "modest" amount. The finished report referred simply to "the savings" with no qualifying adjective.[19]

The Select Committee put an end to the abuse, with their final report deciding that any surpluses from classes II and III should "be transferred to the keeping of the Royal Trustees who would be the Prime Minister and Chancellor of the Exchequer of the day" rather than the sovereign's Privy Purse.[20] This move was motivated less by moral outrage than by the practical necessity to find extra money to plug the persistent £30,000 hole in the budget which had been caused by rising wages and other costs.

As a hedge against inflation, it was decided to establish a reserve fund so that savings in the early part of the reign could pay for the expected increased spending later. This was set at £95,000 a year but £25,000 of it was earmarked for the Queen's personal use to fund the expenses of junior royals not on the Civil List.

This last compromise measure came after heavy lobbying from the Keeper of the Privy Purse, Sir Ulrick Alexander, on behalf of the Queen. Faced with cuts to her private funds in the Privy Purse, she pressed for money "to relieve a hardship which clearly exists" for her aunt-in-law the Duchess of Kent whose husband Prince George had been killed in a plane crash while on active service in 1942 leaving behind three young children to support without any public allowance.[21] She also wanted financial support for the children of her uncle the Duke of Gloucester and possibly her own grandchildren.

In one letter to the Treasury, Alexander proposed that the grandchildren receive "say, £2,000 a year, if possible free of tax… to provide themselves with a motor car and chauffeur besides things such as extra clothing"[22] and in another, he reminded officials that "Civil List Balances have been regarded in the past as the only means by which provision could be made for the Sovereign's grandchildren who are not granted a parliamentary annuity."[23] The word "only" was underlined by a sceptical Treasury hand – possibly that of the undersecretary Burke Trend who in an earlier memo recorded that Alexander had told him that "the Queen Mother is a fairly wealthy woman in her own right."[24] Regardless of tradition, the Treasury clearly had their doubts whether it was right for public money to be earmarked for the unborn offspring of one of Britain's richest families. They also took a dim view of Alexander's other suggestion that a new law be passed exempting the Duchess of Kent (as well as Princess Anne and Princess Margaret) of income tax on any private income used for public duties, before eventually deciding that "this proposal also should be rejected."[25]

When it came to funding the Duchess of Kent, one member of the committee was surprisingly supportive – or at least initially. Hugh Gaitskell, the future Labour Leader and former Chancellor who had found George VI "a fairly reactionary person," said that he personally had much sympathy for the royal widow who was deprived of an allowance due to an oversight in the last Civil List which had been politically impossible to rectify during wartime.[26] In its place he favoured a sum of around £6,000 a year specifically provided for her in the new bill. But when Rab Butler pointed out that this would mean providing for her three children as well, he seemed to change his tune and in the end went along with the committee in backing the less generous scheme of using an unspecified slice of the reserve fund to meet her needs.[27]

In early May the Queen gave her consent to the draft package of measures but made it clear that this was "specifically conditional on our [the Treasury] preserving our freedom to give financial help to the Duchess of Kent and to the Gloucester and Kent children."[28] At the end of the month, the Keeper of her Privy Purse appeared before Gaitskell and other Select Committee members and kept the Kent matter firmly on the agenda by handing over a long memorandum pleading poverty for the Duchess, who could no longer afford to subscribe to many of her late husband's charities, as well as a twelve page list of her remaining sponsored charities and all the public engagements she had performed since 1945.[29]

Backbench MPs would have been unaware of these behind the scenes manoeuvrings when in early July Rab Butler rose to his feet in the chamber of the House of Commons to present the new Civil List. Speaking with his customary brusque assuredness, he declined to talk about the personal circumstances of the Duchess but said that it was surely right that special cases such as hers were given financial support. The Queen's grandchildren were not forgotten either. He reminded members of the warning in the report that one consequence of the end of Civil List savings was that the Queen "may be deprived of the means of making any provision, for instance, for her grandchildren, and some alternative arrangements will be necessary."[30]

In the short term at least, the government did little to help the grandchildren and the Queen was obliged to subsidise her immediate family from private funds in her Privy Purse.

Chapter 9:

Inheriting the Earth and More

One person who could never be accused of failing to provide for her grand-children was the dowager Queen Mary who within 6 months of the Civil List gaining royal assent had catalogued all her personal possessions and rewritten her will leaving all of her wealth to her favourite granddaughter, the soon-to-be crowned Elizabeth.

The bequest in March 1953 came just 13 months after the death of George VI who also left the bulk of his estate to the Queen, a double windfall that highlights another important source of her wealth – family inheritance. What made the two transfers particularly fruitful was that the Queen did not pay any death duties thanks to the Crown Private Estates Act 1862.

The main purpose of the bill was to facilitate the buying of Balmoral but its accompanying tax benefits were the object of close scrutiny by Treasury officials trying to work out how much money to give the sovereign in the new Civil List settlement: "As regards death duties it is considered this Act does not in the view of the Royal immunity involve liability to estate duty, while in the case of legacy and succession duties there are specific exemptions in the relative acts in favour of legacies, etc., bequeathed 'to or for the benefit of the Royal Family'."[1] In other words, some of the family heirlooms were also tax-free.

In fact, Mary's daughter-in-law, the Duchess of Gloucester, let the cat out of the bag when she responded to an innocent question from the dowager Queen's official biographer: "But Ma'am, I always thought no member of the royal family ever paid death-duties?" inquired James Pope-Hennessy. "Oh, no, oh no. That's only the monarch," Princess Alice retorted. "And that is *why* Queen Mary left *everything* to the *Queen*, because she knew this and wanted to avoid death duties."[2]

There was even a suggestion from the Treasury that such tax exemptions should be taken into account when deciding on the level of the Civil List: "we must not overlook the value to the Royal Family of the degree of immunity from tax which they enjoy, in the light of the current very heavy rates of tax."[3]

At the time of George VI's demise in February 1952, death duties were indeed crippling. Under Attlee's post-war programme of wealth distribution, estate tax was raised to 50% on bequests between £100,000 and £150,000 and a chilling 80% over £1,000,000. The tax burden fell hardest on the Queen's aristocratic cousins: the Earl of Harewood was obliged to dispose of two thirds of his Yorkshire land, the Duke of Argyll had to sell his island of Tirée, and the Duke of Richmond reluctantly jettisoned much of his Banff estate. When the Duke of Devonshire died in 1952 with a £2.5m tax bill the diarist Henry "Chips" Channon feared that it could also spell the death of his country mansion: "What dread score has destiny to pay off against the Devonshires? Is this the end of Chatsworth?" It wasn't but by 1956 two thirds of the peerage had no country estate.[4]

George VI left the Queen his two country estates of Balmoral and Sandringham which had been officially valued in 1936 at £300,000 and which by 1952 would have been worth considerably more.[5] This indicates that the tax waiver saved her hundreds of thousands of pounds on the landed assets alone. Some reports suggest that the king's total estate may have been as large as £2m but the exact figure is unknown to outsiders because the 1862 act also made the will of the sovereign closed to public inspection.

What we do know, however, is that she received one family heirloom almost as valuable as the landed estate – a stamp album. This was the Royal Philatelic Collection which is the greatest collection of UK and Commonwealth stamps in the world and has been valued at £100m. But like her Duchy of Lancaster estate doubts persist as to whether the property is public or private.

One of Elizabeth's leading biographers, Sarah Bradford, assumed that the stamps were part of the Royal Collection and thus akin to national property, and certainly the palace gave that impression for a time, with the Lord Chamberlain stating in 1971 that "though they are private collections for practical purposes are regarded and operated in a similar way to the Royal Collection of Pictures and Works of Art."[6] But more recently the Keeper of the Philatelic Collection, Michael Sefi, has set the record straight in a lecture to the Smithsonian Institution in Washington: "the Queen's collection… is a private collection. It is not a public collection and there is no guaranteed public access."[7]

There is also some confusion whether the stamps were obtained purely through the private funds of its main collector George V or with a strong element of public assistance. The official history of the collection goes out of its way to stress that "like any other less privileged collectors he bought most of those that are in the collection"[8] and that "as king he received dozens of unsolicited gifts, including many stamps which he made a point of not accepting unless he knew the donor or the gift was an official one."[9]

But if you put his stamps under the magnifying glass you soon see that a considerable part of the royal collection was built on his royal connections. On marrying Princess Mary in 1893, he received as a wedding present from the Philatelic Society a valuable set of stamps and postal papers. Then on becoming Prince of Wales in 1901, he used his father's position as king to receive all new printings of stamps from the Post Office (for the UK), the Crown Agents (for the colonies) and the Universal Postal Union in Berne (for all foreign issues). As heir to the throne, he was now entitled to extra money from the Duchy of Cornwall which he used to fund his big purchases. In January 1904 he paid at auction a world record fee of £1,450 for the first stamp ever produced for a colony – the Two Pence Post Office Mauritius. At the time he was telephoned by the king's equerry who mentioned in passing: "I know how interested your Royal Highness is in stamps. Did you happen to see in the newspapers that some damned fool had given as much as £1,400 for one stamp?" He replied: "I was the damned fool."[10] Today it is worth more than £2m.

If the stamps were rare enough, he was prepared to waive the rules about taking gifts from donors he did not know. Thus, he accepted from Mr H de Vaux of St Lucia a precious set of St Lucian One and Six penny stamps. Official gifts also found their way into the private collection as happened when he was asked if he wanted a reminder of his state visit to India and he promptly relieved Delhi's postal archives of some very valuable stamps.[11]

Even at the height of the First World War, he had few qualms about enlisting government officials in his collecting expeditions. When in 1916 Harold Nicolson was working at the Turkish desk of the Foreign Office, he was requested by the king to contact the Consul General in Salonika to obtain a block of military stamps with the word "Levant" misprinted on the envelope by the British occupying forces. A disgruntled Nicolson who had more important wartime matters to attend to – and who incidentally would go on to write the king's official biography – got his own back when he recorded in his diary: "for seventeen years he did nothing at all but kill animals and stick in stamps."[12]

But what explains this psychological need to collect? The king claimed that being able to retreat into the absorbing world of stamps "saved his life" during the war. He was known to spend as much as three afternoons a week locked in his stamp room in Buckingham Palace. On some basic level it satisfied a requirement for order in a changing world – a view echoed by the collection's curator Edward Bacon: "it represented a comforting return to the peaceful, quiet period of his life when little or nothing was expected of him."[13] For fifteen happy years he had served in the Royal Navy and afterwards he could never drop overboard the need for everything to be shipshape.

It is difficult to put a precise figure on the value of his collection but his assistant private secretary Sir Alan Lascelles noted that "his stamp collecting resulted in him leaving an heirloom worth God knows how many thousands."[14] In the last years of his life, a persistent nightmare was that his successor Edward VIII might sell his precious collection and he even sought legal advice about making it an inalienable family heirloom. During the acrimonious abdication settlement there was indeed serious talk of the now Duke of Windsor disposing of all the stamps, but thankfully for his successors' family wealth, it never came to pass.

Although not a fanatic like his father, George VI was sufficiently interested in philately to set up a separate collection for his new reign mounted in Morocco-leather blue albums. Like the old king, he did not turn his back on unsolicited gifts. Thus in June 1945 he was happy to receive from the former head of the New South Wales Postal Department a valuable set of twenty forgery stamps depicting the Sydney Harbour Bridge. Today they remain an interesting sidelight of the Queen's collection.

Elizabeth II may not be a passionate collector but she knows her stamps and is prepared to sanction changes to the collection. At the turn of the millennium it was decided to buy for £250,000 the Kirkcudbright cover – a unique block of ten penny blacks on an envelope posted on the date of issue on 6th May 1840. In order to raise the cash, duplicate and surplus items from the collection were put up for sale and the auction at Spink's on 17th May 2001 gave a rare glimpse into the market worth of the Queen's stamps. An 1861 Cape of Good Hope penny stamp with a reserve price of £18,000 went for £74,750 and the auction of the 200 other stamps raised an astounding £745,000.

Another auction at Spink's in June 2008 of just 13 stamps from the collection raised £170,000, double the reserve price. A third sale in April 2017 of four highly valuable Indian stamps helps to put a price tag on the Queen's stamps. A strip of 1948 Gandhi ten rupee Purple-Brown and Lake Service stamps fetched £500,000. Although this batch was not actually owned by the Queen, the royal collection does contain an arguably more valuable square block of the same stamps.[15]

Given these auction prices, it is odd that the official royal website claimed that "it is impossible to say how many stamps there are in the Collection, or to put a value on it." What we do know is that a vast strong room in St James's Palace contains around 350 leather-bound, colour-coded albums and another 200 boxes – all protected from possible light and heat damage by carefully calibrated environmental controls. The heart of the collection is George V's 328 red albums containing 17,500 pages of stamps, proofs and drawings. George VI's collection runs to 10 blue albums and 78 boxes, while the Queen's consists of about 20 green albums with her EIIR cipher embossed in gold leaf on the spine.

In 2001 a leading philatelist David Feldman valued the collection at around £100m but that figure – as he acknowledged – was contingent on market conditions and the timing of the sale: "Selling the entire collection in one go would fetch one price, but breaking it up and selling it over a period of five to ten years would double that price."[16]

George V's part of the collection surprisingly contains many valuable gifts from his wife Queen Mary who was not known as a great collector of stamps. The official record lists 13 sets of rare stamps – including another set of wartime stamps from Salonika with the word "Levant" overprinted on the envelope.[17] Her collecting, though, was mainly focussed on jewellery, and during her 60 years as a leading member of the royal family, she amassed more precious jewels than perhaps any other British Queen.[18]

Like her husband, she was shameless in using her royal position to persuade others to part with their valuables. If her eye were taken by some dazzling piece on a visit to the country house of a close acquaintance, she would drop a strong hint that they might want to make a gift of it to her or at least sell it for a low price. She also enlisted an army of "spotters" or "shoppers" to scour the auction rooms and antique emporia for bargain jewels or under-priced furniture. According to Margaret Bigge, daughter of George V's private secretary, "Queen Mary was the greatest *pincher* eye I knew. She was always pinching and screwing."[19]

It was through family connections that she secured her greatest windfall – the fabulous Romanov jewels. When George V's aunt the Dowager Empress Marie Feodorovna died in 1928, he organised the sale of the treasures she had smuggled out of revolutionary Russia – pearls the size of cherries, massive globe-shaped emeralds and a fistful of huge rubies. So as not to flood the market, the disposal had to be discreet. But by virtue of her position as consort Mary gained inside information about what was on offer and "bagged all the best" pieces for a sum believed to be below the valuation price.[20]

Mary's amassing of gems bordered on the manic. In an echo of her husband's stamp collecting, it reflected a psychological need for order in an unstable world. Throughout her life she had to fight against the double stigma of coming from minor royal stock (her grandfather's morganatic marriage meant that she was originally only a serene highness rather than a fully royal one) and from the penury of her parents (her near bankrupt father had to take the family abroad to escape creditors and he never had the resources to fund his passion for collecting art). Her royal jewels gave her not only enhanced regality but also financial security.

The last two months of her life were devoted to imposing order on her valuables. She updated her inventory of 1946 by cataloguing all her jewels, tracing different family connections and writing in her own hand labels for many items. No wonder Winston Churchill in his parliamentary tribute called her "practical in all things."

When it came to distributing the valuables in her £406,407 estate, the royal practice of passing down jewellery through the female side of the family and giving preference to the next in line was largely observed. The Queen Mother was bequeathed a number of valuable heirlooms and Princess Margaret received a stunning diamond-surrounded sapphire once owned by the Russian Tsarina, but the majority of the jewels went to the new Queen Elizabeth.[21]

One of the most magnificent items was the Vladimir Tiara. Originally crafted from the finest diamonds and pearls by the Russian court's jeweller, it had been Grand Duke Vladimir's wedding gift to his bride Grand Duchess Maria Pavlovna, Tsar Alexander III's sister-in-law. After her death in 1920, it became one of Mary's first purchases of Romanov jewellery, but not content with such riches, she promptly enhanced the value of the piece by adding 15 emeralds from her family's famous collection of Cambridge Emeralds. In her dotage the old Queen had little occasion to wear the piece in public but it soon became one of the new Queen's most popular tiaras.

Often worn with the piece is the Delhi Durbar necklace which she also inherited from Mary and which also incorporates some of the Cambridge Emeralds. Designed specifically for the glittering 1911 Indian pageant for the newly crowned George and Mary, it consists of nine bulbous gems from the Cambridge Emeralds, which had been won in a German state lottery around 1818 by her grandmother, the Duchess of Cambridge. The transfer of the jewels down the generations reflects her family's own rocky history. When her feckless brother, Prince Francis of Teck, bequeathed the gems to his mistress, the Countess of Kilmorey, Mary had effectively to bribe the woman with the offer of money and other jewels in order to get back the family heirlooms. Much later Queen Elizabeth loaned the emerald necklace to Princess Diana who famously wore it as a squaw-like headband on her first visit to Australia with Prince Charles in 1983.

By far the most valuable bequest from Queen Mary was the seven Cullinan Diamonds. Ironically it came as a result of one of the British Imperial Crown's most expensive and ill-conceived colonial adventures – the Boer War. After the peace treaty, the people of Transvaal demonstrated their new-found support for the Crown by giving Edward VII cleavings from the largest diamond in the world which had been discovered at Pretoria's Premier Mine in 1905 and named after the mine's chairman Thomas Cullinan. It was 4 inches long, 2.5 inches wide and weighed 3,106 carats.

Shortly before her father-in-law's death in 1910, the government of South Africa presented Mary with 102 cleavings (or chips) from the diamond and in keeping with the royal family's usual understatement they have been known ever since as "Granny's chips." Of the 9 main cut stones, she turned Cullinan III and IV – known as the Lesser Stars of Africa – into a spectacular brooch which today is probably the most valuable jewel owned by the Queen.

No doubt due to its preciousness it is rarely worn, unlike the Cullinan V brooch which is made from an unusual heart-shaped stone of 18.8 carats and has become a favourite item of Elizabeth thanks to its flexibility. At considerable expense Mary engaged the royal jewellers Garrard's to refashion it so that when it was not being used as a brooch it could be the centrepiece of either a tiara or a pendant. Cullinan IX, the smallest of the diamonds at a mere 4.4 carats and the only one cut in a stepped pear-shaped form, was turned into a platinum-mounted claw ring by Mary before she left it to the Queen in 1953.

"Granny's chips" have been valued at £29m although at least one piece is no longer regarded as the Queen's private property. Since diamonds from the Cullinan III and IV brooch were worn at the 1910 coronation and on other state occasions the item is often described as "crown property."[22] But where do you draw the dividing line between crown and private property?

The last person to try was Queen Mary who with the help of Garrard's made detailed inventories of the royal jewellery collection in 1946 and 1953. Broadly speaking, she distinguished between three types of jewels. First there was the crown property which included not just the Crown Jewels housed in the Tower of London but also all the jewels presented to Queen Victoria up to her death in 1901 and which would pass from one monarch to the next in perpetuity. Then came family heirlooms which comprised of jewellery given formally to senior royals after 1901 which should ordinarily be transferred down to the next generation. Finally there was private jewellery which had been bought with personal funds and could be disposed of freely.

The only problem with these categories is that they are far from watertight. Mary herself was famous for altering and recycling her jewels, muddying the waters of provenance by mixing private jewellery with family heirlooms as happened with the Cambridge Emeralds in the Vladimir Tiara. It is notable that there has been no inventory of the royal jewellery collection during the Queen's long reign. Garrard's would have been best placed to undertake such a task as they had been the royal jewellers since 1843 and stored many of the gems in its Mayfair vaults but in 2007 they lost that role to private jeweller Harry Collins who has maintained a discreet low-key presence.

As with the royal stamp collection, an inventory of the bejewelled Queen's *embarras de richesses* might reveal some embarrassingly high figures. So perhaps it is convenient for the sovereign not to know how much her box of gems is really worth.

Chapter 10:

Milking the Cornwall Cash Cow

The double windfall of two lucrative inheritances in the space of a year may have boosted the Queen's personal wealth but it did nothing to help plug the shortfall in the public finances of her costly court. In the early fifties, Buckingham Palace was leaking money as readily as a grand London townhouse with a hole in its roof. Revenue disappeared through the constant drip of increased maintenance charges and the deluge of rising wage costs caused by a new surge in post-war inflation. With annual palace expenditure mushrooming by £10,000 a year between 1946-52 something had to give.

One possible economy was to cut down on ceremony. The idea of less pomp and circumstance found a champion in the Labour Leader Clement Attlee who, although an admirer of George VI for risking his own fragile health to fulfil his official duties, argued on the 1952 Civil List Select Committee that the workload of his daughter might be lightened if "some of the colour and pageantry of State occasions" were reduced.[1]

In the crosshairs of the Treasury was something as mundane as the £15,000 a year spent on ceremonial horses. Even though the number of animals in the Royal Mews had more than halved in the last reign, the annual cost of forage had risen from £3,000 to £3,200.[2] With the palace apprehensive about the prospect of "doing away with state carriages and horses" the Select Committee gave the matter serious consideration but in the end decided that the loss in grandeur was not worth the candle. Attlee's later amendment calling for "a change in the conventions involving less elaborate ceremonials" was also rejected.[3]

An alternative approach was to transfer some of the Civil List costs to other government departments. This had already begun in the previous reign when the department responsible for public buildings, the Ministry of Works, had grudgingly agreed in 1951 to pick up the tab for the electricity, gas and heating costs of the monarch when in residence at Balmoral and Sandringham. By 1952-3 the annual bill had risen to a hefty £30,000.[4]

But it was now proposed that the Ministry should also pay the wages of the industrial staff working at Buckingham Palace, Windsor Castle and Holyroodhouse which amounted to £24,157 a year. Again there was considerable pushback from the Minister of Works, David Eccles, who argued that there would be no incentive for the palace to economise if it knew that Whitehall would always pick up the bill and that a better approach would be for the royal household to pay it directly through an increased Civil List.[5]

To settle the turf war, the Chancellor of the Exchequer, Rab Butler had to write an emollient letter to Eccles pointing out the presentational benefits of getting the cost off the Civil List books: "there are also obvious advantages of having expenditure of this sort charged to the ordinary vote where the ordinary official machine can take it in its stride."[6]

In the letter Rab acknowledged that the transfer did not bring any actual savings for the public purse since all that would happen is that the money would come indirectly from the departmental vote rather than via the Civil List grant. If the Treasury wanted to reduce the real cost of the monarchy new revenue streams would have to be found. It was even suggested that some of the extra funding might come from Dominion nations like Australia and Canada, although the idea was not pursued fully due to its "major constitutional implications."[7]

It was at this point that the Chancellor decided to raid the Prince of Wales's piggy bank. Charles as heir to the throne was entitled to the revenue from his private estate, the Duchy of Cornwall. In 1952 this was £95,141 – a sum of £2.5m in today's money which many would regard as more than adequate provision for a three-year-old. In search of a precedent for what to do with the income, the Treasury officials naturally looked to the previous Civil List but in 1937 there had been no Prince of Wales and all revenues had reverted automatically to the Exchequer.

In order to find a new set of rules for a new reign, the Treasury next turned to officials at the Duchy of Cornwall. Not surprisingly their wish was to stay with the status quo. They accepted that it was reasonable that while Charles was still a minor half of the Duchy income should go to the Civil List and the other half retained to pay for his education and other needs but insisted that once he came of age he should be entitled to all the revenue again. In what looked like an act of chutzpah they set the age of majority not at the usual 21 but at 18 and also argued that the profits should be exempted from tax and that the strict auditing rules for the accounts should be relaxed.[8]

Unfortunately the Treasury had other ideas. After much internal discussion, they proposed that the lion's share of Duchy profits should go not to Charles but the Civil List: instead of one half of the income, he would receive just one ninth. This would continue until his 18th birthday when he would get an extra £30,000 for the next three years. On his majority at 21 he could draw the revenues in full but would be expected to make a significant voluntary payment to the Treasury in lieu of tax.

The Duchy was forced to accept the new plan when Buckingham Palace privately made it clear that it preferred the Treasury option.[9] Although this appeared as if the Queen was being disloyal to Charles it made perfect economic sense since the extra Duchy money made a significant contribution to her financial settlement. It represented almost 20% of the total Civil List grant in 1952-3 and since the arrangement would run for another 18 years the aggregated revenues were considerable. In presenting the deal to parliament in July 1952 the Chancellor estimated that the total figure would be £1.38m but he miscalculated by almost a £1m as the actual return between 1952-1970 came to a massive £2.28m.

If such a large slice could be taken by the Exchequer, then why not surrender the whole pie? This was certainly the fear of the Duchy whose Receiver General, Sir Clive Burn, told a Treasury official that he was "very anxious" about any change in the status of the estate and "hoped that there would be no suggestion of the Duchy being taken over by the Crown Lands or merged in hereditary revenues."[10] In the parliamentary debate on the Civil List, Labour did table an amendment for all of the Duchy money to be surrendered during the minority, with the shadow Chancellor Hugh Gaitskell going so far as to assert that: "I do not think that one can deny that the revenues not only of the Crown Lands but also of the Duchy of Cornwall, for instance, are really public revenues."[11] But in defeating the motion the Conservative Chancellor advanced strong arguments against surrender based on the constitutional principle that historically the Duchy income belonged to the heir to the throne.

Newly discovered Treasury documents show that from the outset Rab had no intention of altering the status of the Duchy. As early as 20th March 1952 he wrote that "we cannot and should not interfere with the Duchies of Cornwall and Lancaster."[12] His civil servants were clearly on the same page since the Treasury official responsible for drafting the bill, Burke Trend, argued in a memo of March 15th that "any attempt to require their surrender [the Duchy revenues] to the Exchequer, as part of the hereditary revenues in return for a fixed parliamentary annuity to the duke on majority, should be resisted."[13]

The Treasury's defence of the status quo resided on historical precedent. The Duchy had been established by royal charter as far back as 1337 when Edward III created his son, Prince Edward ("the Black Prince") the first Duke of Cornwall. Its purpose was to provide an income from its land rents to the heir to the throne and its status was similar to the trusts used by the landed aristocracy where one generation to the next could live off the income but was not permitted to sell the capital assets. Originally these assets consisted of 17 manors in Cornwall, various smallholdings in Devon, the forest of Dartmoor and several castles (including Tintagel) but in subsequent centuries it gained and lost land, acquiring more Cornish manors after the Dissolution of the Monasteries but having to dispose of manors in Isleworth in exchange for estates in Somerset.

Over the past 650 years, the history of the Duchy of Cornwall has mirrored that of its sister organisation the Duchy of Lancaster. Under Cromwell's Commonwealth some of its lands were seized before being returned with the Restoration and when in 1760 George III decided to hand over the Crown lands in return for a fixed Civil List sum, it – like the Duchy of Lancaster – surprisingly escaped surrender to the state.

But it was during Queen Victoria's reign that the two duchies became especially entwined. When in the late 1830s Prince Albert started to modernise the finances of the Duchy of Lancaster, he did something similar for its Cornish sibling. At the time much of the revenue in Cornwall derived from tin mining and mineral quarrying, but the Prince Consort reorganised the property portfolio so as to exploit the more lucrative rental land in urban areas such as Kennington in London and suburban Surrey. After a parliamentary report in 1838 was highly critical of its amateurish administration, Albert introduced a new management structure called the Prince's Council whose members had real experience in land management. This administrative model was soon copied by the Duchy of Lancaster.

The Prince Consort headed the Prince's Council for twenty years during which time the Duchy was transformed from a sleepy backwater into a wellspring of Windsor wealth. Before his arrival net annual profits were just above £25,000; 25 years later they were £46,000.[14] A year after his death a special 1862 report by the Council acknowledged the key role he had played in turning around the estate's financial fortunes and indeed, by the end of Victoria's reign revenue had surpassed the £70,000 mark reaching £70,455 in 1900.[15]

But how much of this money actually went to the Queen? For the first four years of her reign, Prince Edward ("Bertie," the future Edward VII) was still a minor and as such she received all of his Duchy income which amounted to more than £100,000. Even when Bertie attained his majority which brought him £60,000 in stock and an average income of £14,000 a year, the monarchy still benefited since he used some of the estate's profits to buy Sandringham House in Norfolk which ultimately became the private residence of the monarch.[16]

Bertie's successor as Duke of Cornwall, Prince George (the future George V), was unable to swell the royal coffers with minority money as he came to the title after his 21st birthday, but his own successor, Prince Edward (the future Edward VIII) was a minor Duke for 5 years and contributed £67,000 to the Privy Purse. When he came of age he also gave £20,000 a year of Duchy money to the consolidated fund which financed royal pensions and other annuities.

Following Edward VIII's short reign and abdication, there was no male heir under George VI to receive the Duchy money but again this did not stop the monarchy from benefiting. It was decided that Princess Elizabeth should have first call on the income and what was left over would go to her uncle the Duke of Gloucester and then to the Civil List as a whole. The sums involved were far from small since total net revenues from 1937 to 1951 amounted to £1,608,770 (around £40m in today's prices).[17]

Even after Prince Charles reached his majority in 1969 and received all his Duchy money, the House of Windsor was still a winner. After strong prompting from the Treasury, he agreed to hand over 50% of the income (£105,000) to the consolidated fund which ultimately financed the royal household. Since this was in lieu of tax which at the time was over 90% at the top rate, it was not such a bad deal for the twenty-one-year-old. When in 1981 he married Diana the percentage of surrendered Duchy income was reduced to 25%.

Today, Charles voluntarily pays income tax at the top rate of 45%. In 2018-19 he handed over to Her Majesty's Revenue £4.7m from a total Duchy income of £21.6m. The reason why the net tax take was 25% rather than 45% is due to the deduction of his considerable expenses. He had a 116-strong household (including 1 butler, 2 valets, 3 chauffeurs, 5 chefs, 9 housekeepers and 14 communications workers) and heavy overheads (there was also the undisclosed wages of his 18 gardeners and estate workers; gardening costs in past years have run to over £100,000).[18]

But a significant slice of his expenses went on funding four other members of the royal family. In 2018-19 he gave almost £5m to the two households of Prince William and Kate and Prince Harry and Meghan to perform their official duties (although after 2020 the Sussexes will no longer receive such funding as they will not be working royals – but they will get a £2m parachute payment to soften the transition to civilian life). If the Duchy of Cornwall did not finance this expenditure then the Queen would have to pick up the tab for her grandchildren in the same way as she does for her children other than Charles.

The Duchy of Cornwall has changed out of all recognition since the Queen's accession in 1952 when it comprised of 138,000 acres mainly in the West Country and another 69 acres in London which included the Thames wharf property between Waterloo and Blackfriars Bridges and five pubs in Kennington.[19] Today it has shrunk to 131,620 acres but the property portfolio spread over 23 counties in England and Wales is much more diverse. In addition to the traditional west country holdings including oyster beds in Cornwall's river Helford, the Duchy owns the Oval cricket ground, Guy's and St Thomas's Hospitals, the Poundbury model village outside of Dorchester, up-market holiday cottages in the Isles of Sicily, a £38m Waitrose depot near Milton Keynes, a Holiday Inn site in Reading and Prince Charles's own country pile Highgrove House with its 425 hectare organic farm. In total the assets are now worth over £900m – a hundredfold increase on their value in 1970.[20]

Their profitability has also been transformed since the early years of the Queen's reign. Net revenues have mushroomed from £95,000 in 1952 to £20.7m in 2017 – a growth in real terms of almost £18m.[21] If you plot the figures on a graph, profits straight-lined for all of the fifties and sixties, dipped in the early seventies and then began to shoot up in the nineties. But the most remarkable growth has occurred since the millennium: between 2000-2018 profits tripled, rising by an extra £10m in real terms (although the impact of Covid-19 is predicted to depress profits in 2021).

So what explains this remarkable transformation? The answer from the Duchy is simply that "this has been achieved by disposing of poorer quality assets and investing in higher quality assets." In practice this has meant moving out of low-yield long-term rural leases and into more lucrative commercial property in urban areas – a process which was propelled by the property and stock market boom of the late nineties and early 2000s. By 2018, one half of all its revenue came from the commercial property, with just one quarter from agriculture and another quarter from residential property.

Prince Charles deserves some credit for overseeing this transformation since from the late seventies he has been actively involved in administering the estate which unlike the Duchy of Lancaster allows its royal benefactor a hands-on role – or rather a feet-first role as every tuft of land seems to bear the ecological imprint of his green Wellies. Like Prince Albert 150 years earlier, he chairs the twice-yearly meeting of the Prince's Council and appoints its non-executive members.

But the main reason for the Duchy's profitability is its highly professional management. During the growth years of 1997-2013 it was run by Sir Robert (Bertie) Ross, who brought to the job of Secretary and Keeper of the Records a quarter of a century of experience as head of the agricultural department of Savill's the estate agents. Like many a city manager, he was put on a bonus-related salary which earned him over £1m in his last five years in the post, and today his successor, Alastair Martin, a chartered surveyor and son of a Somerset farmer, takes home an annual salary and pension package of over £300,000.[22]

Even though the Duchy likes to portray itself as a private estate, it is really a highly commercial business. It is engaged in a number of joint ventures with private partners including a half share in a renewable energy company called J.V. Energen LLP which sells electricity to the national grid and a 15% holding in Barrow Shipping Ltd which distributes Biomethane, a green gas made from organic waste. But the most profitable venture is its initial 50% and now 100% stake in QMS (Poundbury) LLP – a property company owning Queen Mother Square of his Poundbury model estate in Dorchester which returned a profit of £482,000 in 2019-2020 with the likelihood of greater revenue in years to come as the building project nears its completion date in the early 2020s.

Since it is not legally a company, the Duchy pays no corporation or capital gains tax and as such possesses a potential commercial advantage over its competitors. Even the Treasury admitted in private to being perplexed by the immunity: "these revenues of are free of tax but there is some mystery surrounding the rationale of that arrangement" and that some select committee members of the review of the Civil List back in 1971 were as a result "rather dissatisfied with this situation."[23]

"If it looks like a duck and quacks like a duck and swims like a duck, you sort of assume it is a duck," the Labour MP Nick Smith said to a Duchy official during a Public Accounts Committee inquiry into the estate in 2014. "Given the Duchy of Cornwall looks and behaves like a corporation, with income from complex investments, and quacks like a corporation, with its council including the great and good from banking, on the face of it, many of my constituents would say that the Duchy should pay corporation tax and capital gains tax."[24]

After taking evidence from all parties – palace officials, republican critics and Whitehall watchdogs – the committee chaired by the redoubtable Margaret Hodge recommended that "the Treasury should examine the impact on the marketplace of the Duchy engaging in commercial transactions while exempt from tax."[25] It also called for greater transparency over its tax affairs after discovering that the Prince of Wales's annual review adopted the most unusual practice of lumping VAT together with income tax when offering a figure for how much tax he pays.

But does Charles receive far more than he requires? This was a question pursued in 2005 by the Public Accounts Committee which investigated the growth in profits of both the Duchy of Cornwall and the Duchy of Lancaster. In what amounted to a damning indictment of palace profligacy it recommended that: "There should be an assessment of how well the surpluses of the two Duchies correspond to the respective needs of the Households of The Queen and The Prince of Wales. The current arrangements stem from the fourteenth century, and the resulting income is to that extent an accident of history."[26]

The history of the Duchy of Cornwall shows that longevity in office can bring enormous financial benefits. Prince Edward (the future Edward VIII) was Duke of Cornwall for 25 years which meant that when he became king in 1936 he had accumulated a nest egg of £1.1m (£74.3m in today's money).[27] As the longest serving duke in history, Prince Charles has held the title for almost seventy years during a period when revenues were considerably higher than in the pre-war era. This means that when he eventually accedes to the throne he will be able to bring to the monarch's personal coffers many tens of millions of Duchy of Cornwall pounds – although on the debit side, he might lose ownership of his beloved Highgrove House as presumably it will remain part of the official estate.

Most valuations of the Queen's wealth overlook the revenues from the Duchy of Cornwall. Neither the *Sunday Times's Rich List* nor the *Mail on*

Sunday's Royal Rich Report – or even the broader *Forbes's World Billionaire List* – mentions the contribution from her son's private estate. They do all reference the Duchy of Lancaster but as we have seen historically the two duchies have been inextricably entwined. But for the Duchy of Cornwall (and a little help from the Duchy of Lancaster), the Queen would not own the £60m Sandringham estate and if it had not been for the Duchy of Cornwall, her official income after the war as heiress presumptive and then young Queen would have been severely curtailed.

Although putting a precise figure on the cash contribution of the Duchy is a task that might challenge the financial nous of Prince Albert, over the course of the Queen's reign it could have added well in excess of £10m to her official coffers.

Chapter 11:

Playing Hide and Seek with her Private Fortune

During the sixties, the buying power of the Queen's money was steadily eroded by the inexorable decline in the national economy. One balance of payments crisis followed another as Chancellors of the Exchequer came and went in symmetry with the falling value of sterling and the rising rate of inflation. The two decades leading up to 1970 witnessed the biggest sustained rise in prices since the Napoleonic Wars with the retail price index climbing by 74% and average earnings rocketing by 126%.[1]

The reserve fund that the palace had established in 1952 as a hedge against inflation proved inadequate. Each year £75,000 had been set aside from the Civil List for investment in government bonds with yields of 3-4% and maturity dates in the mid to late sixties. But inflation had eaten into their real value and with royal household staff now demanding pay rises (a non-unionised delegation literally knocked on the door of the Queen's Treasurer unannounced one day in 1960) spiralling wage costs meant that the contingency fund was needed much sooner than expected. As early as 1962 expenditure exceeded the allotted £475,000 Civil List and the palace had to draw on its reserves for the first time.

If inflation was undermining the Queen's public revenues, it was also doing damage to her private finances. In 1960 profits from the Duchy of Lancaster went down in real terms and then flat-lined for the next five years.

Rab Butler, now the Tory deputy prime minister, observed in his diary in the early sixties that she kept a close practical eye on rising prices and much later remarked that she drove a hard bargain when buying or selling land.[2] This price sensitivity was hardly surprising as she had a growing family with the birth of Prince Andrew in 1960 and Prince Edward in 1964, and growing overheads. As ever Balmoral drained money like a sieve and to keep wages down, cheaper servants had to be recruited from abroad. "The turnover of staff is quite rapid at the Palace," noted Stephen Barry who became a valet in the mid-sixties. "The pay is not very high… and a lot quickly lose interest and go."[3]

In the depth of this downturn in royal fortunes, the Queen came to a surprise decision in 1968. On the urging of Prince Philip and Lord Brabourne, his television producer cousin, she consented for the first time for TV cameras to film her private life behind palace doors. "It wasn't a soap," according to Brabourne. "It was a matter of conveying these people as human. Before 'Royal Family' the public had no idea what they were like."[4] A BBC crew led by director Richard Cawston would be allowed to follow her for a year and record not only her backstage duties as head of state but also her personal responsibilities as head of a family of four growing children. "Royal Family" – an intimate 110-minute television portrait – would prove a media sensation thanks to its emphasis on the family side of the story.

One reason for letting in daylight upon the magic of the monarchy was to reboot the royal family which in the eyes of the swinging sixties generation had grown fusty and irrelevant. Another was to launch into the public realm the coming-of-age Princess Anne and Prince Charles who was to be invested as Prince of Wales in a year's time. But there were also financial considerations at play. With a revised Civil List in the offing, the Queen wanted to demonstrate that she represented value for money and how better to do this than show that her family were normal and ordinary people like the taxpayers who would ultimately foot the bill. At a stroke of a bow, the monarchy would be made middle class.

In one sequence we see Prince Charles learning to play the cello when suddenly a string breaks and the watching Prince Edward is pinged in the face and yelps "what did you do that for?" The Queen is also shown busy with work rifling through her official boxes of state papers even when on "holiday" in Balmoral. We also witness some of the drudgery of her official duties when she receives the newly installed US ambassador Walter Annenberg who in an embarrassed attempt to make small talk explains the difficulties of settling in: "We're in the embassy residence, subject of course to some of the discomfiture as a result of a need for elements of refurbishment and rehabilitation."

But the most famous sequence is the barbecue by the loch at Balmoral. Like many a dad at a family picnic, Prince Philip assumes the role of cook, struggling to light a wrought-iron grill that has seen better days and charring sausages to the amusement of Princess Anne who finds it "an absolute total guaranteed failure." At their side, Prince Charles helps Prince Edward make a special salad dressing from cream which is then tasted by a grimacing Queen ("it's oily!"). Later, we see her entering the local village shop with Edward to buy an ice lolly and ask if they have any bull's eyes. With no trace of a curtsey or any other formality, the sales assistant treats Her Majesty like any other mother wanting to keep her kids quiet with the offer of sweets.

In fact, the Queen's press officer Sir William Heseltine later admitted that he didn't believe that she was exactly a regular at the shop but that it was she who had suggested it because she had done it before.[5] Heseltine himself massaged the message by persuading the BBC not to include any field sport sequences. "The long hours spent by the royal family blasting little birds out of the sky," wrote the Queen's biographer, "did not match the desired image of middle-class normalcy."[6] A courtier acknowledged that "it was an attempt to buy popularity."[7]

With all filming having to be pre-approved by Prince Philip and his media advisors, the programme seemed little more than a piece of PR – a clever ploy to soften up the public for a future pay rise. Some cynics thought the sequences stage-managed, with the TV critic Milton Shulman writing "It is fortunate at this moment in time that we have a royal family that fits in so splendidly with a public relation man's dream."[8] But these were minority voices. "Royal Family" got rave reviews in most newspapers and the viewing figures went through the roof. Shown on the BBC on June 21st, 1969 and then repeated on ITV a week later, the programme was seen by 38 million people – 68% of the British population. It was also distributed to foreign broadcasters and watched by 350 million viewers around the world.

Everything was now going perfectly for the royal reset and the monarchy seemed on course to get more money until on November 9th Prince Philip put his foot in it on American television. "We go into the red next year," was his throw-away response to a reporter's unusually direct question about the royal finances on NBC's *Meet the Press*. Instead of stopping digging, he ploughed on in the same jocular vein:

"Now inevitably if nothing happens we shall either have to – I don't know, we may have to move into smaller premises, who knows? We've closed down – well, for instance, we had a small yacht which we've had to sell, and I shall probably have to give up polo fairly soon, things like that."[9]

Aware of the horrendous optics of the Queen's consort complaining at the end of a foreign tour of poverty at home, the palace tried to suppress the pre-recorded programme but it was too late and the damage was done. It prompted a barrage of criticism in the press and a group of Bermondsey dockers to write to the prince offering to start a collection to buy him a polo pony.

On November 11th – two days after the broadcast – Prince Philip's *faux pas* came up for discussion by the cabinet. The main item on the agenda was the new prices and incomes bill but the Labour Prime Minister, Harold Wilson, announced that he would now have to make a statement in the Commons about how he planned to plug the gap in the royal finances. But not all of his colleagues believed this went far enough. "I think we should make some political capital out of this," fumed Barbara Castle, the Employment Secretary. "Now that Prince Philip has put this all before the public complaining to the government as if we are being unfair to them – at least let's have a Select Committee to look into the private fortune of the Queen," she said before adding: "Why, after all, should the Civil List be increased to enable Philip to play polo when his wife was one the richest women in the world and who enjoyed tax concessions that other people were denied?"[10]

She found an ally in Richard Crossman, the Health Secretary and a fellow republican, who said he thought Philip's speech was "a constitutional breach," recording later in his diary that "the Queen pays no estate or death duties, the monarchy has not paid any since these were invented and it has made her by far the richest person in the country."[11] The divisions in the cabinet reflected the wider social split in the party. Crossman, the judge's son who was educated at the public school Winchester and became an Oxford don, clashed with Harold Wilson, the son of an often-unemployed works chemist who had to win a scholarship to get into grammar school and then Oxford: "[Harold] is a steady loyalist and roughly speaking it is true that it is the professional classes who in this sense are radical and the working-class socialists who are by and large staunchly monarchist," observed Crossman. "The nearer the Queen they get the more the working-class members of the cabinet love her and she loves them. Fred Peart and Harold adore public dinners... It is only Barbara [Castle], Roy [Jenkins], Michael Stewart and I who intensely dislike these occasions."[12]

That afternoon Wilson made his statement to the Commons disclosing for the first time that the Civil List reserve fund had drained down to a mere £30,000 and would run out next year. Discussions had been going on for some time with the palace to resolve the matter and it had now been agreed to set up a Select Committee to review the Queen's income and the expenditure of the monarchy as a whole.

But Labour surprisingly lost the General Election in 1970 and the Select Committee was set up by Edward Heath's Conservative government with Anthony Barber, the new Chancellor of the Exchequer in the chair. Like Wilson, Barber was a grammar schoolboy from Yorkshire who went to Oxford and became a supporter of the royal family. But he was also in charge of the government coffers at a time when money was tight and inflation was about to let rip. If the Queen was to get a pay rise, it would have to be done discreetly.

One of his first acts on 17th May 1971 was to invite Wilson and Roy Jenkins, the Shadow Chancellor, to a private meeting in the Lord President's office in the Commons – along with his private secretary, Bill Ryrie, and the Lord President, Willie Whitelaw. When presented with a range of funding options for the Civil List, Wilson wondered why the Queen's

Duchy of Lancaster (not to mention her son's Duchy of Cornwall) had not been included as a source of finance. Jenkins then put his finger on the Queen's Achilles heel – her private fortune: "it could be argued that this was no business of the Select Committee but it would be [said] that the exemption which the Queen's private fortune had enjoyed for generations from estate duty meant that it was very much larger than it would have been in the hands of a private individual."[13] Although Barber batted away this suggestion by saying that palace officials simply had no idea of its size, this was the start of a game of hide and seek between the government and Her Majesty's opposition to find out the real extent of her private wealth.

Around this time a spate of stories began appearing in the press about how rich she was. Much of this was sheer speculation with figures as high as £100m being bandied around but when some of the mud began to stick and people questioned whether such a wealthy woman deserved a pay rise from public funds, the royal family was forced to act. Unsurprisingly the first to respond was the media-savvy Lord Mountbatten. "Unless you can get an informed reply published making just one point, the image of the monarchy will be gravely damaged," he wrote his nephew Prince Philip on June 5th advocating a planted article in a friendly and authoritative paper like the *Times*. "It is true that there is a fortune which is very big, but the overwhelming proportion (85%?) is in pictures, *objets d'art*, furniture etc. and three state-owned palaces. The Queen can't sell any of them, they bring in no income... So will you both please believe a loving old uncle and NOT your constitutional advisors and do it."[14]

Just five days later, the fight-back began when the *Daily Telegraph* ran an article by the Queen's former private Secretary, Sir John ("Jock") Colville, stating that "it particularly upsets her when she is described as being worth £50-100m... If she has got more than £2m today I will eat my hat."[15] He subsequently wrote to the *Times* repeating the single digit sum and the palace press office briefed that it was "a considerably more realistic guess than some of the absurd figures."[16]

A day after the *Telegraph* piece appeared, Colville's figures were discussed behind closed doors at the Treasury when Anthony Barber met the two palace officials who knew most about her finances: Lord Cobbold, the Lord

Chamberlain who was in overall charge of her official palace expenditure, and Lord Tyron, the Keeper of the Privy Purse who was responsible for her private income from the Duchy of Lancaster. The Chancellor asked for greater transparency on the Queen's private wealth, arguing that "since Her Majesty and her predecessors had paid no personal taxation or estate duty, the private resources could not be regarded as private in quite the usual sense. There was some feeling that it was at least reasonable that the facts should be known."[17] In response Cobbold could only say that "she might be willing to make a statement not on her personal resources but her inheritance… to indicate that what she had inherited amounted to 'not more than x.'"

Where the palace and Treasury could agree, though, was that "firm resistance should be put up against any proposal to ask the Queen's personal bankers to appear." One of those who might have been asked to give evidence was Colville himself who was then a director of Coutts, the royal bankers. In the end no banker was obliged to give evidence, unlike Cobbold who had to appear twice.

On the first occasion – on June 21st – he remained tight-lipped when pressed on the Queen's private wealth: "Her Majesty has been much concerned by the astronomical figures which had been bandied about in some quarters suggesting the value of these funds may now run into fifty to a hundred million pounds or so… she wishes me to assure the committee that these suggestions are wildly exaggerated."[18] Some Labour committee members – including Roy Jenkins – found the answer unsatisfactory and he was called back on July 27th. This time, he was asked by the Shadow Chancellor to be "a little more precise" about the size of the Queen's tax-free private fortune. But all he would say was that "in using the phrase 'wildly exaggerated' Her Majesty had specifically in mind the rumoured figure of £50 million and not the even more astronomical figure suggested in some quarters." But for a clearly-disappointed Jenkins the answer "left certain problems to the committee."[19] Even if the figure had been narrowed down to below £50m, it was unclear whether this sum referred to only her liquid assets and investment income or included all the Duchy of Lancaster and her private estates as well. If it was her cash and not her land, how did this square with the £2m figure that the palace leaked to the papers?

What the royal household also wanted to protect from overzealous MPs were the two Duchy estates. As early as September 1970 Sir John Fiennes, the Parliamentary Council who checked all royal legislation, let the cat out of the bag when he noted that "on all previous occasions one of the things which the palace has insisted on is that there should be no surrender of Duchy comparable to the ordinary surrender of the hereditary revenues of the Crown."[20] Fearful that some Labour MPs might make a grab for the Queen's money, John Boyd-Carpenter, an arch-monarchist Conservative on the committee, warned Anthony Barber "how Jenkins has tried to use it [the Civil List review] as a lever to extract information about her private fortune… [and] how Wilson is trying to use it to get his hands on the Duchies."[21]

Ironically it was Boyd-Carpenter who put the Duchies in danger with a personal plan which had unintended deleterious consequences. In his letter to the Chancellor, he proposed that the Civil List should be funded entirely from the profits of the Crown Estate. This would represent a win-win since the Queen would no longer have to go cap in hand to parliament if she ran out of money and the Treasury would no longer have to administer a complicated taxpayer-funded scheme.

But the proposal caused considerable concern at the palace. If the Treasury funded the Queen's public grant from the hereditary revenues of the Crown Estate, then sooner or later they would want to do the same with the hereditary income from the Duchies of Lancaster and Cornwall. Hadn't the Labour Party been officially advocating such a move for decades?

But to kill the plan, the royal household needed to collude with the Treasury and here Lord Cobbold was able to capitalise on his political experience serving under six Chancellors of the Exchequer while Governor of the Bank of England between 1949-1961. In a meeting on September 20th to discuss the draft Civil List report, Cobbold expressed his concerns about the plan in person to Chancellor Barber and it was agreed that action should be taken "to persuade Mr Boyd-Carpenter to abandon his idea of linking the provision for the Civil List to the revenues of the Crown Estate."[22]

Later that day in a letter marked "Secret" Barber wrote to his cabinet colleague Willie Whitelaw spelling out the Lord Chamberlain's worries and the proposed solution: "Cobbold… would prefer our latest proposals to a link with the revenues of the Crown Estate à la Boyd-Carpenter. His reason – which he would not want to give publicly – is that this might bring into issue the whole question of the revenues of the two Duchies. I told him that this was what you had always feared. He therefore agreed with me that at some stage, together with you and me, the three of us would see John Boyd-Carpenter, and Cobbold would explain to him why he does not favour Boyd-Carpenter's proposals."[23]

On September 24th Barber received a letter marked "Personal and Confidential" from Cobbold confirming that "the point is taken that introduction of Crown Estates revenues [the Boyd-Carpenter plan] into this picture might sooner or later add to pressures to alter the status of the two Duchies." An attached Treasury note warned, "As Lord Cobbold was anxious that no one but the Chancellor should see it, the Chancellor would be grateful if you would treat it with due discretion."[24]

No record exists of Boyd-Carpenter's meeting with Cobbold, Barber and Whitelaw as it was meant to be conducted on Privy Council terms but sometime in the autumn of 1971 the plan was dropped with due discretion.

When the report was published in December 1971 with a new Civil List set at £980,000 several members of the Committee refused to vote for it on the grounds that it had failed to uncover the full extent of the Queen's wealth. "The Chancellor does the monarchy a disservice by not allowing it to disclose the information [about the Queen's private fortune] or to pay tax," argued the absenter Joel Barnett, a qualified accountant who would later win fame for his Barnett Formula for local finance. "On that basis if I am scrupulous I cannot make up my mind whether the sum should be £980,000 or £430,000 because the essential facts have been denied me."[25]

His Labour colleague Willie Hamilton, a firebrand republican who earned notoriety for his *ad hominem* attacks on the Queen ("a middle aged woman of limited intellect") and Princess Margaret ("an expensive kept woman"), observed that "there is no doubt that the establishment worked hard to screen the royal family's private wealth from parliament and the people and of course succeeded"[26] and backed up his argument with a quote from a recent *Financial Times* editorial "the committee has not made any serious attempt to find out all the relevant facts about Her Majesty's private income."[27] Fed up with the financial obfuscation, he issued his own minority report calling for the revenues of the Crown Estate and the Duchies of Cornwall and Lancaster to be put into a single pot to fund the monarchy, for the Queen to be paid a fixed salary of £100,000 a year and for all the income of the royal family to be subject to tax in the same way as for any private citizen.[28]

It was over tax that Hamilton achieved his one victory during the committee proceedings. Helped by the Chancellor's earlier decision that all questions to do with the monarch's tax position would be fielded not by the palace and its tight-lipped representatives but by the Inland Revenue and the Treasury, he noticed in the Revenue's written submission that "the Queen was not liable to an assessment of income tax or surtax and is entitled to claim repayment of any income tax suffered at source (e.g. company dividends)."[29] When the Treasury's Permanent Secretary, Sir Douglas Allen, was asked how much payment she was actually receiving, all he would say was "that is a question we must refuse to answer as being detailed information about tax of an individual."[30]

But others have made a stab at calculating how much it boosted the Queen's investment income. Using historic share data from Barclays Capital, the *Mail on Sunday's Royal Rich Report* estimated that if she had invested £500,000 in 1952 it would have grown (thanks to a 40-year tax exemption) to £352m in 2001.[31] The figure, though, is based on certain assumptions about how much was invested, how little was withdrawn and how long the tax exemption lasted. If the investment was more than £500,000 then the yield would obviously have been far bigger but equally it could have been made smaller by withdrawals for payments to family members and for other outgoings. But most significant is the duration of the tax waiver. If the investment had begun as early as her accession the tax advantages would have been greater since in 1952 dividends were taxed at source at a hefty 47.5% basic rate and a crippling 97.5% top rate. If she had invested more than £500,000 and fallen into the higher tax bracket, then without the exemption almost all the dividends would have been swallowed up by the Revenue.

It is not certain when the tax dispensation actually began but newly unearthed Treasury documents suggest it was early in her reign. According to a 1959 survey of the royal finances – by coincidence, written by the same Inland Revenue official John Strudwick who 12 years later gave evidence to the Select Committee with his boss Sir Douglas Allen – "Repayment of this tax was not claimed in the past, but shortly after the accession of the present Queen repayment was claimed back to that date, and the Treasury agreed that it should be allowed. Similar claims are now made at regular intervals and the tax deducted is repaid."[32]

In his report innocuously entitled "Taxation Questions" but later marked "SECRET" due to its highly confidential contents, Strudwick explained that "there was no liability to taxation" on the Queen's investment income and that the legal justification for this was Crown Immunity: "the Queen is as part of the Royal Prerogative not liable to Income tax or Surtax." In other words, as the embodiment of the state, she could not tax herself. The only caveat was if an act of parliament made her liable or she did not claim it – as was the case with her father George VI.

The overriding priority was to keep all her investments secret. A leaked letter dated 5th December 1973 from Robert Armstrong, the private secretary of Prime Minister Edward Heath, revealed that his predecessor Harold Wilson had attached "great importance to arrangements which protect the Queen's private share-holdings from disclosure," indicating that there had been liaison with the palace on the matter.[33] Then in April 1977 the new Callaghan government announced that her shares would be exempted from the rules of the 1976 Companies Act which required the disclosure of the real owners behind holdings held by nominees.

At the same time as this announcement, Lord Cobbold's former employers, the Bank of England, established the perfect vehicle for monarchs to keep their shares secret. Exempted from the new regulations, the Bank of England Nominees Ltd (a wholly-owned subsidiary of the bank) allowed heads of state and other royal dignitaries to invest in British companies in what was essentially a two-way blind trust. They would not try to influence corporate dealings and in return, their names and the size of their holdings would not be disclosed.

By its nature, this arrangement precluded anyone from knowing details of the Queen's BoEN holdings despite widespread speculation that they were in blue chip companies.

According to an investigation by the *Times*, the Bank of England Nominees had an equity portfolio worth £57.3 million in February 1993 with the most valuable holdings being in Glaxo, Marks and Spencer, Unilever, Tesco and Shell.[34] These are all reliable UK stocks that one might expect a head of state to invest in and indeed the newspaper claimed that "at least 75% of these shares are thought to be owned by the Queen." Although there is no way of proving that the Queen did actually own them since her name does not appear on the register, some credence to her having a large BoEN portfolio is given by the appearance of less well-known companies on the list. There was a £577,000 stake in De La Rue which manufactures banknotes with the Queen's head on them, £137,000 in Anglian Water which supplied water to her Norfolk estate, £76,000 in Thames Water which supplied water to Windsor Castle and £337,000 in Severn Trent which supplied water throughout her realm. None of these regionally-based companies seem an obvious investment target for a Saudi prince or some other foreign potentate.

Even though the anonymity precluded establishing conclusive proof it was possible to track the larger transactions of unnamed holders. At the time of the Charles-Diana divorce proceedings in August 1996 an unusually large volume of share dealing was detected by the *Mail on Sunday's Royal Rich Report* – "Bank of England Nominees built up a £30m stake in BP, selling it months before the final settlement."[35] Since the Queen was responsible for funding much of the £17m settlement and the cash had to be found at short notice, the newspaper suggested it might have been her shares that were traded – although again there is no conclusive evidence linking her to the transaction.

If the value of BoEN was its anonymity, then this became redundant in 2011 when the company lost its exemption from disclosing the name of shareholders with the introduction of tougher regulations and in 2017 it was dissolved altogether. Another way of protecting the secrecy of the Queen's holdings is to invest abroad where disclosure rules are laxer. We now know from the Paradise Papers revelations that the Queen's Duchy of Lancaster had investments in two overseas Crown dependencies – Bermuda and the Cayman Islands – and it is perfectly possible that she also had investments in Commonwealth counties. The discovery that the Queen had £10m in offshore investments taken from Duchy of Lancaster funds in her Privy Purse also makes redundant the statement by her Lord Chamberlain, Lord Cobbold, to the 1971 Select Committee that none of the money going into the Privy Purse "has been used to augment Her Majesty's private resources."

This still leaves open the question of how much her private funds are worth today. In 1993 when another bout of speculation put the figure anywhere between one hundred million and several billion pounds, Lord Airlie, the head of the royal household, had to intervene to set the record straight: "Her Majesty has authorised me to say to that the lowest of these estimates is grossly overstated."[36] According to Robert Hardman, the well-connected royal chronicler who consulted Airlie for his biography of the Queen, "the sum, it emerged, was somewhere around £60m."[37] Converted to today's money, this represents £115m – a figure which rings true since it corresponds to the *Sunday Times*'s rising valuations of her investment portfolio – from £90m in 2011, £110m in 2015 and to roughly £120m in 2017.

But one suspects that the Queen does not know the exact figure either. She might agree with the American billionaire Nelson Bunker Hunt who when asked how rich he was by a congressional committee replied: "I don't have the figures in my head. People who know how much they are worth aren't usually worth that much."[38]

Chapter 12:

Tacking around Thatcherism

The arrival of Margaret Thatcher at Downing Street marked a sea change in the Queen's relationship with her prime ministers who up until then had all been careful not to rock the boat when her finances came up for review. The previous Conservative Leader, Edward Heath, who had acknowledged early on that the money issue was "delicate,"[1] adeptly steered the ship of state through the choppy waters of the 1971 Civil List, never impeding his Chancellor's charted course with policy objections and finally agreeing in cabinet to double the public grant to the monarch. Although the Queen failed to establish a relaxed personal relationship with her buttoned-up prime minister with one former courtier saying "Ted was Tricky – she was never comfortable with him,"[2] Heath himself thought that he got on well with her during their weekly audience: "The Queen is very interested… you can speak with complete confidentiality to her. You can say things you would not say to your number two."[3]

While Harold Wilson held the keys to Number 10, she could be assured of having both a financial friend and a personal admirer. In 1975 – just 3 years after the original Select Committee settlement – he managed to avoid a row over the increase of the Civil List from £980,000 to £1,400,000 by putting it through the royal trustees rather than the cabinet: "When it came to re-doing the Civil List," the Queen's private secretary Martin Charteris remembered, "Wilson was frightfully helpful. He used all his political skills and knowledge to get her what she wanted."[4] He looked forward to his regular audiences at Buckingham Palace and Balmoral where he was addressed informally as "Harold." According to his cabinet colleague Richard Crossman, "he was devoted to the Queen and is very pleased that she likes his visits to her." When he retired in March 1976, she came to *his* house by making a rare visit to Downing Street for his farewell party.

His successor James Callaghan was cut from similar Labour monarchist cloth. A Royal Naval Reservist, he had a father, James senior, who served as a rigger on the first royal yacht *Victoria and Albert* (which junior visited as a young child) and a wife, Audrey, who was enlisted to buy a present for the Queen's Silver Jubilee in 1977 when the cabinet could not agree (she chose a silver coffee-pot in preference to Shirley Williams's suggestion of a saddle and Tony Benn's of "a vase carved in coal by a Polish miner").[5] Although some members of his cabinet were keen for the Queen to pay tax and the palace to be "nationalised" under a new Department of Royal Affairs, nothing so radical ever came to pass on his loyalist watch. Instead he invited the Prince of Wales to attend the cabinet and asked him how things had changed since George III last sat there: "Well, then I would have been in your chair," but according to the Prime Minister's aide Bernard Donoughue who was there for a parliamentary questions briefing "it was a bit stilted."[6] He also attended the NEDO economic planning council and was later offered a programme of instruction in government through work experience in Whitehall but much to the PM's disappointment this was declined by Charles who at that early stage of kingly apprenticeship showed little interest in political affairs.[7]

Like Heath, Callaghan enjoyed his audience at the palace: "what one gets is friendliness but not friendship… But she is very interested in the political side – who is going up and who is going down."[8]

At first sight, one would have expected the Queen to strike up a friendlier relationship with Mrs Thatcher. Unlike previous Tory prime ministers such as the octogenarian Churchill and the sexagenarians Macmillan and Douglas-Home, there was no age gap as they were both in their early fifties with the PM being just 6 months older. And of course there was no gender gap between Britain's first female head of government and one of the then relatively few female heads of state. Indeed, when the Queen came to the throne in February 1952, the future prime minister wrote in a newspaper article: "if, as many earnestly pray, the accession of Elizabeth II can help to remove the last shreds of prejudice against women aspiring to the highest places, then a new era for women will indeed be at hand."[9] But according to Thatcher's official biographer gender may actually have fostered friction since as Princess Margaret once pointed out, neither had much experience of working with women at a high level.[10] As one courtier put it, "they were very different kinds of women. Margaret Thatcher made her way by hard work and bullying. The Queen was handed it all on a plate."[11]

From the start their relationship was characterised by tension and stiffness. When she went to Buckingham Palace for her first Privy Council meeting after becoming prime minister in 1979 she was so nervous that she arrived 45 minutes early and courtiers had to make stilted small talk to her before the Queen was ready.[12] In the actual audiences, she was never able to relax like Wilson or Callaghan: "Why does she always sit on the edge of her seat?" the Queen once asked a Tory peer. Her private secretary, Sir William Heseltine, asked her if the experience was like Queen Victoria being lectured by Gladstone ("He speaks to me as if I were a public meeting"). No, was her reply: "It wasn't at all like that… but I was not given much encouragement to comment on what she said."[13]

Mrs Thatcher devotes little space in her memoirs to her dealings with the Queen, only remarking about the weekly audience: "Anyone who imagines that they are a mere formality or confined to social niceties is quite wrong; they are quite business-like and Her Majesty brings to bear a formidable grasp of current issues and breadth of experience… I always found the Queen's attitude to the work of the government absolutely correct."[14]

But the real problem was political, not personal. Mrs Thatcher came to power with an agenda to cut public spending and shake up public institutions like the Civil Service, the nationalised industries and the BBC. To some of her die-heart supporters this included the monarchy as well. They objected to the Queen's acceptance of Marxist-leaning dictators in the Commonwealth, suspected Prince Charles of social democratic sympathies in campaigning against urban poverty and considered the palace a flabby sacred cow that merited a dose of free market medicine. According to the historian David

Cannadine, "Many Thatcherites regarded the monarchy as another vested interest, an unacceptable amalgam of snobbery and frivolity"[15] and this view was confirmed by John Biffen, the Chief Secretary to the Treasury, when he told parliament in March 1980: "The government's search for economies in public spending applies to the Civil List."[16]

Despite assurances in the 1971 Civil List Report that the palace had made great efforts to cut costs, there was undoubtedly waste in the royal household. Stories went the rounds of how in a throwback to the 1920s people sauntered in at 10 a.m., had dry martinis at noon and then took luncheon in a special dining room separate from other staff. Not surprisingly management was lax and working practices antiquated. Below stairs, kitchen staff worked with Victorian utensils and those in the Royal Mews wore Victorian livery. The lack of collaboration between departments often led to over-manning and even the Queen had to ask "Why have I got so many footmen?"[17]

As her young family grew older, they became more expensive to run. Prince Andrew had come of age and based in Buckingham Palace was beginning to splash the cash on an extravagant bachelor lifestyle, while his now-married sister Princess Anne had to be given an extra £23,000 in public funds in March 1980 to repair the roof of her Gatcombe Park home in Gloucestershire.

All this happened on the watch of Lord "Chip" Maclean, who for fifteen years between 1971 and 1985 oversaw the workings of the royal household as Lord Chamberlain. He hailed from one of Scotland's oldest families being the 27th chief of Clan Maclean of Duart and serving as Lord Lieutenant of Argyllshire as well as Chief Scout of the Scout Association. A perfectionist in royal ceremony who in 1981 organised the wedding of Prince Charles, he came to symbolise the tweedy courtier whose expertise lay more in managing pomp and circumstance than income and expenditure.

No doubt seeing the way the political wind was blowing, in December 1984 the palace decided it might be time for a radical replacement. Partly on the suggestion of the Queen's modernising press secretary William Heseltine, they picked David Ogilvie. Tall, slim and elegantly attired, superficially he seemed another country set courtier. As the 14th Earl of Airlie, he too came from a venerable Scottish family who owned castles in the Highlands and hobnobbed with royalty. His grandmother, Mabell, Countess of Airlie was Queen Mary's Lady of the Bedchamber and closest confidante. He became friends with the future Queen Elizabeth as early as his fifth birthday when she was a party guest and growing up on a family estate neighbouring Balmoral, he was able to get to know her better in an informal setting ("I have known her all my life," he later told her biographer "and she knows me warts and all").[18] He went on to Eton, served in the Scots Guards and developed a taste for pageantry: "He is immensely grand," one former royal aide confided. "He looks wonderful when dressed up in his ceremonial garb. Cecil B. de Mille would describe him as being a bit too much."[19]

But it was his commercial banking background that differentiated Airlie from past Lord Chamberlains. Between 1951 and 1984 he worked for the investment house Schroeders rising to the rank of chairman before taking early retirement aged 58. On joining the palace he readily admitted that he knew nothing about the running of the royal household, but what it needed was a fresh pair of eyes with no emotional baggage and a banker's zeal to cut costs. One of his first acts was to call in a consultancy firm to undertake a radical review of how the monarchy was managed.

He chose Michael Peat, a fellow old-Etonian with a forensic accountant's mind, who had recently done a similar root-and-branch job on Schroeders themselves. Although his family firm Peat Marwick McLintock were already the royal auditors with his father being responsible for going through the books, nothing was sacrosanct with both occupied and unoccupied palaces being put under the microscope. For six months Peat and his small team poured over the ledgers, demanding all departments justify their expenditure and becoming a hate figure to the old brigade who called him "ruthless" and "the axeman." He discovered among other things that the palace was spending £92,000 a year on light-bulbs alone, the unoccupied palaces like Hampton Court were being used as sinecure flats for retired courtiers and the box at the Royal Albert Hall when not occupied by royals was being monopolised by top household officials.

Completed in record time by December 1986, the 1,383-page report contained 188 recommendations for every corner of the royal household. Portion control should be introduced in catering and the five segregated dining rooms be merged into one. On nights when it was vacant the Royal Box at the Albert Hall should be made available to all staff. To reduce energy costs, hydro-electricity from the Thames should be used at Windsor Castle and new combination boilers installed at Buckingham Palace. Each department should re-interview staff to justify their role and a new annual report should record clearly the total expenditure of the household.

Although individually the proposals looked prosaic, collectively they represented a revolution. Some courtiers described it as "ushering in the most radical internal reform for a century" and others put Airlie's earthquake on the same scale as the one in the 19th century: "Prince Albert was a great force for change but after [he] had gone it went to sleep until David Airlie become Lord Chamberlain."[20] He woke up the royal household by reading them the riot act and more importantly he did it with the full backing of the Queen. When presented with the report, she nodded her assent and just said, "Get on with it."[21]

Airlie's main aim was to get the government off his back at a time when there was a real risk that the Civil List money would run out and more household expenditure would have to be transferred to the annual parliamentary vote. "The government was getting too closely involved in the running of the royal household, particularly the Treasury,"[22] he told one interviewer, while his colleague William Heseltine said to another: "More and more the Treasury had become the masters and they were controlling everything from the stable boys' pensions to the salary of the Lord Chamberlain."[23]

The reforms also helped to get the public off his back by dampening popular unrest. The mood of the nation was changing as the traditional deference to the royal family was eroded by the ethos of individualism and social mobility fostered by the Thatcherite revolution. Newspaper speculation that the Queen was worth billions and enjoyed huge tax breaks did not go down well with upwardly-mobile working-class readers who might have just managed to get on the property ladder by buying their first council flat. The Queen's private secretary Martin Charteris detected something in the air in December 1987 when over a lunch with the Victoria and Albert Museum director Roy Strong he talked about the need to restore some mystery into the royal family after they had been almost stripped bare.[24]

What he must partly have had in mind was the striptease that they had performed on nationwide television a few months earlier. In what was arguably the most embarrassing episode in the Queen's reign, her youngest child Prince Edward staged a *Royal It's a Knockout* – a charity version of the wacky TV games show in which Princess Anne frolicked around in medieval dress and Prince Andrew and Fergie joined in silly stunts like tug of war. The optics were made worse when in the subsequent televised press conference, Edward was greeted by a barrage of negative questions and then walked out in a huff. The Queen's press secretary Robin Janvrin later admitted to Woodrow Wyatt: "the 'Knock Out' programme was a disaster and should never have been allowed."[25]

Now that the royals themselves had invited daylight on magic, it was open season for the press. In July 1986 the *Sunday Times* ran an article based on "sources close to the Queen" about how Her Majesty "was dismayed by many of Mrs Thatcher's policies." She considered them "uncaring, confrontational and socially divisive" and in particular the 1984 conflict between striking miners and the government had caused serious damage to the social fabric of the nation. In what seemed like a constitutional breach it alleged that "the Queen was an astute political infighter who is quite prepared to take on Downing Street when provoked." [26]

The story caused a sensation because it seemed to confirm the widespread suspicion that the prime minister and her head of state were at political loggerheads – especially over the on-going Commonwealth row about whether sanctions should be imposed on South Africa. Its source was the royal press secretary Michael Shea who later admitted that there had been no prior briefing with the Queen and he had never heard her criticise the prime minister – although he did tell a colleague at the time that he had "led them [the *Sunday Times*] to publish a very sympathetic picture of the Queen: concerned about the coal miners concerned for the Commonwealth" and he thought it would be helpful in presenting her constitutional role.[27]

When the Queen's private secretary William Heseltine learned that Shea had briefed the press without her authority, he immediately advised her to contact Mrs Thatcher to put the record straight. That evening she rang the

PM at Chequers and explained – according to Heseltine – that she "could not imagine how the story came to be circulated, and anyway it bears no relation to the truth as I understand it."[28]

Meanwhile, Woodrow Wyatt, an acolyte of the Prime Minister and a columnist on a sister paper to the *Sunday Times,* rang her with the encouragement of its owner Rupert Murdoch, to suggest who the real source of the story was and to advise how to handle the issue when it was raised in parliament. "I did [it] in such a way that she knew immediately who it was." I said, "When you have to answer your question in the House I should merely say it is the silly season." But the PM decided not to make any political capital from it whatsoever: "No, I will say that a denial has been issued from Buckingham Palace and I have nothing further to say. I never answer questions affecting the Queen."[29]

The killing of the story might be seen as a minor victory for the palace over Downing Street since it would have been acutely embarrassing to the Queen if the full details had been revealed. A few months later Shea was quietly eased out of his job. "In the end we had to encourage him to move on," explained Sir William Heseltine. "He just went further than he should have done in attributing attitudes and notions to the Queen." But another private secretary Lord Charteris later suggested that he might not have been that wide of the mark in thinking that the Queen's outlook was very different from Mrs Thatcher's: "you might say that the Queen prefers a sort of consensus politics, rather than a polarized one, and I suspect this is true, although I cannot speak from knowledge here. But if you are in the Queen's position, you are the titular, the symbolic head of the country, and the less squabbling that goes on in that country, obviously the more convenient and the more comfortable you feel."[30]

In 1990 the palace chalked up another small victory over the government when it was decided to abolish the Crown Suppliers in the Department of the Environment's Property Services Agency. Responsible for maintenance at Buckingham Palace, Windsor Castle and other occupied palaces, this body had been seen by modernisers like Lord Airlie and Michael Peat as part of the Treasury's creeping control over the finances of the royal household. Weren't they better placed than civil servants to know what needed repairing at the palace? Under the new system, the palace would have charge of some of the budget and thus be able to decide on what was to be fixed when and where.

But a more pressing concern for Airlie was the rigid budget of the Civil List which precluded long-term planning. He could demonstrate to the government that after the Peat reforms the palace was now efficiently run but what was urgently required was a bigger budget to combat inflation and more budgetary control to plan for the future. His and Peat's initial plan was to fund the royal household directly from the profits of the Crown Estate. But would the Thatcher government buy such a radical move?

To make the decision clearer for Number Ten, the Treasury agreed in the summer of 1989 to set up a secret working group on "The Future of the Civil List." It laid out the four options: Remain with the present funding system of an annual parliamentary vote; revert to the system that existed previously of a five-yearly vote; move to funding from the Crown Estate on a five-yearly basis; or accept the full-blown palace plan for direct and long-term funding from the Crown Estate.

The high-powered committee which consisted of Airlie, Peat, the Treasury's permanent secretary, the prime minister's private secretary and half a dozen senior Whitehall officials met four times in late 1989 before concluding that the full palace plan "would raise constitutional issues which ministers may wish to avoid."[31] In other words, a Select Committee would have to meet to consider whether the Crown Estate could legitimately be used in this way and inquire into the Queen's personal wealth and issues of taxation.

It is not clear how the Thatcher government reacted to the report as the official papers from the period have been heavily redacted after this author's Freedom of Information request was only partially successful (on account of the royal family being granted special exemptions), but at some stage in early 1990 the palace's more radical plan must have been quietly shelved.

In passing it is worth pointing out that the final report contained an important piece of new information about the true status of the Crown Estate. Contrary to the widespread public belief that the Queen still "owned" the land in some personal capacity and as such had a right to reclaim its rental income if she so wished, the report stated that it was "not a private landed estate" in the most unequivocal terms. "It is a public estate (which was confirmed by the 1971-2 Select Committee [on the Civil List], and since 1760 the revenue has been 'looked upon as part of the income, not of the sovereign but of the State' ["The Crown Estate." published by HMSO 1960]. As State income, the surplus property belongs to the Consolidated Fund and once there the surplus is no different from any other public revenue."[32] In other words, the money was not the Queen's but the Treasury's – although even today many still erroneously believe that it is hers.

Around this time Airlie came up with a revised scheme: the annual Civil List should be raised from £5m to £8m but it should be set at that amount for a whole decade. Although the Crown Estate link had gone, it remained a highly ambitious plan. In effect, he was betting the farm that inflation in the eighties would not outstrip the pay rise. If he got his sums wrong (based on a 7.5% inflation rate) it would be disastrous for the palace as they would soon run out of money and have to go cap in hand to the government who could demand greater Treasury control over spending as the price for being bailed out. As it happened, inflation went down in the nineties and it proved a generous deal – but Airlie could not have foreseen this at the time and he had sleepless nights worrying about it.[33]

There is no record of the matter being discussed by cabinet in 1990 although ironically in its July 19th meeting, immediately prior to the announcement of a higher Civil List, government ministers had agreed that "with high inflation and low growth it was particularly important to restrain public expenditure… The Prime Minister summing the discussion said that the cabinet… would need to have the will to restrain spending in what was clearly a very difficult year."[34]

This still left the problem of getting it through parliament where some Labour support might be needed. Here the Prime Minister again proved a friend to the palace. To square the deal with Labour she arranged for her private secretary Andrew Turnbull and the Treasury permanent secretary Sir Peter Middleton to meet with the party leader Neil Kinnock who in the seventies had voiced anti-monarchist views but had now moved to the centre of his party. In the end, when it came up for debate on July 24th,

1990, the announcement was only made on the day and only 20 minutes of parliamentary time was allocated. Most of this was taken up by a statement from the Prime Minister saying that the new settlement was "appropriate for the dignity of the Crown" and a response from the leader of the opposition. Kinnock asked one innocuous question about what steps had already been taken to improve efficiency at the palace which was easily answered by Mrs Thatcher who added "I am grateful to the Right Hon. Gentleman for his support."[35] Some potentially embarrassing details about higher allowances for junior members of the royal family – such as Prince Edward's rise from £20,000 to £100,000 – were not even read out by the Prime Minister but buried in a written statement in the official Commons record Hansard. As had happened with the Civil List bills in 1947, 1952 and 1971 – and the Sovereign Grant legislation in 2011 – it was a parliamentary stitch up.

But of course the real winner was the palace. It largely achieved its aim of becoming master of its own financial destiny. During Mrs Thatcher's tenure Lord Airlie had always been ahead of the game, pre-empting any assault on the royal household funding by putting his house in order. The BBC – another public corporation that successfully thwarted Thatcherism – had done something similar under its pragmatic director-general, John Birt. It did not make many friends among the workforce but it secured the long-term survival of the organisation. By making the palace shipshape for coming decades, Airlie and his crew took the wind out of the sails of Thatcherism.

Chapter 13:

Making a Major Tax Concession

After the Queen's money had under Margaret Thatcher narrowly escaped a burning, it would soon be a case with John Major at Number 10 of out of the frying pan and into the fire. A spark at Windsor Castle on 20th November 1992 would set in train a conflagration which would end in Her Majesty being pressed into paying income tax for the first time.

The tinder was an old curtain near the altar in the Queen's private chapel. A picture restorer's lamp came into contact with the fabric shortly before midday and within minutes the fire had swept through the adjoining rooms in the north-east wing of the castle, setting alight the beams in St George's Hall and climbing up to Chester Tower and the Clock Tower. By 1.30 pm the dome above the chapel had collapsed and visiting tourists looked up in horror as clouds of black smoke billowed above the ramparts of this most emblematic of royal palaces.

With the Queen at a reception in Buckingham Palace and Prince Philip away on a tour of Argentina, Prince Andrew was the only royal in residence at the time and immediately took charge of a salvage operation. Putting his naval training to good use, he organised a human chain to carry to safety ancient tapestries, huge canvasses and other precious items (thankfully, many artworks and furniture were already in storage) but serious damage was done to 115 rooms, including the Private Chapel, the Grand Reception Room and the State Dining Room. Later that afternoon, the Queen dressed in a distinctly unregal headscarf and raincoat arrived on the scene to inspect the charred remnants of her home since childhood. As Prince Andrew admitted in the subsequent press conference that evening, she was "shocked and devastated."

Three days later, the Heritage Secretary, Peter Brooke, announced to the House of Commons that the government would pay for the restoration work. In the following debate it emerged that the castle was uninsured and that the repair bill could run to £20m-40m. This triggered an outcry on the opposition benches of the chamber with Alex Salmond MP, the Leader of the Scottish National Party, summing up the mood when he called the government's response "a blank cheque" and argued that if the taxpayer was expected to pay the bill then "the royal family should pay taxes like everyone else."

The debate was soon taken up in the popular press with the *Daily Mail* attacking the royal family for its "wealthy insensitivity" and demanding that "the Queen must now listen." Even the venerable correspondence page of the *Times* made it their top topic day after day: "If Windsor Castle belongs to the state but the Queen regards it as her home, should she not pay rent?" asked one reader, while another argued, "I cannot see any reason why the Queen should not herself pay to repair damage caused to those parts of the castle which are not open to the public."[1]

Ordinarily, the restoration payments might have been accepted without a public row. After all – as the Heritage Secretary pointed out to MPs – the castle was "state property" and it was the responsibility of the government to ensure that such official residences were maintained "in a manner commensurate with [their] status." But these were not ordinary times.

The hostile media coverage did not come out of the blue. It had been brewing for well over a year. In June 1971 the ITV programme *World in Action* provoked a press storm by revealing that the Queen's tax exemption had no historical or constitutional basis. Contrary to what was commonly assumed, it was an exception to the general rule established in the 19th century that monarchs should pay income tax like their subjects. The investigation was based on exhaustive archival research by Phillip Hall whose book "Royal Fortune: Tax, Money and the Monarchy" led to another round of Queen-bashing when it was published in January 1992.

At this time, the behaviour of younger royals also poured fuel on the fire burning into the monarch's money. In February the *Sun* published intimate pictures of the Duchess of York on holiday in the South of France with the Texan millionaire Steve Wyatt. More embarrassing still was the publication by the *Daily Mirror* in August of photographs of the Duchess lying topless on a sun lounger having her toes sucked by her American financial adviser, John Bryan.

That summer the marriage of the Prince and Princess of Wales also went into meltdown after the June serialisation in the *Sunday Times* of Andrew Morton's book "Diana: Her True Story." Based on taped interviews with Diana, it disclosed her heartache over her husband's affair with Camilla and her fraught relationship with other members of the royal family. Then in late August the *Sun* revealed the intimate contents of a recorded conversation between Diana and her close friend James Gilbey which became known as the "Squidgy tapes" after he responded to her calling him darling by referring to her throughout as Squidge or Squidgy.

Brick by brick the traditional deference of the media towards the royal family had been dismantled. Now that their royal romances had been laid bare it was open season on their royal finances too. This coincided with a growing fashion in the press to print rich lists. It began in 1989 with *Fortune* magazine's study of global wealth estimating the Queen's personal assets at £7 billion which if correct – as her biographer pointed out – would have made her "the world's richest woman."[2] This claim was indeed made in a 1991 survey by *Harpers and Queen* and a year later the 1992 *Sunday Times Rich List* dubbed her Britain's wealthiest person.

No wonder that when the Queen delivered her anniversary speech to the Guildhall on November 24th she looked under pressure from all sides. Her voice still weak from inhaling smoke from the fire and the after-effects of a cold, she first made a heartfelt call for understanding: "1992 is not a year on which I shall look back with undiluted pleasure… In the words of one of my more sympathetic correspondents, it has turned out to be an annus horribilis." But in a less-quoted but more significant line she hinted that change might be in the offing: "No insti-tution – City, Monarchy, whatever – should expect to be free from the scrutiny of those who give it their loyalty and support, not to mention those who don't."

We now know from recently-released cabinet papers that the speech was probably co-ordinated with the government's PR fight-back plan which was formally agreed two days later. The minutes of the cabinet meeting of November 26th record that ministers discussed how: "Recent media coverage of the Royal Family had been intrusive and intolerable. Members of the Royal Family were being put under extreme strain... The Government should reinforce the Queen's initiative by strong expressions of support for the institution of the monarchy. The Prime Minister might consider making this the centre-piece of a major speech in due course. Support from other leading figures in public life such as the Archbishop of Canterbury and the Cardinal Archbishop of Westminster, could also be timely."[3]

But the real bombshell coming from the cabinet that day concerned tax: "The Prime Minister said that several months ago the Queen, who was not subject to taxation, had asked him to consider arrangements by which she could pay the equivalent of income tax on her private income... The Queen had also proposed taking personal financial responsibility for some payments currently met from the Civil List."[4]

Later that afternoon John Major announced the details to a surprised House of Commons. The Queen would voluntarily pay income tax on her private fortune and the Prince of Wales would do something similar on his income from the Duchy of Cornwall. She also agreed that the Civil List allowances of other members of the royal family (including Princess Anne, Prince Andrew, Prince Edward and Princess Margaret) would now be paid from her own funds.

One of the great ironies is that the most deleterious reform of the Queen's finances was delivered by one of her greatest admirers. In his memoirs, the fervent royalist John Major acknowledged how helpful her audiences were: "I hope Tony Blair seeks her advice and heeds her response. I found them invaluable on many occasions." He later told her biographer Robert Hardman that he was initially opposed to any tax change: "the fact of the matter is that we would not have required the Queen to pay tax. I did not require the Queen to pay tax."[5]

The process – he explained – had begun "in 1991 on the initiative of the Queen [and] much thought had been given to the matter by Buckingham Palace and the Treasury" and a joint working party (with from the Revenue two officials led by Andrew Turnbull and from the palace Lord Airlie, Michael Peat and Sir Robert Fellowes) was set up in February 1992.

When in March the Queen had a pre-budget meeting with the Chancellor of the Exchequer –according to the diary account of Woodrow Wyatt from his talk with Norman Lamont – she only wanted to discuss the issue of paying income tax and was beginning to believe that she should. Lamont replied that he thought the answer lay in handing over all of the Crown Estates to her and then paying the tax on that income which would be more than she would get from the Civil List.[6]

At this stage the Chancellor was even less keen than his Prime Minister to impose income tax and Wyatt would later tell the Queen Mother that Norman Lamont unequivocally did not want the Queen to pay income tax but the prime minister overruled him on the issue.[7]

Major met with the Queen in September at Balmoral to discuss the conclusions of the Treasury working group. The plan was to announce the measures in the New Year with them coming into effect on 1st April 1993 but the Windsor Castle fire and the media's hostile reaction to the high repair costs changed everything. A sense of panic was detected by the diarist Woodrow Wyatt on November 26th when the Queen's private secretary Robin Janvrin told him that the prime minister was going to announce that the Queen had actually volunteered to pay tax when it had been discussed three months earlier. Wyatt judged this a huge error, fearing that it would create a feeding frenzy among the tabloids and the asking of awkward questions about the amount of tax the Queen should pay.[8]

In retrospect, the palace's handling of the tax issue appears inept in the extreme. The PR car crash was the result of always being behind the curve and allowing the media to set the agenda. The impression was given that the Queen had been forced to pay tax due to pressure from the newspapers with the *Sun* leading the charge and claiming all the credit: "The Queen pays tax and it's victory for people power."

On November 26th – the day of the tax announcement – the PR

consultant Tim Jackson wrote presciently to the *Times*: "The National Heritage Secretary's premature assurance that the government would foot the bill… robs the Queen of the public relations opportunity of the decade by not allowing her to preserve a national treasure and pay for what will undoubtedly be one of the most challenging and impressive restoration projects of our time."[9]

When the palace did eventually get on the front foot, the damage had already been done. On 11th February 1993, it was announced that the royal palaces and their art treasures would be opened up to paying visitors (the money would later be used to finance the Windsor Castle repairs without recourse to public funds). In an unprecedented press conference in the picture gallery of St James's Palace, Lord Airlie, the Lord Chamberlain responsible for running the royal household, announced the precise details of the new tax arrangements that the Prime Minister had given to parliament an hour earlier. Tax would not be charged on what were deemed public assets like the official residences or on bequests from one sovereign to the next like the transfer of Balmoral and Sandringham but the Queen and Prince Charles had agreed on a voluntary basis to pay income tax and capital gains tax on their private income from April 1993. In an equally remarkable interview to BBC News that evening, Michael Peat, the household's director of finances, said that: "The Queen is a very pragmatic person. She appreciates that there is a general feeling she should pay taxes."[10]

"Too little too late" was how the press generally greeted the news with the odd exception. While the *Times* applauded the new arrangements as a step in the right direction to "pay as you reign", the *Independent* thought them "not as tough as they should be" and *Daily Mirror* moaned that "the Queen is set to become Britain's biggest tax 'dodger.'"

The reaction of the Queen Mother was equally unenthusiastic – but for different reasons.

When the diarist Woodrow Wyatt met her at Newbury racecourse on 28th November 1992, she put much of the blame on the Prime Minister for her daughter having to pay tax. According to this account, the Queen let John Major persuade her – something that would never have happened under Mrs Thatcher who was more of a patriot.[11]

Before the decision was formally announced on November 26th, the tricky task of breaking the news to the Queen Mother was given to the Queen's private secretary Sir Robert Fellowes who was a member of the joint Treasury-palace working party. He was right in anticipating that she would not be pleased as when he explained the details during an early evening appointment at Clarence House, there was a long pause before she said, "I think we will have a drink." The resort to a Martini for her and a whisky and water for him was her way of saying that she did not blame him personally but nevertheless thought that the decision was wrong.

According to her authorised biographer William Shawcross, "she was concerned lest acceptance of such reform should imply criticism of the Queen and her predecessors, particularly the King, for not having paid tax earlier."[12] When Shawcross was later asked to cast more light on her embarrassment (and respond to related financial questions), he felt that he was not "the best qualified person to answer them."[13]

The reason for the sensitivity was that George VI stood out from monarchs who preceded him by enjoying the privilege of being totally exempt from income tax. The question of whether he should or should not pay much exercised the minds of the Treasury which in the spring of 1937 began the process of setting his public grant for the rest of the reign. The issue of "the King and taxation" came up in the first meeting of the Select Committee on the Civil List on April 8th which was chaired by the Chancellor of the Exchequer Neville Chamberlain and included members who were committed royalists like Sir Winston Churchill and David Lloyd George as well as leading figures in the Labour Party like Clement Attlee and George Benson who might be expected to ask awkward questions about the king's private income. Treasury officials helped to avoid the disclosure of any embarrassing information by providing Chamberlain alone with an updated version of a secret report which was written a year earlier for Edward VIII's Civil List. Entitled "Taxation Questions" and marked "SECRET", the document spelled out the monarch's legal liability to pay tax since the days of Queen Victoria.

In a note accompanying the report, one Treasury official asked "You dealt with the taxation questions orally last year – and I assume you will deal with them… similarly this year." The Chancellor responded in a scrawled barely legible hand "I do propose to deal with it orally."[14]

The fact that there is no further written reference to the tax issue in the National Archives does suggest that Chamberlain wanted to keep under wraps any formal record of his decision-making. Ordinarily a decision as important as relieving the sovereign of income tax would not be taken by a senior Treasury official or even a Select Committee but would need the agreement of the Chancellor or even the Prime Minister. To add to the mystery, one of the relevant files "Royal Family: Civil List: 12 October 1936-23 May 1937" was destroyed due to "a clerical error."[15]

One consideration that probably swung his decision in favour of a tax exemption was the cost of the abdication settlement for the new king. The original deal struck on the 10th December 1936 had begun to unwind. At the time, it had been agreed that the Duke of Windsor who claimed to be short of funds would be paid £25,000 a year in return for handing over to his brother Balmoral, Sandringham and the royal heirlooms. The plan was for the government to be responsible for the payments with the future king agreeing to underwrite the deal if there were any difficulties with the Treasury. Many expected the details of the annuity would be written into the new Civil List.

But in the spring of 1937 it emerged that the Duke had lied about his personal wealth. Instead of "being badly off" as he claimed, he had – as the king's treasurer Ulrick Alexander later revealed – a private fortune of £1.1m. He had deceived both his brother and his greatest friend in parliament Sir Winston Churchill who mindful of the political consequences warned Chamberlain in a letter: "The moment this is disclosed the Labour Party could hardly help drawing the moral of the very large savings which it is possible for Royal persons to make, and argue that the existing Civil List should be reduced."[16]

The Chancellor clearly recognised that once the Duke's private fortune became known it would be impossible to persuade parliament with its large contingent of Labour MPs to vote any public funds to him. For this reason there was no mention of his annuity in the Civil List Bill which was laid before parliament on 24th May 1937. The Bill was the last legislative measure presented to parliament by Baldwin's government. He resigned on May 26th and was replaced by Chamberlain who unlike his predecessor held little residual sympathy for the ex-king.

As Prime Minister, Chamberlain had more opportunity to meet face to face with the new monarch and early in his tenure he would have had to explain in person that the Duke's annuity could never be paid from the public purse. At some point in the next 6-9 months they must have agreed on an informal deal. The king would finance his brother's allowance out of his own pocket and in return he would be exempted from paying income tax. This tax break enabled Chamberlain to avoid the political row that would have ensued if he had gone back to parliament to ask for an increase in the Civil List and it relieved the king of some of the financial worries of finding the money to bankroll his brother.

George VI's total exemption can be been seen as the culmination of a process beginning in the previous century of a succession of monarchs chiselling away at the scope of income tax.[17] It had originally been introduced between 1798-1815 as a temporary measure to fund the Napoleonic Wars, but in 1842 the newly-elected Prime Minister Sir Robert Peel brought it back to plug a black hole in the public finances. This presented a dilemma for Queen Victoria who could have invoked the traditional defence of Royal Prerogative which asserts that the monarch is above the law and is not liable to tax unless an act of parliament expressly makes him or her so.

But initially at least Victoria raised no objection to paying the tax. Sir Robert Peel told the House of Commons in March 1842 that she had "stated to him that if the financial condition of the country was such that, in a time of peace, Parliament should think it necessary to subject all incomes to a certain charge, it was her determination that her own income should be subjected to a similar burden."[18] She would set an example – even though she was not obliged to pay.

One reason why she was so amenable was that she regarded the tax as temporary. Another was that she was hopeful that her Civil List might be increased as compensation – particularly since Prince Albert had been persistently lobbying the government for the grant to be raised from £30,000 to £80,000 a year. A further factor was that the level of tax was not especially onerous, being levied at a rate of only 3% on income over £150.

When it came to her Civil List, the tax was imposed on Class I which paid for her private expenditure from the Privy Purse and Class III which funded the expenses of her household. There was originally no tax to the Queen on Class II which was deducted at source on the salaries of her staff, but from 1872 tax was extended to her on any savings she made from this category of expenditure. By 1886 she was paying about £6,675 a year in income tax on her Civil List with the total sum between 1886 and 1896 amounting to £73,405.[19]

With her private spending outstripping her public grant, the Queen now began to have second thoughts about the wisdom of her earlier decision. "I believe the Queen always regretted having given way to Sir Robert Peel in this matter," wrote Sir Edward Hamilton, a senior Treasury official at the turn of the century. "And no wonder; for when the tax was re-imposed in 1842 it was avowedly a temporary tax. The Queen was asked to set Her subjects the example of submitting to a temporary burden."[20]

But it was not until Victoria died in January 1901 that battle between palace and Treasury was well and truly joined. Edward VII was the first to throw down the gauntlet in a discussion about the new Civil List with Hamilton on February 2nd: "He liked the idea of being relieved (if it were possible) of such charges as the payment of income tax, postage and telegraph charges."[21] Hamilton agreed that the tax was "on the whole wrong and unnecessary" and in May tried to press the Chancellor of the Exchequer, Sir Michael Beach, to be more conciliatory.[22]

But on 18th June in response to a backbench MP's question about any possible changes to the tax arrangements, the Chancellor made it clear that his government would not back down: "When Sir Robert Peel introduced the Income Tax in 1842 he was authorised by the late Queen to announce to parliament that Her Majesty would pay income tax on the Privy Purse and on Class III of the Civil List. It was so paid during her late Majesty's reign. We have advised that a similar course should be taken now and that course will be followed."[23] The significance of this statement was that Treasury now regarded the temporary liability as permanent. After almost sixty years of the monarch paying tax, a short-term measure had become set in stone as a royal convention.

The king soon found that the newly taxable income inadequate for his extravagant lifestyle and in 1904 he rallied his troops to fight for a revision of the Civil List. Hamilton who found the king's overspending on such matters as Sandringham estate "appalling" argued that increasing the public grant was no solution and that "if anything has to be done it would be best to terminate the arrangement whereby the king pays income tax."[24] But the government stood its ground and for the rest of his reign Edward grudgingly paid tax on his Civil List at a rate of about £18,000 a year.[25]

His successor George V proved more successful at chipping away at the tax liability. By 1910 the power dynamic between the palace and government had changed dramatically with the Asquith administration now needing the acquiescence of the sovereign to get its controversial reform of the House of Lords through parliament without provoking a constitutional crisis. In the early months of the reign, a deal was struck whereby the Civil List would no longer be liable to income tax in return for it being responsible for the cost of state visits, which previously had been paid by the Treasury.

When David Lloyd George, the Chancellor of the Exchequer, announced the terms to the House of Commons in July 1910 he admitted that setting off against each other "these two troublesome difficulties" could not exactly be called "a bargain" but argued that it was illogical for the state to tax the maintenance grant of the sovereign since "It is either adequate or it is not adequate for that purpose. If you deduct the sum of Income Tax it seems to be giving me with one hand and taking away with another."[26] Again and again he emphasised that the payment was a voluntary act by the monarch: "It was levied as a result of quite a voluntary undertaking by Queen Victoria when income tax was enacted in 1842. It was purely a voluntary promise on her part to pay the income tax which was then understood to be a temporary charge."

It has been pointed that Lloyd George was being disingenuous in both these arguments.[27] By suggesting that the Civil List was only used for public expenditure he conveniently forgot how the Privy Purse element of the grant funded the private spending of the sovereign and by concentrating solely on Victoria's voluntary payment of tax, he turned a blind eye to the way her son Edward VII was effectively forced to pay tax.

But the statement was significant in what it showed about the informal connections between income tax and the Civil List. Strictly speaking there should be no linkage; if it is right to tax kings and queens like any normal citizen, then they should be taxed irrespective of any external financial considerations. But in practice income tax has been used as a balancer against the Civil List swinging one way or another according to how high the grant is set. When the Civil List was expected to be generous, Queen Victoria was obliged to pay tax and did so willingly. When the Civil List was lower than anticipated, Edward VII wanted to be relieved of the tax burden but eventually had to relent. It was only when Baldwin's government wanted to add new obligations to the Civil List (and gain political favour) that the tax was taken off the public grant – although George V continued to pay tax on his private investments.

Total exemption from tax was granted to George VI mainly because the government wanted to avoid the embarrassment of raising the Civil List to pay for his unexpectedly costly abdication settlement and the most likely reason why his daughter Elizabeth II inherited this tax dispensation was that that the government calculated that if they did away with it, the Civil List would have to rise causing a public row during a period of national austerity.

In a newly-declassified and highly revelatory 1989 note on taxation, the Treasury admitted that this was indeed their general thinking: "in practice it should be noted that immunity from taxation has enabled the Government to pay a small Civil List confined to the specific official aspects and thus keep the whole issue of financing the monarchy in a rather lower key than would otherwise be the case." Tax was one half of the dual funding approach: "the State provides for the monarchy in two ways: first through explicit finance (currently votes and the Civil List) and secondly by foregoing tax on the Sovereign's private wealth."[28]

In this sense the tax has always been arbitrary, dependent on the swings both in the public grant and in the public mood. It was public pressure that caused the tax to be re-imposed in 1992 – although people forget that the Queen only agreed to do this on a voluntary basis rather than as of right. This allows some flexibility in a future financial settlement for the balance to be changed again between being fully taxed or being fully funded by the state.

Chapter 14:

Counting the Cost of Divorce

When the Queen called 1992 her *annus horribilis* she was not just thinking of the Windsor Castle fire and its financial consequences. In that year the marriages of all three of her elder children collapsed bringing with it equally calamitous financial consequences. As one of her courtiers earlier remarked presciently: "Those girls are going to cost the Queen a lot of money."[1]

The two girls in question – the self-styled "wicked wives of Windsor" – were Sarah Ferguson and Diana Spencer. Unlike Diana, Sarah came to marriage with "a past", having had a well-publicised live-in relationship with the divorced motor racing entrepreneur Paddy McNally. She had strong royal connections through her father Major Ronald Ferguson who was both a relative of the Queen's private secretary Robert Fellowes and the polo manager of the Prince of Wales. She had met Charles when she was 18 and been a guest at his wedding to Diana who became a friend and on-and-off confidante.

Boisterous and unstuffy with an earthy sense of humour, she seemed the perfect match for Charles's younger brother Andrew who with his dashing good looks and wandering eye had developed a reputation as a playboy prince since joining the navy after schooling at Gordonstoun and seeing action in the Falklands War as a helicopter pilot. On her wedding at Westminster Abbey in July 1986 the "fun-loving Fergie" – as the press labelled her – was greeted into the royal family as a breath of fresh air.

The young couple were themselves able to sample some country air when as a belated wedding present in 1987 they received Sunninghill Park in Berkshire. Using Duchy of Lancaster money, the Queen paid around £3m to the Crown Estate for the 150-year lease to 665 acres of parkland between Ascot and Windsor and then provided further funds to build a twelve-bedroom house with a five-acre walled garden, swimming pool, tennis court, billiard room and security guardhouse ("luxuries granted," Sarah would later acknowledge, "but a big house must have its finishing touches if it is not to look half-baked.")[2] It soon became known as South York due to its resemblance to the Ewings' Southfork ranch in the popular US television series *Dallas*, although it would have evoked very different memories to the Queen as the erstwhile regency mansion was earmarked to be her first married home before it burnt down a few months ahead of her wedding in 1947.

To build the Duke and Duchess of York's dream house took another three years during which time their marriage started to crumble. Sarah grew bored living alone in Buckingham Palace while Andrew was away at sea. "Andrew and I were home together roughly one day out of ten," she explained later. "My husband grasped the problem as well as I. 'I am a prince, then a naval officer, then a husband,' he would say. Those were the priorities put upon him and one of the three had to lose."[3] After he spent only 42 nights at home in one year (1988), she began to be seen socialising with wealthy Americans who "weren't the right sort of people" in the view of palace officials as quoted in Sarah's memoirs.[4]

In February 1992 the *Sun* splashed pictures of her holidaying in the Mediterranean with the Texan oil millionaire Steve Wyatt which led in March to the palace formally announcing the separation of the royal couple. Informally it was made clear to royal correspondents that it had been her decision and that now "the knives were out for Fergie at the Palace."[5]

For Andrew the final straw came on August 20th when the *Daily Mirror* published photos of her topless and having her toes sucked by the American financier John Bryan while on holiday with their two daughters, Beatrice and Eugenie. To add to the embarrassment the story broke when Sarah and Andrew were at Balmoral with the Queen. That morning Sarah had to confront her mother-in-law: "The Queen was furious. I had to apologise of course but penance and contrition have their limits – there are things that cannot be put right."[6] She departed a few days later recognising it was now all over. Legal proceedings were quickly set in motion and the divorce became absolute on 30th May 1996.

Since Andrew was on a naval officer's salary of less than £45,000 and had relatively few financial assets of his own, the Queen had to underwrite much of the divorce settlement – particularly those parts dealing with her two grandchildren to whom she was devoted. Although formally the Duke agreed to pay Beatrice's and Eugenie's private school and university fees, the Queen set up a £1.4m trust fund for the princesses. She also provided a lump sum of £350,000 which had no restrictions on its use. In addition Sarah was granted a modest monthly allowance based on Andrew's naval pay.

The issue of where they would live proved trickier. Ordinarily under English law the divorced wife was entitled to a half share of the marital home but Sunninghill Park was not – according to some accounts – fully owned by Andrew. It had belonged to the Queen who had reportedly bought it in 1987 through a trust-like holding company whose directors worked for her lawyers, Farrer and Co.[7]

As compensation Her Majesty agreed to give £400,000 for Sarah to buy a new house for the children and herself with the proviso that it was in their name and could not be sold to raise capital.[8] But the proposed home – Birch Hall in Windlesham, Surrey which was acquired for £1.5m in 1998 – proved too costly to maintain with its overheads running to £80,000 a year and eventually Sarah moved back to live in Sunninghill Park in an unusual arrangement whereby she occupied one wing and her former husband the other.

In 2000 the Queen reportedly agreed to hand over the property to Andrew and in the same year, a new trust known as the Sunninghill Park Settlement was established.[9] When the Queen Mother died in March 2002 he moved into her Windsor Park house Royal Lodge (where Sarah and the children eventually joined them) and put Sunninghill Park up for sale. The initial asking price was thought to be £12m but in September 2007 it was sold for £15m to Timur Kulibayev, the son-in-law of the authoritarian president of Kazakhstan, Nursultan Nazarbayev. The transaction was not made directly in his name but involved two trusts, as a Buckingham Palace statement later confirmed that the sale of Sunninghill Park "was a straight commercial transaction between the trust which owned the house and the trust which bought it."[10] The buyer was reported to have been represented by Kulibayev's business partner, Kenges Rakishev, and the seller by the Queen's Treasurer, Sir Alan Reid, and a lawyer from Farrer and Co.[11] Unusually for a high-end property in fashionable Ascot, Sunninghill Park was left derelict for almost a decade before it was finally demolished in 2015-16.

If the outlay for this wedding gift were added to her generous contribution to the divorce settlement, the Queen could have lost over £3m on Andrew's failed marriage. Yet this was chicken feed compared to what Charles's marital breakdown would cost her.

Just 13 days after his statement to parliament that the Queen had agreed to pay tax, on 9th December 1992, John Major stood up before a hushed House of Commons to announce that "the Prince and Princess of Wales have decided to separate." Given recent press speculation about the precarious state of their marriage, the news came as no surprise but there were sighs of disbelief in the chamber when after saying that "their constitutional positions are unaffected" he added that "there is no reason why the Princess of Wales should not be crowned Queen in due course." In the upper house Lord St John of Fawsley commented wryly that "there would be no constitutional bar but it certainly requires… a strong imagination."[12]

The statement had been discussed in cabinet that morning. From newly-released government papers, we now know that legal guidance had been given by the Attorney General, Nicholas Lyllel, QC, who advised that "the separation of the Prince and Princess of Wales… did not affect their constitutional positions… There was no legal impediment to their being crowned king and queen in due course." After the cabinet was advised that in the view of the Archbishops of Canterbury and York "the separation would not affect the Prince of Wales becoming Supreme Governor of the Church of England on succession to the throne," the Prime Minister warned his colleagues that "it was important that in any public comment on this matter Ministers should follow closely the Attorney General's clear guidance on the constitutional position. They should not be drawn into speculation about the consequences of further decisions about the marriage of the Prince and Princess of Wales which were entirely hypothetical."[13]

It later emerged that John Major's statement was drafted by his cabinet secretary Robin Butler with significant palace input from Richard Aylard, Prince Charles's private secretary, Robert Fellowes, the Queen's private secretary, and Charles Anson, the Queen's press secretary. According to Charles's recent biographer Tom Bower, the Prince of Wales had encouraged Aylard to include in the statement that "their royal highnesses have no plans for divorce" to which was added "and their constitutional positions are unaffected."[14] Robin Butler would later admit: "With hindsight it was a mistake to have said that. It was seen as softening the blow, showing that she was not being thrown into outer darkness."[15]

Following the announcement, Diana was allowed to stay in Kensington Palace with William and Harry and a full complement of staff, while Charles moved to more cramped premises in York House in St James's Palace which he immediately redecorated at considerable expense. Over the next three years, "the War of the Waleses" was played out in the popular press and on the airways. Diana got her views across by lunching with Fleet Street editors such as Max Hastings and David English and leaking information to favourite reporters like Richard Kay and Andrew Morton, whereas Charles countered by releasing private details of his marriage to hopefully sympathetic biographers like Penny Junor and Jonathan Dimbleby and contributing to the latter's ITV documentary on his life where he admitted to being unfaithful but only after the relationship had irretrievably broken down.

The turning point, however, was Diana's interview to BBC *Panorama* on 20th November 1995 during which she famously said that "there were three of us in this marriage" and then made the even more damaging suggestion that Charles might not be suitable to be king.

Seeing how this now undermined the monarchy and an orderly succession, the Queen wrote to Diana and Charles on December 18th requesting they divorce as soon as possible. The problem for the palace was that Diana – as she hinted in her *Panorama* interview – "would not go quietly." After Charles engaged the divorce lawyer, Fiona Shackleton from the traditional royal lawyers Farrer and Co, Diana seemed to turn her back on the establishment by picking Anthony Julius from Mischon de Reya, a firm with strong Labour Party connections. "I had no divorce experience and no interest in doing divorces," Julius recently recalled. "And I said this to her and told her it would be my first divorce case. She said 'this will be my first divorce too, so we'll learn together'."[16]

The 39-year-old solicitor benefited greatly from the experience of the Duchess of York who was aggrieved about the apparent meagreness of her recent divorce settlement and willing to share information on how to best the palace. "Sarah Ferguson was a very, very useful friend to the Princess during the months before the divorce," admitted her media advisor Jane Atkinson. "If she hadn't had her house to go to she would have gone mad."[17] The information was shared over Sunday lunches at Sarah's rented home on the Wentworth Estate. Julius later described her role as that of "a yellow canary," a reference to the birds used by coal miners to warn of poison gas ahead.[18]

"Women leave the royal family in only one mode: with their heads cleaved from their shoulders" was how a bruised Sarah summed up her divorce experience, and as a result, Diana was determined not to capitulate.[19] She was careful to pick the brains not just of her former sister-in-law but also of two other royal divorcés, Lord Snowdon and Mark Phillips, who advised her "to get the money first."[20] Learning from Sarah who was eventually granted a settlement of £2m, Diana asked for £46m up front.[21]

"We negotiated in a suitably tough way," recalled Julius with lawyerly understatement.[22] When in February the Queen wrote Diana a letter concerned about the slow pace of the negotiations, she refused to be rushed or intimidated in any way. When she began to have second thoughts about her earlier agreement to lose her title Her Royal Highness she leaked information to the *Daily Mail's* Richard Kay that "the princess had wanted to remain HRH the Princess of Wales but the other side had refused and that had been the sticking point for the past two weeks."[23] This in turn prompted an unprecedentedly blunt rebuke from the Queen's press secretary: "The decision to drop the title is the Princess's and the Princess's alone. It is wrong that the Queen or the Prince asked her. I am saying categorically that is not true. The Palace does not say something specific on a point like this unless we are absolutely sure of the facts."[24]

The legal wrangling continued for months until on 13th July 1996 a final settlement was announced. It was a more than generous deal worth around £17m to Diana. She received a lump sum of £15m as well as £400,000 a year to run her office. She also got to keep her rent-free residence at Kensington Palace and to retain use of all the royal jewellery which would eventually pass to the wives of her sons. Prince Charles agreed to pay the children's expenses and school fees. Her one reverse was to lose her HRH style, being known as Diana, Princess of Wales, but she would still be regarded as a member of the royal family and have access to the state apartments at St James's Palace for entertaining and the Royal Flight for overseas engagements.

When it came to paying for the £17m settlement, Charles found his personal wealth inadequate. Although in 1996 his Duchy of Cornwall estate had assets worth over £300m which provided him with an annual income of around £5m, strict sales rules prevented him from dipping into its capital. As a result he had to borrow from the Queen whose Duchy of Lancaster assets were more liquid.

Charles was also obliged to sell all his private investment portfolio. "Princess Diana took every penny he had," his financial consultant Geoffrey Bignell later disclosed. "I was told to liquidate everything, all his investments, so that he could give her the cash. He was very unhappy about that. That's when I stopped being his personal financial adviser because he had no personal wealth left. She took him to the cleaners."[25]

The palace disputes that Charles was ever seriously strapped for cash. After 1997 his Duchy of Cornwall profits were able to provide him with a growing annual income stream of over £6.5m from which he could begin to pay back the loan and if he had really been left without a bean he could always have relied even more on the Queen who in 1996 received an income of £5.7m from the Duchy of Lancaster.

Back in 1992 the Queen also had to oversee the divorce of Princess Anne. 19 years earlier her daughter had married Captain Mark Phillips, a Sandhurst-educated Queen's Dragoon Guard who shared her passion for horse-riding having won an Olympic gold medal in eventing. Prince Philip famously noted of his daughter: "If it doesn't fart or eat hay, she isn't interested", but other members of the royal family were known to have misgivings about the match, with Prince Charles being credited with nicknaming the groom "foggy" on the grounds that he was thick and wet.

For a belated wedding present the Queen bought them, as she would Andrew and Sarah, as well as Harry and Meghan, a country estate – in this case, Gatcombe Park, an 18th century mansion set in 733 acres of Gloucestershire countryside. It was the home of Rab Butler, the former Chancellor the Exchequer who had granted her a generous Civil List in 1952. But she did not return the compliment, disappointing the seller by paying via her representative the Earl of Carnarvon £500,000 for a property some thought worth closer to £700,000. "The royal family, you know, drive a very hard bargain," Butler remarked afterwards although he might also have been alluding to the way in January 1957 the Queen had done him no favours in accepting the verdict of the Conservative Party's "magic circle" that Harold Macmillan and not Rab should replace Anthony Eden as prime minister.[26] At the time he began referring to the Queen as "our beloved monarch" in a distinctly sardonic tone of voice and if he did feel any bitterness it would have been reinforced in 1962 when once again he would be passed over for the premiership as Tory grandees manoeuvred the monarch into accepting Sir Alec Douglas Home instead.[27] For his pains, he was in 1967 given the dubious pleasure of mentoring the student Prince Charles at Trinity College, Cambridge where Rab was then Master.

The Queen also bought Anne and Mark the neighbouring Aston Farm for around £800,000 but wisely kept Gatcombe Park registered not in their name but in that of a trust. By the late eighties their marriage was unravelling as they began to lead separate lives. In April 1989 tabloid newspapers published intimate letters between Princess Anne and the Queen's equerry Commander Timothy Laurence. Mark Phillips also had a brief relationship with a New Zealand teacher, Heather Tonkin.

They separated in the spring of 1989 and their divorce was announced in April 1992, a few weeks after the news that Andrew and Sarah had agreed to split. As part of the settlement, Mark got to stay in Aston Farm and commercially manage its 500 acres. He also reportedly received a half share of the wedding gifts including a gold watch, Purdey guns and antiques valued at over £1m, as well as reportedly a lump sum of £200,000.[28] Although Princess Anne had money of her own from a family trust, some of this settlement must have represented a loss for the Queen who traditionally takes responsibility for looking after the divorced non-royal partner. When Princess Margaret's marriage ended in 1978 the settlement involved Her Majesty having to provide new accommodation for Lord Snowdon and in due course on August 31st, £75,000 was paid for the freehold of a townhouse in South Kensington.

Three days after John Major's announcement that Charles and Diana would separate, on 12th December 1992 Princess Anne married Commander Timothy Laurence. Unlike her first wedding in Westminster Abbey, it was a discreet affair arranged at short notice and attended by a small gathering of guests including her grandmother, mother and three brothers, although not her sister-in-law Diana. It had to be held in Crathie church, Balmoral since Anne wanted a religious wedding and the Church of Scotland was more accommodating to divorced people than its English counterpart.

The cost of the three marriage breakups in 1992 was compounded by the fact that in the same year the Queen agreed to fund the public duties of her three children from her own private resources. Part of the financial settlement in November with John Major was the agreement that the £870,000 Civil List payments to Princess Anne, Prince Andrew and Prince Edward (as well as Princess Margaret and Princess Alice, Duchess of Gloucester) would end.[29] The palace later confirmed to the BBC that she had to dip into her Duchy of Lancaster income to reimburse them.[30] So 1992 was a bum year not just for her public standing but for her private estate as well.

Chapter 15:

Looking a Gift Horse

If the marital problems of her bloodline cost the Queen many millions, then another form of bloodstock would prove equally expensive. Her reputation for frugality was belied by her one indulgence – horses. Over the course of a long reign, she has spent a small fortune on equestrian pleasures – whether riding, racing or breeding.

At its high point, the annual outlay on the sport of kings reportedly surpassed £600,000, with the bulk of the money going on keeping 30 expensive thoroughbreds in training.[1] Racing is often viewed as a means of escape, or as her trainer Henry Cecil once put it, "her form of relaxation." But there are other factors at play too. Horses unlike humans do not know she is Queen and allow her to interact normally. In addition it is surely no coincidence that the head of an institution based on the hereditary principle is interested in bloodstock. "You're a brood mare if you're a royal wife,"[2] observed the TV presenter and sometime royal chronicler Jeremy Paxman: "The first duty of any Queen is to ensure the dynasty lives on and to bang out a healthy heir."[3] The "virgin" Queen Elizabeth I famously died childless and the Tudor line had to pass to the Stuarts. But when it came to Elizabeth II a passion for bloodstock was well and truly in her blood as she hailed from a long line of lovers of the turf.

Perhaps the most enthusiastic was her great-grandfather Edward VII. When Prince of Wales he could only watch from the stands as the non-horse loving Queen Victoria broke up the Royal Stud at Hampton Court on her accession, revived it in 1862 on Prince Albert's advice and then in 1892 dispersed it again. On his own initiative he established in 1886 a separate stud on his Sandringham estate, but his commitment to racing was less an act of rebellion against his strait-laced mother and more a way of fitting in with his new circle of rich friends – plutocrats like Leopold de Rothschild and Sir Ernest Cassel and politicians like Lord Rosebery who all owned and bred racehorses and liked to socialise at the Epsom Derby or the Newmarket Jockey Club.

Following in their hoof prints he started acquiring a string of racing horses. The most successful was Perdita II which after winning the 1886 Liverpool Summer Cup became a valuable brood mare supplying him with two Derby winners, Persimmon in 1896 and Diamond Jubilee in 1900.[4] In the same year Ambush II won him the Grand National.

But "Bertie" found that racing was fraught with financial risks as a few high-profile wins could often be negated by the more frequent losses. In his best year, 1900, he had earnings as the leading owner of £29,585[5] but between 1888 and 1896 total prize money was just £5,904, and if you ignore the one exceptionally good year of 1891 the annual average was a paltry £250.[6] It did not help that he had a habit of giving away some of his winnings to his mistresses.[7]

In April 1896 his two closest advisors – his private secretary Sir Francis Knollys and the soon-to-be auditor of the Civil List Sir Edward Hamilton – decided that something had to be done to avoid a financial crash: "we all feel that what HRH ought to do is to give up racing – perhaps if Persimmon is nowhere in the Derby this year, he may get disgusted and leave the Turf."[8] Unfortunately for them the horse at odds of 5-1 against won the race and Bertie survived to live another day.

The matter came up again in 1901 on his accession as Edward VII. "Will he sell his horses... Will he become desperately serious?" wondered Winston Churchill suggesting that his old extravagant lifestyle might no longer be appropriate to his new status.[9] But the king would have nothing of it, expressing over dinner to Sir Edward Hamilton his anger with a lower than expected Civil List: "He was afraid he would not make ends meet; and if that proved to be the case nobody, he said, could attribute it to an extravagance like racing because his racing paid for itself owing to his valuable sires."[10]

He would later claim that the purchase of Perdita II for £900 brought him in stud value a return of a quarter of a million pounds over 20 years.[11] This was just as well since prize money earnings from the Royal Stud dried up during his decade on the throne forcing him to write to his trainer: "We have a number of bad horses, Marsh. I consider it my duty as your master to get rid of these animals to save your reputation as trainer."[12]

His only win of note was the 1909 Derby victory of Minoru who had to be leased from an independent stud rather than the traditional royal one. His fixation with racing success continued to the very end. On being told on his deathbed that his horse Witch of The Air had won the 4.15 at Kempton Park by half a length, he replied: "yes, I have heard of it. I am very glad." He then fell into a coma and never spoke again.

This final piece of racing news was delivered appropriately enough by his heir, the Prince of Wales. After being crowned George V, the new king added horseracing to his other leisure activities despite the initial concern of others that he might not share his father's passion for the turf due his preference for stamp collecting and his reservations about betting. He adored the Sandringham estate, however, and was determined to make its stud a success. After winning the 1,000 Guineas at Newmarket with Scuttle in 1928 he wrote in his diary: "I am very proud to win my first Classic and that I bred her at Sandringham. She is certainly a game filly."[13] But during his 25-year stewardship of the Royal Stud that was to be his only classic victory. With a total return of just 100 guineas "he was", in the words of one royal racing chronicler, "a singularly luckless owner."[14]

Where he proved more successful was in passing on his enthusiasm for horses to his granddaughter, "sweet little Lilibet." When the future Queen was two, he named a foal "Lilibet" and for her fourth birthday he gave her a Shetland pony called Peggy. During holiday stays at Sandringham, he would take her on a tour of the stud and introduce her to Scuttle who was now a much-valued mare. Famous for being stern to his own children, he was quite happy to play horsey games with his favourite granddaughter, allowing her to lead him by the beard while on all fours on the floor – a sight that once proved embarrassing when they were interrupted by the visiting Archbishop of Canterbury.[15]

Her father too was an important influence ensuring that she was taught horsemanship from an early age. Her first instruction came at just three and a half years under the supervision of the Crown Equerry and then when she was twelve she received twice-weekly lessons at Buckingham Palace from the renowned equestrian master Horace Smith who among other skills taught her the essential ceremonial art of riding side saddle. Over the next 5-6 years of tuition, she would be able to open up to him in a way that she could with few others. "She confessed to me once", he later wrote, "that had she not been who she was, she would like best to be a lady living in the country with lots of horses and ponies."[16]

By his own admission her father George VI "knew nothing about breeding" or other equine matters when he came to the throne in 1936 and for the first years of his reign the Royal Stud fared badly. With more than 20 horses in training, it managed only 6 wins in 1937, 2 in 1938 and 5 in 1939. His fortunes improved, though, during wartime when horse-racing was allowed to continue to gee up the national spirit and the stud produced two promising thoroughbreds, Big Game and Sun Chariot which were strongly tipped for success at the Derby and Oaks. In the spring of 1942, the king took his daughter to visit them at the Beckhampton stables in Wiltshire and as soon as the young princess stroked and patted them down she was smitten – so much so that she admitted to not washing her hands for the rest of the day.

She attended her first horserace in 1945 and acquired her first racehorse in 1947. This was the chestnut filly Astrakhan, a wedding present from the Aga Khan which had been bred on his Sheshoon Stud at the Curragh. But the gift horse proved a headache from the off. It soon had to be withdrawn from training for physiotherapy on its weak knees and forelegs. When this seemed to do the trick, in October it was entered in the Sandwich Stakes for two-year-olds at Ascot and came in second winning the princess her first purse money of £81 12s. After coming third at Windsor, it went on to win the Merry Maiden Stakes at Hurst Park, raising hopes that it could run in next year's Oaks for three-year-olds. Unfortunately, it failed badly in the next trial race and a decision was taken to retire it from all competition.

Her other horse proved equally unlucky. Perhaps as compensation for the Astrakhan disappointment, in July 1949 she and her mother paid £1,000 to joint-buy an eight-year-old bay steeplechaser called Monaveen. In October 1949 it won by 15 lengths at Fontwell Park, marking her first racing victory in her own colours of scarlet, purple hooped sleeves and black cap and gaining her £204 in prize money. On New Year's Eve it went on to win the Queen Elizabeth Chase (and a purse of £2,328) at Hurst Park but when it tried to repeat the feat a year later, it fell at the water jump, broke a leg and had to be put down. "This has been a very sad day," said Queen Elizabeth (the later Queen Mother) whose only comfort was that her daughter had not been present to witness the death.[17]

When George VI died in 1952, the Queen inherited his racing colours of a purple jacket, scarlet sleeves and gold-fringed black cap – along with his racing enterprise. This was split between the main base at Sandringham with its 20 brood mares, 7 yearlings and 3 two-year-olds and the royal trainer's Freemason Lodge with its 2 three-year-olds and 4 juvenile racers. The most valuable bloodstock were the nineteen-year-old mare Feola and her 3 daughters, Hypericum, Angelola and Above Board who was the king's last major winner. When it came to racers, the prized asset was Aureole, the three-year-old son of the Derby winner Herperion, who combined a lightning speed with a moody temperament.

The Turf was never far from the Queen's thoughts even in the build-up to the coronation. "You must be feeling nervous, Ma'am," a lady-in-waiting innocently asked her at a grand luncheon at Buckingham Palace on the eve of the big day of 2nd June 1953. "Of course I am, but I really do think Aureole will win," she is supposed to have answered. In fact her horse came second to Pinza in the Derby which was run 4 days after her crowning.

Aureole would, however, prove her worth the following year, winning four successive major races (including the Coronation Cup at Epsom) and earning £30,000 in prize money. By the end of 1954 the Queen was the leading owner with total earnings of £41,000 from 19 wins. This was the start of a winning streak as the monarch became the leading owner again in 1957, runner up in 1958 and third in 1959.

But, as had happened with her grandfather and great-grandfather, the Queen discovered that prize money can dry up just as quickly as it appears. In 1960 she had just two winners from a string of 22 horses in training and her fortunes continued to spiral downwards during the first half of the sixties. By now her two main trainers Captain Charles Moore and Sir Cecil Boyd-Rochfort had been in charge for 25 years and new blood was urgently required.

In 1970 she appointed Sir Michael Oswald her stud manager and in a more significant move made Henry (Lord) Porchester her first racing manager. His formal task was to bring a clearer, systematic approach to her equine empire but he also performed a more personal role in being her eyes and ears on all developments and decision-making at the stables. "Porchey" – as she liked to call him – had known her since 1944 when he was a lieutenant in the Royal Horse Guards and regularly attended functions at Buckingham Palace, most famously sneaking out into the Mall with her to celebrate VE night in 1945. His father had been a successful racehorse owner and breeder whose Highclere stud had bred the 1930 Derby winner Blenheim, while his grandfather, the fifth Earl of Carnarvon, had won fame by co-discovering Tutankhamun's tomb. Over the decades he became her closest confidant outside of her immediate family. According to Princess Anne, "Porchey" was the only one who could be guaranteed of being put through to her mother on the phone at any time of the day and without question.[18]

On his watch, the Queen's horses began to have better luck in the seventies as a string of promising racers came on stream. The highpoint was 1977 when Dunfermline won the St Leger and the Oaks, earning the monarch £170,000 on her Silver Jubilee, her best year ever in terms of prize money. But making a profit from the unpredictable world of racing remained a precarious business. In 1974 the Queen won 11 races and £140,000 in prize money from her 22 horses in training, while a year later she achieved only 7 victories and £8,000 in earnings from the same number of horses.[19]

During this period, the royal stables and studs had to be reorganised. In 1971 the Queen bought Polhampton Lodge, a stud on the Hampshire Downs which she had leased since 1964 for breeding purposes before turning it into a training ground for injured or mature horses. In 1976, the practice of sending thoroughbreds to the royal stud at Hampton Court was ended to pre-empt any possible criticism that public money in the state-run palace was cross-subsidising her racing venture. Then, in 1982 she bought the West Isley stables in Berkshire where Major Dick Hern had long trained her horses. As part of the restructuring strategy, Porchester decided that he must move out despite the fact he had recently suffered the double blow of a crippling riding accident and major heart surgery. This caused uproar in the racing community and reputational damage to the Queen, with another of her trainers, Ian Balding, warning her private secretary Robert Fellowes, "If you do not make some new sort of arrangements for Dick Hern it will be the most unpopular thing the Queen has ever done and she risks having her horses booed at the winning enclosure."[20] The decision was eventually reversed but not before the damage had been done.

The purchase price demanded by the West Isley owners Lord Weinstock and Sir Michael Sobell was a hefty £750,000 and to afford it she had to sell one of her most prized assets, Height of Fashion who had won five of its seven races in 1981 and 1982. Sheikh Hamdan al Maktoum of the Dubai royal family paid £1.2m for the filly, but given that it went on to produce a Derby and 2,000 Guineas winner for its new owner and that its old one achieved few major victories in the rest of the eighties, many believed that it would have been better business to have retained it as a brood mare to supply the next line of royal racers.

But the fact of the matter was that she was no longer one of the major players in the racing world and was obliged to sell to balance the books. In 1999 she sold the West Isley yard for £1.7m to the former England football player turned racehorse trainer Mick Channon, prompting one racing correspondent to remark: "a man born in a two-up and two-down council house in a tiny hamlet has just bought the Queen's magnificent stable... in the Royal County of Berkshire."[21]

The Queen now had the added financial burden of covering some of the Queen Mother's racing losses. Ever since the fatal fall of the steeplechaser Monaveen in 1950, she had prudently decided to give National Hunt racing a wide berth but that had not stopped her more cavalier mother from buying a string of 16 jumpers which were trained by her friend Peter Cazelet at his private stables at Fairlawne House in Kent. In her dotage, she became famous for never selling a horse, however old or lame. Eventually the costs caught up with her and she had to rely on her mother to pay her trainer's invoices. After one particularly bad season, she accepted the offer with gratitude, signed the bill and before sending it back to Buckingham Palace wrote under the large sum "Oh dear."[22]

Unlike her daughter who, apart from buying the compulsory sweepstakes ticket in the royal box, never bet on the races, the Queen Mother was an inveterate gambler. She was one of the few private individuals to have had installed in her home a betting shop Tannoy system known as "the blower" which relayed the latest racing results and odds from courses around the country. In the wake of one disappointing afternoon, she sent her Treasurer Arthur Penn a sheepish note saying, "I have lost all your money at Ascot – I do hope you do not mind." [23]In fact, she had probably lost some of her mother's money since we now know that much of her £4m overdraft at Coutts bank in the late nineties was paid off by the Queen – with a little help from Prince Charles too.

The racing costs did not end with her death in March 2002. She bequeathed her daughter her string of 11 horses, worth an estimated £1m. But there was never a question of the Queen selling them as, regardless of the high maintenance fees, it was thought inappropriate for the royal family to lose its presence in National Hunt racing. The Queen Mother's racing manager Sir Michael Oswald was kept in his position and in November he entered his old charge First Love in the Hygiene Beginners' Chase at Uttoxeter. It was the first time a steeplechaser had carried the Queen's colours for over half a century, but although odds-on favourite, it finished second.

Around this time a study of her flat racing stable revealed just how expensive her equine enterprise had become. According to the *Mail on Sunday* report, her total outlay in 2000 was an eye-watering £600,000. £489,000 went on training her 30 racehorses and another £104,000 was spent on her 26 broodmares and the running of her two studs at Sandringham and Polhampton Lodge. When it came to their capital value, the string of racers and the brood of mares were each estimated to be worth £1.8m.[24]

Offsetting some of the costs, the Queen earned £256,587 in prize money from 11 wins in 2000. This proved a fairly typical year. A later study of a longer period found that between 1988 and 2017 she won 451 races and gained £6,704,941, averaging out at 15 wins and £223,498 per year.[25] When asked whether the Queen's racing business made money, the former royal press officer Dickie Arbiter could not give a definitive answer although he did stress that "horse racing is a very expensive business and you do not normally make much money."[26]

But simple arithmetic suggests that her racing operation must have lost hundreds of thousands of pounds, if not millions. Assuming that it costs roughly £18,000 a year to run a racehorse (the mean figure derived from £14,000 in 1992, £16,000 in 2001 and £22,000 in 2017) and that she had roughly 20 horses in training (34 in 1991, 30 in 2001 and 20 in 2008) then over thirty years she would have spent a total of £10.8m in maintenance charges – which is £4m more than her prize money winnings during the same period.

This meant that the Queen – like Edward VII a century earlier – would have to rely on stud income to lessen the losses. By the turn of the millennium, she owned three studs: one at Polhampton Lodge and two on the Sandringham estate – the main one just a few hundred yards from the Big House and the other three miles away at Wolverton (she also bred polo ponies on the Balmoral estate but that brought in little revenue). When Lord Porchester died from a heart attack in 2001, his son-in-law John Warren became the monarch's bloodstock and racing adviser. With a reputation for running a tight ship, he merged the two Sandringham studs into a single operation and gained additional revenue by opening up the facilities to outsiders so that about half of all the foaling was done by non-royal breeders. Some of the foals were then transferred to the Polhampton Stud which came to be used more for young or injured horses than stallions.

As one of the best bloodstock agents in the world, he won the trust of his employer who was herself an acknowledged expert in breeding and racing. "If the Queen wasn't the Queen, she would have made a wonderful trainer," he later told the *Daily Telegraph*. "She has such an affinity with horses and is so perceptive." [27]According to the former stud groom Bob

Rowlands, "She's very knowledgeable about horses. That was the main thing you had to be careful of was not trying to pull the wool over the Queen's eyes because you knew that she was more knowledgeable than you were." [28]

Over the decades she has put her stamp on her stud. She turned Sandringham's old Walled Garden into luxurious paddocks complete with a sculpture of her stallion Royal Applause which complements the bronze statue of her Gold Cup winning mare Estimate standing outside the Big House. No expense has been spared to ensure that her stables provide five star accommodation. Each stallion is now housed in a spacious box with tiled walls, high windows and a reed roof. There is even infra-red lighting for drying off and twenty-four-hour surveillance from digital cameras.

The remote technology permits the Queen to monitor the breeding process on her private device when she was away. "We've got CCTV cameras here that basically can be accessed on any iPads, iPhones and even televisions to watch the foalings and these are on 24/7," explained her stud manager David Somers. "The advantage of the CCTV is that once it's happening I can also be on the phone at the same time, explaining what is going on and talking through the process." [29]

All these mods cons do not come cheap. The heavy investment costs inevitably eat into the income generated from the breeding facilities and the sale of foals. Although the stud probably breaks even, the same could not be said for the racing business which for all her undoubted knowledge of horse-stock and the turf remains an exceedingly expensive hobby. In the 2019 season she had just seven winners over jumps and twenty-nine on the flat.

The one prize that has eluded her is a Derby winner, with Edward VII remaining the only monarch in her recent bloodline to have achieved that honour.

Chaper 16:

Cheating Death Duties

Within the space of six weeks in 2002, the Queen lost her sister and her mother but gained a fortune in art treasures. From Princess Margaret she received nothing, but from the Queen Mother she inherited the entire estate – tax free. The story of the two estates is instructive for showing what happens to the Windsor wealth when it is subjected to death duties and when it is not.

Princess Margaret died, aged 71, at 6.30 am on February 9th, 2002 at the King Edward VII's Hospital for Officers, London. She had been rushed there in the night on the instructions of doctors who were alarmed at her worsening heart condition. The previous day she had suffered a stroke – one of four over the last six years which together left her semi-blind, bed-ridden and dependent on steroids and other pain-relieving drugs. She had spent her last months locked away in her Kensington Palace apartment depressed by her physical appearance and refusing most visitors (particularly male ones). Prince Charles echoed the view of many of her close friends when he told the Queen Mother that her death had probably been a merciful release. One erstwhile acquaintance, Sir Roy Strong, lamented in his diary that her finale was "tragic" after half a century of drinking and smoking had taken its toll.[1]

Throughout her life she had been careful with her own money and her funeral on February 16th was, by royal standards, a relatively modest affair. She had decided on a private service in St George's Chapel, Windsor and personally choreographed all its contents – from the introductory organ music of Tchaikovsky's "Swan Lake" to the final lament of a piper playing "The Desperate Struggle of the Bird." The 450 mourners included show business acquaintances like Judi Dench, Cleo Laine and Maggie Smith, as well as almost all members of the royal family. "It is the saddest I have ever seen the Queen," observed the princess's friend Reinaldo Herera.[2]

Despite her extreme frailty, the 101-year-old Queen Mother managed to get there with the help of a helicopter and a wheelchair. When the coffin was carried out of the chapel to the sound of the piper, she insisted on struggling to her feet to bid her daughter farewell.

In a departure from royal tradition, the princess had wanted to be cremated and not buried. Her body was duly transported to the municipal crematorium at Slough where for the fee of £280 it was turned to ash with little ceremony. She had left instructions that she did not want her children or sister to attend and that her casket should later be interred next to her father's remains in the vault at St George's Chapel.

In keeping with royal protocol, her will was not made public but a later briefing made it clear that apart from a few gifts to friends and former staff members she had left her entire estate to her two children, Lord (David) Linley and Lady Sarah Chatto. The Queen was not a beneficiary.

Since most of her property was made up of family art treasures, it seems at first sight odd that she did not leave any of them to her elder sister. A large part of the explanation must be that she thought her children were more in need of them than the Queen, but it is possible that she thought they might appreciate them better than their aunt given their undoubted artistic leanings. David Linley trained as a carpenter at the Parnham House School for Craftsmen in Wood before setting up his own furniture business and later becoming a non-executive director and then chairman of Christie's UK, whereas Sarah Chatto trained at the Camberwell School of Art, became a professional artist and later married a fellow artist and one-time actor Daniel Chatto. Both benefited in their unroyal-like career path from the active encouragement of their mother.

But Princess Margaret had a less than exalted opinion of her sister's artistic sensitivities. During a dinner engagement in Oxford, she told fellow guests that the Queen did not trust her own judgement in aesthetic matters and that whenever there were designs for new stamps and coins, she invariably showed them first to her sister and her mother.[3]

The Queen Mother also had a low opinion of her appreciation of the high arts. When once asked her own views on a National Portrait Gallery exhibition of paintings of the Queen, she replied: "I have not been to the exhibition, but I have seen most of the pictures, I expect. There have been no nice portraits since Annigoni, and that is for two reasons. One is that the Queen is devoid of egotism, so she does not care about how they depict her; the other is that she has no aesthetic sense – as she'd be the first to admit – and so she does not notice that they are all bad paintings."[4]

The royal reporter Richard Palmer witnessed something similar in 2012 when on a first engagement for the Diamond Jubilee celebrations the Queen visited a special exhibition of artworks in a pavilion near Redbridge: "the guy introducing it to her said – 'this is one of the finest collections of art ever assembled in Britain.' She just went 'oh really' and then walked off. That was it. She showed absolutely no interest."[5] On another occasion at the Turner Contemporary Gallery in Margate, she failed to recognise Tracey Emin and reportedly asked the former enfant terrible of Young British Artists and later Royal Academician if she had ever exhibited internationally as well as Margate.[6]

The first inkling of the size of Margaret's treasure trove came with the granting of probate in 2002 which revealed her gross estate to be worth £7,700,176 (£7,603,596 after the payment of liabilities). Some newspaper commentators judged this a fraction of her true wealth as a recent valuation in 2001 had calculated her assets at nearer £20m. But being careful with money and being a planner by nature, Margaret had undertaken some astute estate tax planning. In November 1988 she had given her beloved holiday home on Mustique – *les jolies eaux* – to her son, David, who later sold it for £1.5m. The transfer fell into the category of a tax-free living gift as it took place more than seven years before her death.

With death duties at 40% in 2002 her two beneficiaries were still left with an estate tax liability of around £3m and to pay it they felt compelled to put some of their mother's treasures up for auction. "I had the sale for a very simple reason, which was an inheritance tax situation, and wanting to build for my family's future and my children's education – normal family requirements," Lord Linley explained in a later interview. "The sale rationalised the collection. We still have some of the best pieces, which we will always treasure, but it was an opportunity to put everything on an even keel."[7] Even Kenneth Rose, a family friend who wrote a well-publicised article critical of the auction, acknowledged that the "children cannot be expected to pay inheritance tax on a hoard of rarely used chattels."[8]

Held at Christies on June 13th and 14th, 2006, the auction of 896 items from the princess's estate inadvertently provided through the sales receipts and the provenance records a revelatory window into the value of the royal family's inherited wealth and how it was passed down from one generation to the next. Despite the bad blood between them (Margaret regarded Mary as insufficiently royal, while the dowager queen thought her spoiled), the princess received a veritable cornucopia of art treasures from her grandmother. Jewellery like the deco pearl and diamond necklace (sold for £276,800) and an art deco sapphire brooch (£66,000). Bejewelled silver items like a George V mother of pearl cutlery set (£312,000) and a gold-rimmed Fabergé clock (£1.2m). On one of the labels Queen Mary described this gift-bestowing process as "giving by degrees" – a reference to the fact that as more often than not it happened incrementally at birthdays, confirmation dates or Christmases. Overall Princess Margaret received at these rites of passage £800,000 worth of presents from her grandmother and if you include the Fabergé clock which was given on an unspecified occasion the total gift bag could be worth £2m at today's prices.

As a life-long smoker, Margaret also received a big batch of cigarette-related gifts. It seemed the only answer to the question of what do you give a princess who seems to have everything. In all, there were 37 cigarette-related lots including fifteen ashtrays, a Cambodian cigar box, a Channel Islands cigarette lighter and array of cigarette boxes and cases. The two most valuable were a gilt cigarette box that fetched £10,200 and a filigrée cigarette case and cigarette-holder, given by President Tito of Yugoslavia on a state visit to the UK, which went for £6,600. As her most recent biographer put it, "the 37 cigarette-based items… stand as a testament to the Princess's prodigious devotion to nicotine."[9]

In the course of the two-day auction it emerged that at least 40 lots were not the princess's private property but official gifts. For instance, a pair of silver model kiwis had been given as a wedding present to the princess in an official capacity by the New Zealand government. As soon as the Queen became aware of this – according to newspaper reports – she got in contact with Lord Linley and asked him to double check whether any public possessions had got mixed up with private ones. She also made it clear that if any items had been given to her sister in a public capacity then the proceeds of their sale should go to charitable causes.[10] Not long afterwards, the revenue from the sale of 47 lots was donated to two of Margaret's favourite charities – SOS Children's Villages UK and the Stroke Association.

This cost Lord Linley £314,700 overall and he paid another £680,000, buying back lot number 793 – an Annigoni portrait of Princess Margaret (one of a pair with the more famous painting of the Queen) – after there was an outcry in the press and the art world at the prospect of such an iconic item of national heritage being lost to a foreign buyer. Many believed that it should have been given to the National Portrait Gallery or at least kept in the family.

Margaret's heirs could afford to be generous as the auction as a whole realised a massive £13,658,728. From this they had to pay the Revenue around £3m in estate tax and another £2m-£3m in capital gains tax on the extra income gained from the auction. Linley certainly did well from his mother's estate (one tabloid dubbed him "the Del Boy of the Palace" and called the auction "a car boot sale") but his critics forget that there was an extremely large tax bill to pay – something that would not be the case with his grandmother's estate.

David Linley and Sarah Chatto were at the Queen Mother's bedside in the Royal Lodge when she died on March 30th, 2002. They had been staying at nearby Windsor Castle as part of the traditional Easter family gathering and the Queen was out on one of her customary rides in the Great Park when she was told that her mother was fading fast. All three rushed to the lodge where they were joined by the Queen Mother's cousin Mary Rhodes and the chaplain Canon Ovenden. Death came peacefully at 3.15 pm. She was 4 months short of her 102nd birthday.

She had had plenty of time to prepare for her final exit and decide what to do with her personal property. In the week before Easter, while bedbound from a recent fall and only able to consume scrambled eggs and a glass of champagne, she made farewell telephone calls to her racing manager Michael Oswald and to Princess Anne in the hope that her equestrian-loving granddaughter might take some of her horses. On Good Friday as a token of thanks for their devoted service, she gave her page Leslie Chappell a pair of cufflinks and her dresser Jacqui Meakin a brooch engraved with her "ER" cipher.

Royal jewellery of a different magnitude was on show when her body was later laid in state in Westminster Hall. On top of the coffin draped in her personal flag sat the crown used in her 1937 coronation which contained the 105-carat Koh-i-noor-diamond, one of the most valuable gems in the world. Next to it, below a wreath lay a simple card from her daughter: "In Loving Memory, Lilibet."

During the four-day lying-in-state an estimated 250,000 people filed by the coffin. The size of the public response took the palace, parliament and government all by surprise and some ceremonial duties had to be rearranged or expanded. On Monday April 8th, the four members of the Company of Archers standing vigil by the catafalque were replaced by the Queen Mother's 4 grandsons, Prince Charles, Prince Andrew, Prince Edward and Lord Linley. So great was the public demand to show their respects that it was decided to lengthen the opening times to 22 hours a day, with entry only stopped at six in the morning. Among those standing guard was Captain James Blunt, a 28-year-old reconnaissance officer in the Life Guards, who 3 years later would record the hit single "You're Beautiful" and attain his own world-wide fame as a pop star.

Blunt also took part in the funeral procession on Tuesday April 8th. Again the public turned out en masse with an estimated one million people lining the route of the royal cortege from Westminster Abbey in Parliament Square where the formal service was held to St George's Chapel at Windsor Castle where the private committal of her remains was completed. The body was placed next to the coffin of George VI and the casket containing the ashes of Princess Margaret.

It usually requires three to four months for probate to be granted, giving executors the legal authority to distribute the assets of the deceased, but in the case of the Queen Mother this was achieved in about a fortnight of her death on April 15th. The reason for the record quick time was that it was simply a formality since royal protocol dictated that the king or queen was not subject to the normal legal requirements to disclose the size of their estate or pay inheritance tax on all their property.

As a scion of Scottish landed aristocrats, the former Elizabeth Bowes Lyon would have had her own personal reasons for disliking death duties. She was born the daughter of Lord and Lady Glamis who owned Glamis Castle in Angus (the site of Shakespeare's "Macbeth"), Streamlam Castle in Durham (the county of much of their mineral wealth) and the manor house of St Paul's Walden Bury in Hertfordshire (the official place of her birth, although most now think she was born in London). Like many landed upper-class families before and since, the Bowes Lyons had to duck and dive using trusts and any other hereditary devices to avoid a crippling blow from estate tax.

"NO DEATH DUTIES!" was how the Queen Mother in a letter to a friend summed up the pleasure of visiting the new federation of Rhodesia and Nyasaland in July 1953.[11] Its status as neither a colony nor a full part of the UK state allowed it tax advantages similar to those in the Channel Islands today. Like many of her class and generation, her views veered to the right: "[she's] much more pro-Conservative than the Queen or the Prince of Wales," wrote her friend Woodrow Wyatt.[12] She expressed her annoyance at some of the fiscal policies of Harold Wilson's government (particularly over Selective Employment Tax) and did little to hide her admiration for Margaret Thatcher's no-nonsense approach to statecraft and her opposition to John Major's eventual decision that the Queen should pay tax.

Given her deep-rooted conservative views, it is hardly surprising that she may have undertaken some estate tax planning of her own. If she did not leave it to the Queen who was sheltered under the sovereign's tax immunity, the Castle of Mey was her most vulnerable possession. Although she stayed in many residences including Birkhall, Clarence House and Windsor

Lodge, it was the only house she actually owned. In 1952 she bought the derelict property at Caithness on the northernmost tip of Scotland for a token £100, but after spending a small fortune in renovation work over the next two decades it would have been worth by the nineties as much as £1m and probably more when you factor in the added value of the royal connection. With an eye to both its high maintenance costs and its likely exposure to tax after her death, she decided in her 96th year in 1996 to put the property into a trust. Prince Charles was made one of the trustees and over the subsequent two decades, he has regularly rented the castle for a week in August. Harry and Meghan also made a surprise visit in the summer of 2018. The current rate for an exclusive weekend is reportedly as high as £50,000 which includes butler service, high-class chefs, fine wines, salmon fishing and deer stalking.[13]

The Queen Mother also used trusts to protect her financial assets for her great-grandchildren. It was reported that in 1994 she placed many millions in a number of family trusts whose beneficiaries were Prince William, Prince Harry and the children of Prince Andrew and Princess Anne.[14] The transfer of such large sums of money (one report put the figure as high as £19m) might explain why in the last years of her life she was seriously short of cash. She ran up a £4m bank overdraft which, as noted earlier, had to be serviced by her mother.

When she eventually died in 2002, the most valuable part of her estate was thus not cash but art treasures. After a lifetime of collecting and inheriting, she had turned Clarence House into a cross between a museum of curiosities and an Aladdin's cave, overflowing with Fabergé eggs, silver cutlery, Chinese porcelain, gilded clocks and Chippendale furniture which were collectively valued at £15m.[15] There was also her fabulous collection of jewellery – thought to be worth another £15m-16m – which included the diamond tiara given as a wedding present by her father and all the valuable gems bequeathed by Dame Margaret Greville.

But even greater riches – perhaps as large as £30m – lay in her collection of paintings. Under the watchful guise of Sir Kenneth Clark, the surveyor of the king's pictures and director of the National Gallery, she developed a good eye for fine art. Immediately after World War Two she bought wisely in a depressed market and, over the decades, amassed an impressive collection of modern British painting – with works by Augustus John, William Sickert, Duncan Grant, John Piper, Graham Sutherland and Edward Seago. Most were bought on the open market but, as with Seago, a few were gifts from the artists themselves. She also got a bargain from John Piper who painted her fifteen magnificent watercolours of Windsor Castle during the Blitz for just £150.

The stand-out painting was probably Paul Nash's Landscape of the Vernal Equinox – a visionary depiction of a pre-war Thames Valley landscape which could be worth well over £500,000 today. Foreign and semi-British painters were not forgotten either. On her walls hung important works by John Singer Sargent, Philip de Lazlo, Alfred Sisley and Claude Monet.

"A veritable art gallery" was how Labour MP Chris Mullin responded when he visited Clarence House after the Queen Mother's death. "A Sickert of George V at the races, an unusual Monet depicting a stark granite mountainside, various portraits of the Queen Mother, a large one of her as a young woman hangs over the fireplace, a series of bleak paintings of Windsor commissioned at the outbreak of war because the King and Queen feared that the castle would be destroyed and wanted to preserve the memory."[16]

Mullin's surprise seemed mild compared to the reaction that greeted the palace announcement on 17th May 2002 that these great art treasures would be going to the Queen tax free. This was due to a 1992 government agreement that exempted from death duties all transfers from one sovereign (or a former sovereign's consort) to the next sovereign. Given the size of her estate (estimated at £50m) and the then rate of inheritance tax (40% after the £242,000 threshold), it was calculated that the tax dispensation could have been worth over £20m to the Queen – a figure that the palace informally accepted.[17]

Not unsurprisingly there was a furore in the tabloid newspapers. "Queen is a tax dodger" screamed a headline in the *Sun*, while "DEAD GOOD IDEAS" and "Queen is left it all by Mum" fumed the *Mirror*. The broadsheets ploughed in too, with the *Guardian*'s complaint ("Tax loophole will save Queen £20m on her mother's will") being mirrored in the *Independent on Sunday* ("Queen's Mother's estate to avoid tax") and the *Sunday Times* ("Queen avoids £20m inheritance tax").

The anger was echoed in parliament – particularly in left-wing or republican circles. "The Queen should pay inheritance tax," wailed Scottish National Party Leader Jim Sweeney, "it's a tax we should all be liable for" before clarifying that it was stated party policy that the royal exemption from paying tax would be ended in an independent Scotland. "There should be utter transparency," argued Alan Williams, a Labour MP on the Public Accounts Committee. "The Queen Mother whose family has benefited from the most remarkable deal on taxation in decades should be treated the same as everyone else." His Labour colleague Paul Flynn, a republican, added more graphically: "If some of the richest people in the country can avoid inheritance tax, why not the butcher or baker, or anyone on a lower income than the royal family. Anyone who owns a house in London these days will be liable to have inheritance tax levied on their estate. This bullshit must end."[18]

The palace did their best to fight back. "The reason for the provision is that the Queen and senior members of the Royal Family can't get a job and earn lots of money," one courtier told the *Daily Telegraph*. "It is also important that our head of state, the sovereign, lives to a certain standard."[19] Another source close to the palace explained to the *Sunday Times*: "The sovereign… needs to have a degree of financial independence to be able to live in a way commensurate with being head of state… If inheritance tax was paid, the money would go and go and go. Balmoral and Sandringham, the Queen's own houses, would go."[20]

Many of the critical articles focused on the most valuable item in the Queen Mother's estate which was also her greatest bargain. This was Claude Monet's Study of Rocks, Creuse: "Le Bloc" (1889) – a 28" x 36" oil painting depicting a stark mountain scene above the river Creuse in Fressline, central France. She had snapped it up for reportedly £2,000 at the Wildenstein Gallery in Paris in late 1945 when prices were low due to the war. By the time she died, Monet was one of the most popular artists in the world and the painting was worth – as all the newspapers noted – £7m.

To dampen down the negative press, the palace made a conciliatory move, announcing in a media release on May 17th that: "The Queen has decided that the most important of Queen Elizabeth's pictures and works of art should be transferred to the Royal Collection. Some of these items, including works by Monet, Nash and Carl Fabergé, from Queen Elizabeth's collection will be on display in the 'Royal Treasures' exhibition, which is due to open at the new Queen's Gallery, Buckingham Palace, on 22nd May."

The Monet was duly put on public display at the new exhibition but its promised transfer to the Royal Collection got lost in a fog of obfuscation. Had it indeed been handed over to the Trust or was it still the property of the Queen?

When as part of an earlier investigation in 2015 this author could find no reference to the painting in the Royal Collection online catalogue, he contacted the Trust for clarification.[21] After a series of telephone calls and emails to various departments, the matter was eventually made crystal clear in a communication from Lucy Whitaker, the senior curator of pictures:

"Her Majesty The Queen inherited the collection which belonged to Her Majesty Queen Elizabeth The Queen Mother and as such it is the private property of Her Majesty; Royal Collection Trust cares for the Collection on behalf of The Queen. The painting by Monet is on display at Clarence House (open in August 2014). As the late Queen Elizabeth's collection does not form part of the Royal Collection it is not included in The Royal Collection Online on the Royal Collection Trust website."[22]

In other words, the Monet and the rest of the Queen Mother's paintings had not been transferred to the Royal Collection as was first suggested. The palace was later criticised for giving – as one newspaper punningly put it – "a misleading impression."[23]

A similar charge of misleading the public could be made about the presentation of the original inheritance tax deal and how it appeared to misrepresent the sort of property that was supposed to be protected for the nation. The agreement was announced by John Major in February 1993 as part of the wider package of financial reforms that saw the Queen paying income tax for the first time. The Prime Minister explained that any bequest from the sovereign (or a former sovereign's consort) to the next sovereign would be exempted from inheritance tax under a new memorandum of understanding.

The immunity did not come entirely out of the blue. It already had some grounding in law since the 1862 Crown Private Estates Act allowed Queen Victoria to escape death duties – although strictly speaking there was no estate tax until 1894 when the government of Lord Rosebery first instigated it. In 1952 when the new Queen's financial settlement was being worked out, Chancellor Rab Butler felt in need of legal guidance on the immunity matter and was informed that under the 1862 legislation the monarch was indeed exempt from inheritance tax. Something similar happened with the Civil List review in 1971 but the wording of the original legislation was in parts vague – particularly when it came to the tax liability of a former monarch's consort. Hence the need for a new Memorandum of Understanding in 1993 which was intended to eliminate any ambiguity and which was the subject of lengthy negotiations between the Treasury and the palace.

When in February 1993 John Major justified the special tax deal to the House of Commons on the grounds of "the unique circumstances of a hereditary monarchy", the Labour Leader John Smith challenged him on the need for a blanket exemption. "Although it is accepted that the assets held by the Queen as sovereign should not be liable to inheritance tax, will the Prime Minister explain why all private assets passing from one sovereign to the next should also be exempt? Although private assets such as Sandringham and Balmoral could well be regarded as having at least partial official use, which could be recognised, is it necessary to exempt all other private wealth from inheritance tax?" [24]

The Prime Minister had no answer to this killer question and could only fall back on the broader argument that the deal was there "to protect the independence of the monarchy" and to prevent its assets from "being salami-sliced away by capital taxation through generations."

No questions in the debate were raised about why the assets of a former sovereign's consort were also granted immunity for the good reason that the Prime Minister did not mention it in his statement – although the matter was referred to in passing in the formal Memorandum of Understanding on Royal Taxation published on the same day. But what was not explained in the report was why consorts required tax privileges in the first place. The most likely reason is that private royal jewellery tends to get passed down the non-male side of the family and so all the valuable gems of female ex-consorts like the Queen Mother were liable to taxation without the waiver.

In justifying the overall tax dispensation the memo stressed that "Sandringham and Balmoral have official as well as private use" reinforcing the impression that the exemption existed principally to protect items of national heritage. It is worth noting on this point that the memo acknowledged that the arrangement had been "drafted in general terms" and warned that "the provisions included in this memorandum will not be used to reduce tax payments by themselves [the Queen and the Prince of Wales] or other members of the Royal Family in circumstances which the provisions were not supposed to cover."

Many wondered whether parts of the Queen Mother's estate overstepped the line. Could her Monet – a painting by a French artist bought in France – really be classified an item of national heritage? Wasn't it odd that she left her entire estate to the Queen rather than just a few choice items and didn't that suggest that she was seeking to stretch the tax blanket to the limit?

The royal commentator Stephen Bates argued that "it was at least questionable whether the Queen Mother's private property was taxable but the issue was not pressed." A year after her death a report by the Fabian Society on reforming the monarchy examined the matter and concluded that "special exemptions, such as those made for the Queen Mother, are not appropriate and should not be made in the future." [25]

An opportunity arose to alter the tax deal when the 1992 Memorandum of Understanding came up for revision in 2013. The new version updated a few minor arrangements to take into account the introduction of the Sovereign Grant in 2011 but left unchanged the section on inheritance tax. It merely reiterated that the tax "will not be paid on gifts or bequests from one sovereign to the next" or "on assets passing to the Sovereign on the death of a former Sovereign."

The drafters of the memo would have been mindful that Prince Philip – although five years her senior – could conceivably outlive the Queen. He was obviously in no way as rich as his wife but in the course of seven decades as royal consort he had accumulated, according to one report, more than two thousand pieces of art. [26] We saw earlier how through his friendship with Edward Seago he built up an impressive collection of paintings by the now fashionable Norfolk artist. Less well known are his 150 artworks by contemporary Scottish painters. Each year he used to buy eight or nine paintings at the Royal Scottish Academy's summer exhibition and then mount them on the walls of Edinburgh's Holyroodhouse Palace which today is home to over one hundred of his canvasses.

On overseas tours he was able to pick up many interesting items of Commonwealth art, and his Australian collection contains some fine pieces by William Dobell and Sidney Nolan and a number of aboriginal works by the highly collectable Albert Namatjira. He also owns two family portraits by the renowned Hungarian artist Philip de Laszlo, as well as some important works by Paul Nash – which must push the total value of his art collections in the direction of £2m plus.

Whether or not he outlives his wife, these artworks will one way or another eventually end up with Prince Charles. The inheritance tax waiver dictates that the Queen will almost certainly follow in the footsteps of her mother and leave her entire estate (including all her art treasures and other private property) to the next sovereign.

In many respects, this process is already well under way – as anyone can discover if they visit Prince Charles's London residence, Clarence House during the month of August (outside of Covid pandemic times). After reserving your place online and clearing the elaborate security checks, you and a party of 20 tourists – largely from Commonwealth countries and the United States – are taken on a 45-minute tour of the private apartments by a Royal Collection guide. The formality of its classical, stuccoed façade designed by John Nash in the 1820s for the future William IV belies a more homely interior. The experience is more like being immersed in a Victorian emporium than visiting a grandiose royal residence. Cosy and chintzy, each room is stuffed to the rafters with antiques, clocks, tapestries, rare books, framed family photos, grand and upright pianos, not to mention a Welsh harp, and every inch of wall space is taken up with fabulous paintings as if on display at the Royal Academy's summer show.

The first waiting room you enter – the Lancaster Room – is wallpapered with seven watercolours of Windsor Castle by Piper along with an Annigoni drawing in black chalk of Prince Philip and an impressive group portrait by Winterhalter. After crossing the Entrance Hall and passing through a gilt-edged white door, you find yourself in the Morning Room overlooking the garden with its lighter pastel-coloured décor and more feminine feel with its silk damask curtains where the Queen Mother's main collection of paintings is hung. The three walls of stunning British art – an Augustus John portrait of George Bernard Shaw, a James Gunn study of Queen Elizabeth, a Lowry and two excellent Sickerts – almost dwarf the more famous Monet painting which is tucked away in the right-hand corner near the window. In the flesh, "Le Bloc" looks as bleak as the stark French landscape it depicts. The guide explains that it reminded the Queen Mother of Scotland and that was why she went ahead and bought it despite naysayers arguing it was not worth the money. When asked how much it might be worth today and whether it is insured, the representative from the Royal Collection can give no clear answer although she will point out that it is occasionally lent out to travelling exhibitions.

More great art is served up in the Dining Room where a sumptuous (although surprisingly svelte) portrait of the Queen Mother by Augustus John stares down on the banqueting table and barking at the heels of the diners is a scene painted by Edwin Landseer of Queen Victoria's three dogs. Across the hallway in the Garden Room alongside one of Prince Charles's own watercolours hang two magnificent landscapes by the Hungarian master Jakob Bogdani depicting exotic birds outside their Windsor aviary. Originally owned by the Admiral George Churchill, the Duke of Marlborough's brother, the pair was bought from his executors by Queen Anne in 1710.

Ultimately it is thanks to the tax dispensation that Prince Charles is able to enjoy this inherited art in the privacy of his home. Other members of the upper classes are not so lucky.

It is common on the death of many an aristocrat for their paintings to be given to the state in lieu of inheritance tax. Over the last decade the National Gallery in London has received a cornucopia of major works under this art in lieu scheme. If Queen Elizabeth (née the aristocrat Elizabeth Bowes Lyon) had not benefited from the generous tax waiver but been treated like the simple aristocrat she once was, then her Monet could well have ended up in the National Gallery rather than 600 yards down the Mall at Clarence House.

The public can visit Clarence House for the price of a £10.30 ticket between August 1-31st; the National Gallery is free and open all year round.[27] In 2018 Clarence House received 11,000 visitors, the National Gallery 5.7m.

Chapter 17:

Trains and Boats and Planes

The Queen's preferred mode of transport will always be the horse but as a lover of outdoor pursuits, she has long been a big fan of off-road vehicles. Her favourite car is thought to be the Land Rover Defender of which she has been the proud owner of around 30 during her lifetime. When in the country, the monarch is often photographed behind the wheel of her trusted Landy – most notably in May 2018 when the then ninety-two-year-old monarch wearing not a crown but a headscarf, green gilet and spectacles was snapped on her way to the Windsor Horse Show. In past years, she has used it to trail Prince Philip in his horse-carriage races in the park. But her 4x4 really comes into its element in the rough terrain of Balmoral where she is not averse to driving at a fair lick.

On one famous occasion in 2003, she invited the then Saudi Crown Prince Abdullah for a spin around the estate. "Women are not – yet – allowed to drive in Saudi Arabia, and Abdullah was not used to being driven by a woman, let alone a Queen," explained Sir Sherard Cowper-Coles, the former UK ambassador to the country, in his memoirs. A little surprised, the future king agreed to get into the front seat of the Land Rover with his translator in the back. The Queen was soon bombing along the narrow estate roads while idly chatting to her guest who became more and more agitated as the speed went higher and higher. "Through his interpreter," the diplomat continued, "the Crown Prince implored the Queen to slow down and concentrate on the road ahead."[1] His blood pressure would have gone through the roof had he known that by law the sovereign was not required to hold a driver's licence.

Her car, though, came with custom-built features. The Defender bought in 2002 included raised suspension to help it drive across the estate as well as electric windows, heated seats and green leather upholstery instead of the customary lambswool. Its fittings were made suitable for hunting parties and when in 2004 it was sold at auction for £30,240, shotgun cartridges were found in the glove compartment.[2]

Today, Balmoral is forging commercial ties to Land Rover in a relationship that appears to benefit both parties. As noted earlier, it offers throughout the year special Land Rover Self Drive treks where owners of those vehicles can pay to go on a 3-hour convoy drive led by a Discovery 4 Land Rover through the stark Highland scenery of the 50,000-acre estate.

In 2018 Balmoral was the venue for two Land Rover events to mark its 70th birthday anniversary. In April it staged a Land Rover Gathering allowing owners to enter "their pride and joy" into a best in show competition, and in the autumn it mounted an exhibition to highlight what the company described as "Land Rover's historic and ongoing relationship with the House of Windsor." Land Rover holds royal warrants as a supplier to the royal household and is the only car manufacturer to have held all three warrants from the Queen, the Duke of Edinburgh and Prince Charles – although in February 2019 Prince Philip had to hand in the keys to his Land Rover Freelander (as well as his driving licence) after he was involved in a crash near Sandringham in which two other motorists were injured and his car ended up on its side.

But the first warrant was granted by George VI in 1951. In a brilliant marketing ploy, Land Rover gifted him the ceremonial 100th vehicle to come off the production line in 1948. His daughter famously rode on top of one during a royal celebration in Hyde Park in 1951 but had to wait another year before she took delivery of her first 4x4. It had special memories for her as it was the car she drove when she served in the Women's Auxiliary Territorial Service during World War Two.

Joining the ATS in March 1945 – as No. 230873 Second Subaltern Elizabeth Alexandra Mary Windsor at the Mechanical Transport Training

Centre, Aldershot – was another clever PR move since it boosted wartime morale by showing that the royals were doing their bit. All the newsreels and magazines were full of images of the uniformed eighteen-year-old undertaking her training in driving and car mechanics – one minute at the wheel of a first aid truck, the next under its bonnet with an oily spanner in hand. Glossed over was the fact that she only served for four months and never stayed in barracks, returning every evening to Windsor Castle. Nevertheless it was a formative experience for the shy princess. In an unguarded comment that revealed just how sheltered life had been until then, she told the Employment Secretary Barbara Castle in 1968 that "the first time she had ever joined in any collective activity was when she joined the ATS during the war. 'One had no idea how one compared with other people,' she said simply."[3] She later confided to a friend that "I have never worked so hard in my life. Everything I learned was brand new to me – all the oddities of the insides of a car."[4]

Her interest in cars has paid dividends over the decades. Largely through family inheritance she has assembled a valuable collection of automobiles with an estimated worth of around £10m.[5] Her most precious motors are housed in a special museum on the Sandringham estate. The jewel in the crown is undoubtedly the 1900 Daimler Mail Phaeton – the first ever royal car and thought to be worth well over £3m. It was acquired by the future Edward VII who developed a fancy for this new mode of transport (as well as some of its female passengers) when at the turn of the century firms began offering him their latest four cylinder models.[6] The other stand-out vehicle is the 1924 Daimler shooting brake – now valued at £600,000 – which was bought by George V to transport members of his shooting party after it had been fitted with special features to accommodate his guns and other shooting accessories.

The Queen's state cars, which are reserved for official functions, are housed in the Royal Mews at Buckingham Palace. The two showpiece vehicles of the fleet are a pair of state Bentleys, the first of which was given to the Queen to commemorate her 2002 Golden Jubilee. No ordinary limo, each car weighs 4.4 tonnes and at 6.22 metres in length is almost a metre longer than the standard Bentley. The pair come equipped with a bullet proof body, an interior shell that can be sealed off against a gas attack and blast resistant Kevlar-reinforced tyres. All that is lacking is a number plate and tax disc of any form which are exempted under the royal prerogative along with the requirement for the Queen to take a driving test.

These two behemoths have been almost overshadowed by a new Bentley Bentayaga billed as the most powerful SUV in the world and one of the most expensive at a list price of £160,000. These are also complemented by three Rolls Royces. Two are relatively recent – being made in 1988 and 1977 – but the third dates to before the Queen was crowned. In 1949, the young Princess Elizabeth was given a Rolls Royce Jubilee Phantom IV in celebration of the car company's golden jubilee. Now worth close to £1.5m, "the Beast" has the honour of being not only Her Majesty's first "Roller" but also the car that transported Meghan Markle and her mother from her Cliveden hotel to her wedding at Windsor Castle in May 2018.

When it comes to the Royal Mews cars, it is far from easy to establish which are privately owned and which are not. The Bentleys would no doubt be classified public property as they are exclusively used for state functions but the Rolls Royce Phantom as a gift before she was Queen might at least be regarded as semi-private. The one car that has definitely been described as "privately-owned" was her Jaguar Daimler V8 which she used to drive around the Windsor Castle estate to visit friends and relatives[7]. In addition to a radio in the boot to communicate with Downing Street, the Jaguar comes equipped with two special features: the arm rest has been customised at the monarch's request with a sliding holder designed to fit her specifically-shaped handbag and on the dashboard next to the cigarette lighter is a secret 007-type button that triggers hidden neon lights alerting her security officers in the event of a smoke or gas attack.[8]

Perhaps the most customised of her private cars is the Aston Martin Volante DB6 that she gave Prince Charles for a 21st birthday present. As a committed environmentalist he felt compelled in 2008 to convert it to run on special bioethanol fuel made from wine produced on his Highgrove farm. This meant that the car consumed the equivalent of four and a half bottles of wine for every mile travelled. Its most celebrated outing occurred in April 2011 when it was borrowed by Prince William for his wedding to

Kate and the happy couple famously drove out of Buckingham Palace after the reception with number plates reading "JUST WED." The DB6 is one of the rarest Aston Martins ever made with only about a dozen vehicles in circulation and when an identical model to Charles's was put up for auction in 2008 its estimate price was £600,000-£700,000. In September 2018 the prince took delivery of his first all-electric car – a Jaguar I-Pace – which he hopes may serve as a totally green replacement for the Aston Martin.

After cars, the Queen's favourite means of transport was probably the Royal Yacht. Part floating embassy, part country house at sea, *Britannia* was like Balmoral and Sandringham a place of refuge for the sovereign. "It represented freedom to her," confided one courtier.[9] No wonder that during its decommissioning ceremony on a cold afternoon in December 1997 as the Royal Marines Band played an impromptu Auld Lang Syne and the Queen stood shoulder to shoulder with Prince Philip and Princess Anne on the Portsmouth dockside, cameras caught her wiping a tear from her eye. According to one of her most recent biographers, she cried more openly a little earlier as she took her final private tour of the ship and said her goodbyes to the crew.[10]

After forty-four years of service, *Britannia* harboured many fond family memories. While it was being constructed, Prince Philip used his naval expertise to advise the interior designer Sir Hugh Casson on its décor, while the Queen offered practical tips on such small details as the shape of the lampshades or the choice of door handles.[11] The ship was fitted with tall mahogany double doors through which heads of state and dignitaries could move from the official receptions rooms to the state dining room before exiting through the grand staircase. The private apartments on the top deck were more stripped down Scandinavian in style, with the Queen and Philip having their own bedrooms with single beds and a connecting door. In 1953 the total bill for the construction and fit-out came to £2.15m.

Although always referred to as a yacht, *Britannia* could more accurately be described as an ocean-going liner. Powered by two steam turbine engines, it was 125 meters in length, 6,000 tons in weight and required a ship's company of 21 officers and 251 ratings to keep it fully operational. To protect the decks from scratches and royal ears from the noise of their footsteps, they were all issued with soft-soled plimsolls.

From 1953 to 1997 *Britannia* clocked up 1,087,623 nautical miles on 968 official voyages where with its capacity to accommodate 56 guests at a table, 120 for a buffet meal and 250 at cocktail parties and receptions where it hosted world leaders of every conceivable personality trait and political stamp. When it docked at San Diego in March 1983, President Ronald Reagan and his wife Nancy were welcomed aboard for dinner to celebrate their 31st wedding anniversary, and as a special treat, the Queen invited them to overnight there. After a Royal Marines band had played for the delighted couple, the president beamed "I come from Hollywood, the entertainment capital of the world, but I don't think we could beat this."[12]

The on-board banquet that the Queen laid on for Boris Yeltsin in St Petersburg in October 1994 made waves of a different sort. After the wine had begun to flow freely, the famously drink-loving Russian President buttonholed Her Majesty and demanded to know whether he should stand for office again. Eventually, following considerable um-ing and ah-ing, she was obliged to ignore the normal protocol of political neutrality and told him to his face: "Mr President, from what you have been saying you will certainly stand again"– a comment which a guffawing Yeltsin took in typical good spirits.[13]

A much trickier guest was King Hassan II of Morocco who in 1980 turned up for a state dinner on *Britannia* almost an hour late and then made matters worse by bringing along some uninvited members of his family and insisting on eating from an icebox of his own food for fear of being poisoned. The Queen later wrote him a thank you letter saying how touched she was by "the way in which Your Majesty took such a personal interest in our programme."[14]

But *Britannia* had a personal family use on top of its official state one – and here it steamed into stormier waters. There were mutterings in parliament in 1960 when the taxpayer-funded boat was used for a six week honeymoon cruise in the Caribbean for Princess Margaret and Lord Snowdon and further disquiet when Princess Anne and Mark Phillips did something similar after their wedding in 1983. Most famously it was used for the honeymoon of Prince Charles and Diana in 1981 – although on this occasion the waves were caused by the young princess's boredom at being cooped up on a ship in the middle of the Aegean and Ionian Seas with only the sailors to chat to while her husband was engrossed in what he described as the "pure joy of one of Laurens van der Post's books."

The Queen also used *Britannia* for her own private excursions. Most summers she would sail in it up to Aberdeen for her annual hibernation at nearby Balmoral. It would also be used for jaunts to visit the Queen Mother in her Castle of Mey by John O'Groats and for the annual cruise round the Western Isles where the family could picnic in privacy on isolated beaches. The Queen Mother herself would occasionally commandeer it for summer voyages in the Mediterranean or day trips to Cornwall and the West Country. One way both mother and daughter could justify use of their own personal yacht was that not only did it offer them much needed privacy but it was also much more secure than overnighting onshore in a hotel or a friend's house. With its full crew of naval officers, it was a floating fortress.

In fact, the vessel was so secure that during the Cold War it was earmarked for use as a nuclear bunker in the event of a Soviet missile attack. Under the so-called Python system, it was decided that the head of state must be kept separate from the war cabinet in case they all got wiped out in a single strike. The best way to ensure that a new prime minister or other minsters could be appointed was to whisk the Queen, the Duke of Edinburgh and a Privy Councillor in the shape of the Home Secretary onto *Britannia* which had excellent communications equipment and then hide in the waters off Scotland. According to Professor Peter Hennessy who first unearthed the secret plans, "she was going to lurk in the sea lochs of the North West coast of Scotland, moving at night from one to other, because the mountains would stop Soviet radar getting to her."[15]

But by the seventies, word of the yacht's high costs was seeping into the public domain. In 1971 the Select Committee Review of the Civil List had revealed that since 1953 it had consumed £8,377,195 of public money from the Ministry of Defence with maintenance costs then running to £757,300 a year.[16] By the mid-1990s, running costs had mushroomed to around £10m a year and on top of that, there was the prohibitive cost of regular refits for the ageing ship. A hefty £19m had been spent on the last major overhaul in 1987 and the next one was estimated to cost a similar amount.

What to do with a yacht leaking money would become a running sore of John Major's premiership with ministers split between economic pragmatism and their emotional bond to royalty. After much debate, the government decided in 1994 that it would decommission *Britannia* when it reached its next refit but left open the option of building a new one which would cost more than £50m. Not surprisingly it was the Treasury who was most opposed to such a course. The Chancellor Kenneth Clarke later wrote: "I adamantly refused, though, to contemplate spending £60m of public money on anything as nineteenth century as a royal yacht at a time when we were cutting back on public spending. I thought that the public reaction would be very negative, and difficult to manage, with every lobbyist citing the yacht when complaining about constraints in their areas."[17]

He was "unpersuaded" by arguments that the amount of money it generated in extra trade (put as high as £700m a year in some quarters) more than compensated for its £10m running costs. But after he faced opposition in cabinet and the Queen made known her "distress" about not receiving a new yacht, he was forced to give way – although in his memoirs he provided a fascinating insight into how governments often felt compelled to defer to the monarchy: "Most politicians are so in awe of the royal family that expressions of displeasure from the Palace about issues bearing directly on the family can usually produce quite significant policy shifts."[18]

The Queen was not above doing some discreet lobbying of her own. According to a recently discovered letter dated 5th May 1995 from her deputy private secretary, Sir Kenneth Scott, to the Cabinet Office Secretary, Richard Williams: "The question of whether there should be a replacement yacht is very much one for the Government and since the last thing I should like to see is a newspaper saying 'Queen Demands New Yacht.' At the same time, I hope it is clear to all concerned that this reticence on the part of the Palace in no way implies that Her Majesty is not deeply interested in the subject; on the contrary, The Queen would naturally very much welcome it if a way could be found of making available for the nation in the 21st Century the kind of service which BRITANNIA has provided for the last 43 years."

In a revealing aside about the palace's attitude to public money, he went on to argue that he hoped that the feasibility of the idea should take precedence over the question of cost and where the money was to come from: "It would not, I suggest, be a sufficient answer to all those who have contributed ideas to say simply that there is no spare money in the Defence Budget."[19] This final remark drew a sharp rebuke in an internal memo from another senior civil servant, Mark Powell: "I am afraid that I disagree with Sir Kenneth Scott's suggestion that the funding aspect should be considered last; I think that all issues should be considered in tandem."[20]

The prime minister was much more torn on the issue. On the one hand, John Major as an ardent monarchist was sympathetic to the idea of having a new royal yacht that could be used by the Queen to promote Britain – or as the former royal press officer Dickie Arbiter argued: "It performed a useful function for selling UK plc." But on the other – as a politician who had been burnt by the furore over taxpayers' money being promised for the rebuilding of Windsor Castle – he recognised that he was playing with fire again. The last thing he wanted was another public backlash against the royals at a time when his own premiership was under attack. "Would I, personally, have wished to retain her? Of course, I would," he told one recent royal chronicler. "But one has to be pragmatic about such things and I don't think such a decision would have been very helpful to the monarchy at that particular time."[21]

In the event, Major dithered – or so his critics claimed. It was not until a few months before the May 1997 General Election that the government announced that if re-elected it would build a new yacht. What they failed to do was square the decision with the shadow Labour cabinet. "I blame myself somewhat", Lord (Douglas) Hurd later admitted, "because as Foreign Secretary I ought to have made sure that the Opposition – Blair and Robin Cook and so on – had some experience of *Britannia* and knew what it was all about. But they didn't."[22]

As a result, when Tony Blair was swept to power in a landslide victory, he turned a pragmatic New Labour eye on what looked like an expensive royal appendage and decided to scrap it entirely without ordering a replacement. Some – including Dickie Arbiter – suspect that "he now regrets the decision." There were valid arguments on both sides about whether or not a new ship should have been built but at the end of the day, an ocean-going royal yacht was an anachronism. It may have made sense in the fifties and sixties as an extremely secure mode of transport to sail royals around the world but the subsequent growth of air travel made it increasingly redundant – as even John Major now largely accepts. The failure of recent attempts to get private sector funds or even lottery money to finance the building of a new royal yacht and turn it into a post-Brexit showcase for UK goods and services does seem to vindicate the earlier arguments of Kenneth Clarke that it was simply uneconomic.

One of the great ironies of *Britannia* is that since its decommissioning it has become a big money-spinner. In 1998 it was converted into a floating museum and permanently berthed at Leith docks near Edinburgh. For the past decade it has regularly been rated Scotland's best visitor attraction. In 2018 it welcomed on board 390,482 people at £25 a ticket with all the money going to its new owners, a charitable trust designed to keep it preserved for future generations and of course economically viable.

Unlike the Royal Yacht, the Royal Train has managed to escape the chop. In 1997 there were plans to send it to the scrapyard but after an efficiency audit by its owner Railtrack it was given a reprieve – although for how long was a moot point. Like *Britannia*, the reason for its popularity with the Queen is privacy. It provides a sanctuary from public view where she can quietly work on her official papers or simply relax and have something to eat or drink in a familiar environment. With all its carriages painted in the claret livery of the royal household, it has been called "Buckingham Palace on wheels" and the nonagenarian Queen is thought to prefer it to travel by car or air.

But there are also practical considerations for why it may be preferable to go by rail. Sleeping on the train reduces the security costs of having to overnight in a private house or hotel. According to the former Keeper of the Privy Purse Sir Alan Reid, "It does offer a very safe, secure and effective way – particularly as the Queen has got older – of having her go up the country in order to do engagements first thing the next morning."[23] Typically she would board the train at Euston, journey to a siding about an hour's travelling time from the final destination and overnight there, allowing her to arrive early the next day right in the centre of town without delays from traffic or bad weather.

Something similar happened when the Queen went to Cheshire for an away day on June 14th, 2018. The visit was made special (and turned into a major media event) by the fact that she was accompanied by the newly married Meghan, the Duchess of Sussex, in her first official engagement without Harry. The two stepped off the train at 10.45 (an hour later than expected) at Runcorn station to a rapturous reception from a throng of flag-waving schoolchildren. Ten minutes later they took a short drive towards Liverpool and the Mersey Gateway Bridge which the Queen declared open. At 12.15 they were back in Chester to open the new Storeyhouse Theatre and watch a special performance before joining the mayor at 1 pm to unveil a plaque, lunch at the town hall and go on a joint walkabout through the city centre. By 3 in the afternoon it was all over and they boarded the train back to London. The next day all the papers were full of photos of Meghan sharing a joke with a smiling Queen, although much later they would report that the trip had cost almost £30,000.

If the former movie actress had expected a locomotive straight out of *Murder on the Orient Express*, then she would have been sorely disappointed. The Royal Train is more functional than flamboyant. Most of its 9 carriages were furnished in the mid-seventies in a G-plan style with few frills. The 12-seater dining coach is narrow and relatively Spartan although it can be spruced up into a state banqueting room for a rare official function. Prince Philip's personal saloon is characteristically shipshape and practical: the bathroom has a shaving mirror specially mounted next to the toilet seat so that he can sit on the loo while shaving; the sitting room with its sofa, chairs and extendable table and desk can be turned into a mobile office; and there is also a mini-kitchen to provide light refreshments without bothering the galley.

The décor in the Queen's quarters is slightly more colourful. Decorated in pastel shades with a few paintings of Scottish landscapes and prints of old royal trains dotted on the walls, her 75-foot saloon of sitting room and bedroom contains a 3-foot wide single bed in one corner with lace-trimmed pillows bearing the sovereign's cipher. The adjoining bathroom is fitted with a full-sized bath and rumour has it that the train must slow down around 7.30 each evening to stop Her Majesty from being sloshed with water during bath-time.

Meghan's invitation was a real privilege considering that the Royal Train is normally reserved for the Queen, Prince Philip, Prince Charles and Camilla. Non-senior royals (including by all accounts William and Harry too) are not allowed to travel on it nor are commoners. The one exception to this rule occurred during the G8 summit in 1998 when with the Foreign Office's agreement, the prime minister's wife Cherie Blair used it to transport the spouses of seven world leaders (including Hillary Clinton, Bernadette Chirac and Naina Yeltsin) from Birmingham to her husband's official private residence at Chequers. The bill came to £11,382.[24]

Historically the Royal Train has also been employed for state funerals. In 1901 it was used to transfer the coffin of Queen Victoria from Paddington to Windsor and in 1936 a special royal train took the body of George V from Sandringham to Paddington – a journey that was repeated in 1952 when George VI also died on the Norfolk estate and had to be transported to London and then on to Windsor. The deaths of the sovereign have a habit of occurring on their private estates and if the Queen were to die at Balmoral, according to recent reports, the Royal Train would be put into service to transport her coffin from Edinburgh to King's Cross.[25]

With the Queen well into her nineties, she now lets the Prince of Wales take some of the strain of the train. In 2018/19 she made two rail trips to her son's three, while in 2017/18 she undertook three journeys (from London to Hull, Leicester and Taplow and back) which together cost (when one connecting flight is included) £67,928. In the same period Charles made seven trips (London to Durham, the Lake District, Llanelli, Newport and two trips from Ayr to London and one from Ayr to Manchester) which came to £141,263.

The publication of such a large figure in the Sovereign Grant's annual report prompted critics to ask whether the train was – as the *Sun* described it – "an unnecessary expense" and should be scrapped. When the same question was put to Sir Alan Reid back in 2013 by the Public Accounts Committee, he said: "it probably had another five to ten years' life in it" adding that "it would then be a major decision whether to invest in a new royal train. I think the numbers would be quite staggering." [26]

As it turned out Reid's first prediction was overly pessimistic. Tests were later carried out on the rolling stock at its storage shed in Wolverton, near Milton Keynes and it was discovered that with regular overhauls its life could be extended many years. "There's no end in sight of its use," promised a palace spokesman, "and no fixed, agreed horizon in terms of when it will become inoperable or be decommissioned." [27] Reading between the lines, one suspects that the Royal Train may not go before the Queen does.

Nevertheless there is no denying that mile for mile the train is the most expensive form of royal transport. When the matter was first investigated by the National Audit Office in 2001, rail travel was found almost twice as expensive as air. By 2016 the differential had widened to an estimated £52 per mile by rail, compared to £12 per mile by air. Part of the problem lay in the high maintenance costs relative to the low usage. In 2018/19 the train cost £800,000 a year to run and was used only 5 times on major trips in 12 months. [28]

The trend in recent years is to travel more by air, but flight still does not come cheap. The Queen's helicopter budget faced forensic scrutiny from the Public Accounts Committee when between 2008 and 2013 it rose by a third from £1.2m to £1.6m and by 2018 it was hovering around £1.8m. [29] But most media venom was directed at Prince Andrew (dubbed "Air Miles Andy") for his cavalier use of aircraft in the Queen's Flight, the RAF squadron set up by Edward VIII in 1936 creating history as the first dedicated air service for a head of state anywhere in the world. He came under fire in 2004 for spending £2,939 on a short helicopter hop to Oxford for an official lunch when he could have gone by train – although he claimed he needed to get back quickly to London for another engagement. Critics noticed how his public duties seemed to coincide neatly with his private pastimes. On one celebrated occasion in July 2013, the golf-loving prince was flown by charter at a cost of £14,692 from Farnborough to Edinburgh to visit the Royal Scottish Fusiliers and the families of those deployed in Afghanistan. This conveniently allowed him to attend the British Open Golf Championship which was being played at neighbouring Muirfield. [30]

Some politicians like the Rhonda MP and former Foreign Office Minister Chris Bryant have in parliament openly criticised Prince Andrew's extravagant travel expenses – both when he was an official trade envoy and when he was pursuing domestic duties. "The Queen has been to the Rhonda twice in my time and she arrived by car. When he arrived he had to arrive by helicopter which cost more than all the money that the local organisation he visited spends in a year." Now, of course, with his "stepping back" from public duties in the wake of the Jeffrey Epstein sex trafficking scandal he will no longer be able to claim any travel expenses from the Sovereign Grant.

When any member of the family used the Royal Flight for purely private purposes they have to pay a reimbursement at the full market rate. In 1999, for instance, the Queen repaid £4,061 for chartering a large 21-seater jet when she required its extra space for her voluminous set of luggage. [31] In 2019 she spent £34, 520 on two charters to fly her up to Aberdeen and back for her annual Balmoral retreat, but this would have been charged to the public purse as she does official work while relaxing on her private estate. [32] This summer sojourn came after a shorter return air trip to Balmoral in May 24-29th which cost £32,734 – although no reason for the journey was given in the official records. [33]

In recent years the Queen has left all the long haul flying to Prince Charles who now stands in for her in most of her overseas duties. In 2019 he came under attack for spending £416,576 on an 11-day trip with Camilla to Cuba and the Caribbean Islands. They travelled on RAF Voyager A330 which was nicknamed Cam Force One after its instigator the former Prime Minister David Cameron who sanctioned its £10m refit and made it available to senior cabinet ministers and royals. In defence of the expense, a palace aide pointed out that the tour was undertaken at the request of the Foreign and Commonwealth Office and Voyager was the most efficient and appropriate form of transport in terms of both cost and security.

One reason why the air costs are sky high is that Charles flies with a large entourage. He often travels with a retinue of over ten staff including a valet, hairdresser, a secretary, a press officer and a private secretary. Some of his officials also undertake pre-trip recces – to sort out the itinerary and security arrangements – which inevitably boost costs. For instance, his swing-round the Caribbean was preceded by two staff planning visits to Havana and Grenada, each lasting about a fortnight. Another two week staff recce to Banjul and Lago preceded Charles and Camilla's ten day tour of The Gambia, Ghana and Nigeria in November which came to a total cost of £216,312.

But even without leaving these shores the Prince of Wales has chalked up a lot of air-miles.

Like the Queen, he has a soft spot for the tranquil charms of the Balmoral estate and in 2018-19 he and Camilla spent a total of £113,467 on seven flights between London and Aberdeen.[34]

With the cost of travel for the royal family hitting £4.6m in 2018-19, it is no wonder that many now regard transport as the Queen's Achilles heel.

Chapter 18:

Giving the Sovereign a Generous Grant

If we now have the facts and figures about royal travel at our fingertips it is due in large part to the reform of the funding system in 2011 which saw the Civil List replaced by the Sovereign Grant. As part of the new deal the royal household was obliged to open up its books to scrutiny from the National Audit Office and publish a comprehensive yearly report listing all its expenditure.

Much like earlier years, the 2019 Buckingham Palace report card made for an interesting read. In the course of carrying out her 140 official engagements and running her large household, the Queen spent from her core Sovereign Grant budget (excluding the Buckingham Palace refit) a total of £49.6m of which almost a half, £23.2m went on wages. In 2018-19 there were 463 full-time employees on the payroll in contrast to 116 who worked at Clarence House for Prince Charles and who were separately funded by him. Despite much talk of achieving efficiency savings, the staffing levels had remained constant in the last decade – as had the pay gap. Just over half of the workforce was female but according to one earlier separate report in 2018 on gender equality, they were paid 12% less than the men.[1]

The median salary for both sexes was £27,000 although that bald figure belied a significant differential between the low earners and the high rollers. On the bottom rung was an unspecified staff member on just £17,633.

According to an earlier study that did give job descriptions, there were employees such as a trainee butler earning £15,000, an assistant gardener on £18,000 and the groom for the Queen's horses on £20,000 (casual staff brought in for the Buckingham Palace summer opening got around £10 an hour).[2]

At the top end there were five senior managers – all on the Lord Chamberlain's Committee and all men – taking home more than £100,000. These were the Lord Chamberlain, his Comptroller, the Master of the Royal Household, the Keeper of the Privy Purse and the Queen's Private Secretary who was by far the highest paid. In 2018-19 Sir Edward Young took home a generous salary package of £211,000, £18,000 more than the last full remuneration of his predecessor, Sir Christopher [now Lord] Geidt. The next highest paid was the Master of the Household, Vice Admiral Tony Johnstone-Burt, on a total package of £166,000. Deducted from his salary was what the report euphemistically called the use of "housing for the better performance of his duties" which was known in the past as a grace-and-favour apartment and which used to charge peppercorn rents until censure from the Public Accounts Committee put an end to the abuse.

For a high-earner Johnstone-Burt had kept a relatively low public profile. He had been in the job since 2013, and when first interviewed by the Queen he had to admit that he had no knowledge at all about how the household was run and had never even set foot on the Royal Yacht despite his naval background. He had joined the service in 1978, seen action in the Falklands, Iraq and Afghanistan and climbed the ranks to being captain of several ships and then vice admiral in charge of NATO liaison in the United States. As he neared retirement he was approached by the palace who traditionally liked to recruit its top managers from the armed forces.

He was required to fine-tune his management approach to suit his new largely civilian workforce. "You have to change your leadership style a bit," he told Kate Gerbeau from Forces TV. "In the military if you say, Kate, I really want this done, NOW, please. It is done… In the civilian world you have to say 'please' a huge amount more and ask if 'you could possibly spare the time etc.'"[3] But he still believed that the two worlds were alike in many ways: "There is quite a lot of similarities in terms of planning and insistence on the very highest standards of excellence." During the coronavirus lockdown he helped organise the quarantine of the Queen at Windsor Castle – complete with 22 loyal royal staff in isolation – a mission which he dubbed "HMS Bubble" because of its "parallels with being at sea away from home for many months."

In normal times his duties included organising huge state banquets at Buckingham Palace and Windsor Castle involving intricate seating plans for dozens of diners who all had to be seated in the right place according to diplomatic rank and protocol. To assist him in this and putting on other official events in the royal residences, he had a staff of 161 in a separate household department responsible for housekeeping and catering. In 2018/19 it consumed £6.3m in payroll costs and another £2.1m in housekeeping and hospitality. Entertaining is an important part of palace life and in the same year, £1.6m was spent on food and drink and £400,000 worth of wine and spirits was held in stock in the royal cellars.[4]

Presentation and communication is another fundamental function of the royal household. First set up as early as 1997, the stylish official website – www.royal.uk – now attracts more than 12m visitors a year following a major revamp in 2016. In 2018-19 a total of £3.7m was spent on IT and Telecoms including an upgrading of cyber security and a costly replacement of the old analogue telephone system with new technology. When it came to snail mail, a further £1.1m went on postage, printing and stationery.

After the staff payroll, the costliest budget item was palace maintenance. Leaving aside the ring-fenced £32.9m for the Buckingham Palace refit, the big ticket item was the £2.4m renovation of Frogmore Cottage, the new home on the Windsor estate for Harry, Meghan and baby Archie. Initially, courtiers tried to sweeten the pill by pointing out that "substantially all fixtures and fittings were paid for by their Royal Highnesses" and that the 19th century grade II listed property was already earmarked for renovation.[5] But as a fuller picture emerged – with talk of a complete redecoration, a luxury kitchen and bathrooms, new guard rooms for their security staff and more expensive work still to come – many wondered why they could not have stayed within the Kensington Palace grounds where the compound was already well secured and where a large apartment had recently been vacated by the Duke Gloucester which would have made an ideal replacement for their rather cramped Nottingham Cottage. If they were still determined to have a place of their own, couldn't they pay for it themselves – particularly since they were not short of money? With the shock announcement of the departure of the Sussexes from public duties in 2020, the Frogmore controversy resurfaced and Harry and Meghan have now reportedly agreed to pay for the costs through a surcharge on their monthly rent.

While most press coverage focused on the refurbishment of Harry's home, what went largely unreported were the repairs to his grandmother's quarters just down the road at Windsor Castle. £700,000 was spent installing new boilers and central heating in the Queen's private apartments. Another expense that slipped under the radar was the £359,000 annuity paid by the Treasury to Prince Philip to maintain a private office to keep in contact with his charities and various patronages even though he had long since retired from public duties.

But all this expenditure was partly offset by one stream of income. In 2018/19 the royal household received around £7m from the Royal Collection as a facility fee for opening up Buckingham Palace and Windsor Castle to paying visitors. Given that the Royal Collection generated almost £46m in admissions and shop sales from the two palaces, this was not as generous a sum as it first appeared. It was, though, an increase of £1m on the previous year and this revenue stream today represents over 10% of the all the money that goes to the core Sovereign Grant. In fact, we now know from a leaked staff email in May 2020 from the Lord Chamberlain that around a third of the royal household's funding comes from non-public grant sources, of which by far the most important is the Royal Collection.

Ironically the reason why the Sovereign Grant was set up in the first place was to simplify the myriad of revenue streams. Prior to 2012, the monarchy got its money from four sources. The official expenses of the royal household were paid out of the Civil List grant from the Treasury and then there was a grant-in-aid from the Department of Transport to cover royal travel as well as two other grants from the Department for Culture, Media and Sport, one to fund the maintenance of the royal palaces and the other for communication and information.

Having so many separate income streams made it difficult for the palace officials to plan. If they underspent on travel, for instance, they could not use the money on property maintenance. To a business consultant turned royal treasurer like Sir Alan Reid this was economic myopia: it fostered short-termism and bred inefficiencies by failing to manage spending on a holistic basis. Around 2010 the Keeper of the Privy Purse devised a scheme to simplify these revenue streams into a single source and took it to the government. The Treasury under the Labour Chancellor Alistair Darling was unresponsive because the timing was tricky. This was the spring of 2010 and a General Election was in the offing. Gordon Brown's cabinet thought it better to postpone such a politically sensitive decision until after the May 5th poll.

But Labour lost and the Conservatives led by David Cameron formed the next government in coalition with the Liberal Democrats. The Treasury under George Osborne were now able to give Reid's ideas their full attention and discussions started immediately because the deadline for the Civil List's ten year review was about to expire. According to his blueprint, better long term management could be achieved by decoupling the source of cash from regular government funding which was negotiated on a short term basis every year. What he proposed with a nod to Lord Airlie's 1989 idea was that the money should come from the profits of the Crown Estates which historically belonged to the monarch but which had been surrendered to parliament at the start of each reign since the time of George III. To ensure that the new mechanism worked as planned, parliament would receive a regular report from the Royal Trustees consisting of the Prime Minister, the Chancellor and the Queen's Treasurer.

Osborne saw the logic of the plan and was particularly struck by the idea of linking the funding mechanism to a "sort of measure" of growth in the economy over the long term. In other words, if the Crown Estates did well like the rest of UK plc, then the royal household's funding should benefit accordingly. Another reason why George Osborne agreed to the plan was that it chimed with Tory policy favouring decentralisation and removing as much funding as possible from direct state control (indeed a palace aide suggested that one of his special advisors was already working on a scheme similar to Reid's). But one suspects that its real appeal was that it kicked a long-standing contentious issue out of politics for good. Instead of having a parliamentary row each time new funds had to be voted by MPs, from now on the money would go through almost automatically without a whimper. In the words of one royal commentator, "it was a neat solution to try to take the heat out of a pay rise for the Queen and all the annual suffering."[6]

Perhaps mindful of the mistake of his Tory predecessor who wrecked the chances of a new royal yacht by failing to secure early on cross party support, the Chancellor made sure that he squared his scheme with Labour before he went public. A full week ahead of the formal announcement in the Commons, the Prime Minister had a private discussion about it with the leader of the opposition, Ed Miliband. Then five days later, the Chancellor gave precise details of the new arrangement to his Labour opposite number, Ed Balls.[7] In the subsequent fortnight, the shadow Chancellor expressed reservations about the proposed length of time before the scheme was reviewed by the Royal Trustees. The government subsequently took his views on board and agreed to reduce the period from seven to five years.

The frictionless passage of the legislation was further lubricated by introducing the bill in late June at the end of the parliamentary session when debating time was limited and MPs were in a relaxed, demob-happy mood. It is noticeable that many sensitive royal matters are slipped out in the summer. The annual reports of the Crown Estate, the Royal Collection, the Duchy of Cornwall, the Duchy of Lancaster, the Royal Household and Clarence House all come out in June-July when parliamentary scrutiny and media coverage tend to be at their most perfunctory due to the approach of the summer break and the silly season for the press.

So it was on two hot afternoons in June/July 2011 parliament met to debate the new Sovereign Grant. Standing before a far from packed House of Commons chamber the Chancellor spelt out the three reasons why the old Civil List had to go: it was too inflexible, too untransparent and too underfunded in its financial reserves. The latter were now so depleted that the royal household was in effect running on empty – although he did go out of his way to "thank the current Keeper of the Privy Purse, Sir Alan Reid, and his predecessors for doing such a good job [in making savings]."[8]

He then went on to put flesh on the plan first proposed by Reid. The Sovereign Grant would be financed by 15% of the profits of the Crown Estate. There would be a floor in that it would never go lower than the previous year's grant and a rough ceiling in that if its reserves reached more than 50% of expenditure they would be deducted from next year's grant. And to make sure everything was above board, the National Audit Office would be allowed to inspect the books and the Royal Trustees would be allowed to review whether the Crown Estate was providing the correct amount of money.

In reply Ed Balls said that the Labour opposition would support the package of reforms which was hardly surprising given his prior involvement in amending the legislation. His only concern was whether 15% of Crown Estate profits was the right level to set the grant. His Labour colleague and Chair of the Public Accounts Committee, Dame Margaret Hodge, also welcomed the changes, particularly the unprecedented access it gave parliament to audit royal expenditure: "This is a truly historic occasion. For the first time ever, we are placing the royal expenditure financed by the taxpayer on a proper footing – transparent for all to see." Again Sir Alan Reid got a name check as she looked forward to taking evidence from him in the future.

Later in the debate Ed Balls quoted her 2010 warning while on the Public Accounts Committee that "if there is to be serious assessment of efficiency and economy and effectiveness (of the monarchy), one has to look at the total income and expenditure. It is difficult to look at just a part." Yet the new arrangement left totally untouched one of the Queen's most important sources of revenue, the Duchy of Lancaster, which in 2011 supplied her with £13.2m (although interestingly Osborne did go out of his way to stress that the Duchy would *not* be audited by the National Audit Office). Also left out of the equation was the £19.1m that the heir to the throne received from the Duchy of Cornwall. No MP in the debate noticed these key omissions despite the fact the Sovereign Grant was described by Balls (and others) as "the most significant reform to the financing of the royal household since the accession of King George III in 1760."

With parliament granting the new legislation a relatively easy ride, it was left to the *Financial Times* to give it a good kicking. In an editorial entitled "Casino Royale," it argued that the scheme bore a disturbing resemblance to the generous performance related pay plans voted by indulgent corporate boards. By guaranteeing that the annual budget would never be lower than the previous year's, the Chancellor was sending the wrong signals to the Queen and her family: "when the Crown Estate does well, royals win; when it does not, taxpayers lose… The perverse incentives in this system are nothing short of frightening."[9]

In fact, the nightmare never materialised in so far as the Crown Estate profits did not dip in the next few years and the taxpayers did not have to intervene directly to top up the grant. But the *Financial Times* was accurate in predicting a win-win for the Windsors since their income climbed in line with the rising Crown Estate revenues which were well above the rate of inflation. From £31m in its first year, the grant grew to £36.1m in 2013-14, £37.9m in 2014-15 and £39.8m in 2015-16 – a rise of more than 25% in three years. "[It] turned out to be a generous settlement," acknowledges its instigator as Prime Minister, David Cameron, in his memoirs.[10] "I think it is very generous," also argues the former Labour Minister Chris Bryant MP. "And at a time of austerity I feel as if my constituents have had to pay much more of a price than the royal family. Interestingly both Labour and Conservative governments have been very timid about ever saying boo." He recalls when the policy was first being discussed within the party by Ed Balls: "He was going 'right we are not going to say boo on any of this' and I was thinking that he was very generous."[11]

Some now wondered whether it was correct to link the Queen's pay package to the income of a property portfolio which was hardly representative of the economy as a whole. As Lord Turnbull said in the October 2011 House of Lords debate: "the revenues of a property company… seems an odd benchmark to determine the appropriate level of funding for the monarchy"[12] – echoing a remark he had made back in November 1989 as a Whitehall mandarin when a similar scheme had been considered: "There was no obvious reason why head of state expenditure should move with Crown Estate revenue."[13] Since it was only an index mechanism and the money did not actually come from the Crown Estate but from the taxpayer, would not the Retail Price Index or some similar measure provide a better benchmark? The government's original answer to that was that there were sufficient checks in the system and if the grant was set too high it could be corrected at the next five yearly review.

When this date arrived in November 2016, some commentators anticipated that the Royal Trustees (Theresa May, Philip Hammond and Sir Alan Reid) would lower the 15% figure by a few points. In fact, they went the other way and raised it to 25%, thus appearing to bear out the 2011 warning of MP Ian Davidson that "the grant would be on, as it were, a golden ratchet – a bit like EU expenditure, it would always go up, and never down."[14]

The reason for the hike in the grant was to pay for the huge bill of refurbishing Buckingham Palace. It was put at £369m and the extra 10% of funding was earmarked for the essential repair work to avoid the risk of what the report ominously called "a catastrophic failure." It spelled out in almost apocalyptic terms how close the palace was to collapse. There was a serious danger of fire due to the faulty electrical wiring system, with sections of the 100 miles of cabling over 60 years old. After more than three decades of use, the ancient boilers were also about to blow – unable to heat the palace properly or more worryingly preserve at the desired temperature some of the Royal Collection's precious artworks. Much of the 20 miles of lead and cast-iron piping needed replacing with the danger that a drainage failure could wreak irreparable damage to the fabric of the building. Alarmingly, a few years earlier, a chunk of masonry had fallen from the façade and narrowly missed Princess Anne's car.

After weighing up all the alternatives, the trustees decided that the Queen should stay in the palace during the phased repair work. The Full Decant option where the building was emptied of everyone and the work completed within six and a half years was rejected on the grounds that it was too disruptive and the cost of lost visitor income too prohibitive. On the other hand, the Full Occupation option where the palace remained fully occupied and the work was done on a piecemeal basis over twenty-one years was judged too lengthy and too risky since fire or flood might occur before its eventual completion.

The decision to go for the Phased Work option with one wing at a time over a ten-year period seemed to strike the right balance between risk and reward. Tony Johnstone-Burt, then just a couple of years into the job of Master of the Queen's Household, told the media that it offered "the best value for money" while keeping the palace open and that by making the investment now "we can avert a much more costly and potentially catastrophic building failure in the years to come… On completion of the work, we'll have a palace fit for purpose until 2067."[15] The former royal press officer Dickie Arbiter defended what he preferred to call "a refurbishment rather than a refit" on the grounds that the building was "part of our national heritage" where the constitutional functions of the head of state took place.[16]

Critics wondered why the work had not been done earlier. In 2013 a Public Accounts Committee report had flagged up the problem. "We were very critical about the lack of investment," its Chair Dame Margaret Hodge later explained. "There was a massive capital investment programme required to maintain the fabric of their buildings and it was outrageous that they had not planned better and spent the money in a more rational way. And so, did it need the money spending on it? Yes, we said so. Should they have planned better? Yes. Had they planned better, would there have been a lesser demand on the public purse? Yes, undoubtedly." [17]

What made the announcement of the £369m programme politically sensitive was that it came at a time of cuts to public spending. When the austerity issue was raised at the press briefing, the palace officials said that they were alive to the possibility of a hostile public response to the scheme but hoped "it will appeal to their sense of nationhood." [18] The initial reaction was far from positive. 145,000 people signed an online petition calling for the royals rather than the taxpayers to fund the refurbishment. "I am all for protecting Buckingham Palace, but at a time when the public purse is so pressured, and on a day that temperatures dropped overnight, when the elderly are freezing… to fund it publicly is something out of a Charles Dickens novel," argued copywriter Mark Johnson who established the petition. "It's up to the royal household how they fund it privately, I don't think it will be hard to find the money."[19]

In an attempt to curry favour with the public, the report promised "a significant increase" in the number of people visiting the palace with greater access to schools and a new learning centre focussed on teaching the history of the British monarchy and UK citizenship. It also guaranteed that the already popular summer opening would be extended beyond the existing 78 days.

But did they miss a trick by not going the whole hog and agreeing to open up the palace all year-round? The demand is certainly there despite the sizable entry charge of £25. When this author tried to get a morning ticket to visit the palace in the relatively quiet period of a mid-weekday in mid-September, the entire booking sheet was full except for one session at 2 pm where just 3 places remained. After weaving through the crowds on the two hour audio tour through the state apartments he was told by an attendant that even at the end of the season they were regularly getting 8,000 people through the palace each day. Most, according to palace attendants, were not UK nationals but overseas visitors with China now supplying the greatest number of tourists followed by the United States and Japan – although whether foreigners will return in the same volume in the post-Covid-19 world is a moot point. Since 1993 when the palace first opened its doors, more than ten million people have taken the paid tour.

Back in 2013, the Public Accounts Committee under Dame Margaret Hodge had grilled palace officials on why they could not at least have a winter opening. Sir Alan Reid's reply was that "we would love to open it for more days but there are restraints on what we can do."[20] On the one hand, there were big set up costs for opening up the palace in the summer which would be prohibitive if repeated in the winter or on weekends when the royal family was not in residence. On the other, there was the restriction of Buckingham Palace being an operational palace with a range of official activities going on there – from investitures and garden parties to state visits and day-to-day administration. According to Dickie Arbiter, "it is very much a working palace and [opening it up all year round] would provide difficulties including undertaking revolving maintenance."[21] The household had thus concluded that "a winter opening was not commercially viable" as it would not generate additional profit.

What went unremarked in these discussions was an attractive Swedish model. *Kungliga Slottet*. This was the name of the official royal palace in the centre of Stockholm that the Swedish King Carl XVI Gustaf decided to vacate in 1981 so that he and Queen Silvia could bring up their young children in the homely surroundings of *Drottningholms Slotten*, a smaller private residence on the outskirts of the city. Located on an island overlooking a lake with lush gardens and extensive woodlands it was family friendly unlike the austere 18th century Baroque Stockholm fortress which was one of the largest palaces in Europe with more than 600 rooms stretched over 7 floors and a warren of cellars and royal vaults.

Not surprisingly this all made the Stockholm palace the perfect tourist attraction – helped by its prime location opposite parliament in the Gamla historic quarter. When the decision was taken to open it to the public for 12 months a year (except Christmas Eve and Christmas Day), visitors soon came in their droves to get a taste of royal splendour. Housed under one roof were the Royal Apartments, the Throne Room, the Cabinet Meeting Room, the Royal Chapel, the family's Bernadotte Library and several separate museums. But the biggest draw by far – as the author can testify from following the snaking queue down the steps – was the Treasury in the cellars where tourists could marvel at the priceless royal regalia: Erik XIV's magnificent golden crown, sceptre and orb – along with Queen Lovisa's sumptuous coronation cloak made from white ermine and red silk velvet. This was Sweden's equivalent of the Crown Jewels with the Stockholm Palace standing in for the Tower of London. Prices were pitched at a reasonable level – 160 Krona (£13) for general admission and extra charges for special site or group tours – and this all made a positive contribution to the household's finances, helping to make the Swedish monarchy one of the most cost efficient in Europe.

While British courtiers hum and ha about the impracticality of maintaining a working palace in a tourist environment, their Swedish counterparts have managed to strike a balance between retaining state functions and keeping the place open to the public. The palace is still home to the royal court (Sweden's royal household), the press office and many other administrative facilities. The changing of the guard continues on a daily basis and the state apartments are used for official duties such as cabinet and foreign affairs meetings with ministers or the king accepting the credentials of a new ambassador. When there is a state visit, the foreign dignitary normally attends a formal banquet in the palace and sleeps in its state apartments. The king has his own private rooms there but prefers to overnight at his Drottningholm residence.

Could King Charles copy King Carl? Might not a thoroughly modern monarch adopt to live in nearby Clarence House and just use Buckingham Palace as his workplace? Such ideas were seriously discussed as far back as February 2002 when in a private lunch at the palace with the Lord Chamberlain Sir Richard Luce, the former director of the Victoria and Albert Museum Sir Roy Strong proposed that Charles, when king, should reside at Clarence House and in the manner of the King of Spain use Buckingham Palace for office work and official functions.[22] Both King Juan Carlos and his successor Felipe chose to live in a private Madrid residence rather than move into the official Zarzuela Palace.

By all accounts, Charles is more than content residing in Clarence House and as someone now past seventy, somewhat set in his ways. If necessary he could always point to the precedent of the original owner of the property – William IV – who never lived in Buckingham Palace, spending instead the whole of his eight-year reign ruling from his private house a few hundred yards away on the Mall. Queen Victoria also preferred to reside elsewhere as did Edward VIII.

If King Charles eschewed Buckingham Palace as a live-in residence, it would be much easier to open it up to visitors all year round. With the private apartments vacated there would be more space to put on show some of the hidden treasures of the Royal Collection which are often left to gather dust behind closed doors at Windsor Castle. The Leonardo drawings could be relocated, all the Canaletto canvases assembled under one roof, the Raphael cartoons returned from the Victoria and Albert Museum and the Queen Mother's collection of modern paintings put on permanent display. With a little creative input from ad-men, the whole experience could be marketed as the London Louvre and Paris-level admission prices charged *en plus*.

But how realistic a business proposition is this? After all, the French were only able to get their hands on the Louvre and its treasures because they guillotined its previous owner, whereas the British king-in-waiting is very much extant and might not be willing to stick his neck out. If the past is anything to go by Charles is not someone who likes to downsize his real estate or cut down on his high living. During his long wait for the throne, he has added to his property portfolio Highgrove, Birkhall and Clarence House – not to mention houses in Wales and Romania. So, it is entirely possible that he might want the best of both worlds. For the benefits of comfort and privacy, he lives mainly in Clarence House but for reasons of state, he relocates to Buckingham Palace whenever there is a major public engagement like Trooping the Colour or the overnight visit of a head of state.

The other drawback of this business plan is that the envisaged changes come too late. The time to make the decision to turn the palace into a year-round visitor attraction was back in 2016 when the Royal Trustees were deliberating on how best to refurbish the place. That would have been the perfect moment to agree to a reconfiguration rather than a refit – as any opposition to spending such a large amount of taxpayers' money could have been dampened by arguing that some of the £369m was to be used to allow all-year public access to the palace. Plans could then have been drawn up to turn the private apartments into a venue for the public display of furniture and artworks, so saving money that would otherwise have been spent refurbishing them for personal use.

To have achieved this in 2016, however, would have involved the tricky task of persuading a nonagenarian monarch to vacate her official home of the previous 62 years. The Queen might conceivably have been up for it – since she nowadays spends the majority of her time at Windsor Castle, not Buckingham Palace and she has always shown flexibility when faced with reforms – but would Charles? He would probably have realised that he was onto a loser since the media would accuse him of kicking his mother out of her house so that he could rule the roost.

If they tried to do it today, it would make no economic sense as some of the money has already been spent doing up the private apartments. The makeover programme began relatively unobtrusively in April 2017 with the upgrade of the plumbing and electrical services in the basement and then in April 2019 they moved on to the major overhaul of the East Wing which included the Yellow Drawing Room, the Chinese Dining Room and the Bedroom Floor. Prince Andrew, Prince Edward and his wife Sophie – who all had overnight accommodation there – had to be rehoused in other parts of the palace. Their private offices had to be transferred to St James's Palace and a temporary home had to be found for 10,000 precious artworks which were handed over to the Royal Collection for safekeeping.

Once the East Wing is finished the work will rotate clockwise around the palace to the South, South West and North Wings, while the West Wing and the State Apartments will be incrementally refurbished room by room so as to cause the minimum disruption. It should all be completed in 2028 by which time the building might well be under new ownership.

Chapter 19:

Ditching the Duchy for a New Deal

The Queen's death is expected to be so seismic as to surpass Diana's in terms of widespread national mourning and world-wide media coverage. "It will be quite fundamental," said one courtier to the *Guardian*. All the preparations are already in place laid down in an elaborate plan codenamed "London Bridge" which choreographs every detail of the nine-day period of mourning from the initial pinning of the death bulletin on the gates of Buckingham Palace to the final entombment of the body at Windsor Castle. But the proceedings will be as much about Charles as his mother. "There are really two things happening," as one palace aide admitted. "There is the demise of a sovereign and then there is the making of a king."[1]

If all goes to plan, Charles will make an address to the nation on the day the Queen dies. On the following day, he will be proclaimed king by the Accession Council at St James's Palace and then will leave London for a tour of his new realm. The first port of call will be the home nations. He will travel to Belfast, Cardiff and Edinburgh to take part in remembrance services for the Queen and have meetings with leaders of the devolved national governments. But there will also be civil ceremonies where he can meet and greet more ordinary professional people and local townsfolk. The rationale of the tour – stress palace aides conscious, as one put it, that "he divides opinion more than his mother" – is for the new king to connect with the mass of the people.[2]

Just as newly-installed prime ministers are often encouraged to take the most unpopular decisions during the honeymoon period of their first days in office, so Charles may be tempted to use the rupture in public life caused by the nine days of mourning to if not bury bad news then at least put to bed a few tricky issues. Many believe he will use that interval to announce that Camilla will be Queen Consort. This is likely to be a controversial move since at the time of his marriage in 2005 his private secretary, Sir Michael Peat, made it clear to the media (and by extension to the wider public who were then less than enthusiastic about the woman chosen to replace the beloved Diana) that when Charles was King, Camilla would become Princess Consort, not Queen. If necessary, Clarence House would support legislation to ensure that she did not get the title as under common law the sovereign's wife automatically goes by the name of Queen. But since then Camilla has been elevated to the ranks of the Privy Council (allowing her to attend the Accession ceremony) and Charles has dropped strong hints that he wants his wife to have the top title. When asked in 2010 by NBC News if Camilla would be Queen, he hesitated before replying "that's well… we'll see, won't we? That could be."[3]

Charles could use the cover of mourning to change not just the status of his wife but also the composition of the royal household. It is expected that he would want to put in place his own choice of media secretary, Keeper of the Privy Purse and personal secretary, perhaps with an enhanced role overseeing both Buckingham Palace and Clarence House. According to royal correspondent Richard Palmer, "when he becomes king his people will move in and most of the people who work for the Queen will be out of a job."[4]

All of the Queen's senior officials must know that they are on borrowed time since the appointment of the top brass is in the gift of the sovereign. "By tradition it is the monarch who decides who is employed," explains the former royal press officer Dickie Arbiter.[5] The Master of the Household, Vice Admiral Tony Johnstone-Burt, was not the only courtier to have a personal interview before his hiring as something similar (but on a grander scale) happened to Dickie Arbiter in the eighties. "It is customary for senior people joining the royal household to receive an audience with the Queen, their ultimate boss… Such meetings can take place at Buckingham Palace or Windsor Castle. That I was granted a 24-hour dine-and-sleep audience at her Scottish retreat was a gift I will never forget."[6]

Charles as king might also have designs on changing Balmoral. Back in October 2008 in a discussion he had with Alex Salmond, the First Minister of Scotland, the idea was floated over dinner of gifting the private estate to the Scottish nation. Under the scheme, Charles would be allowed to stay in nearby Birkhall but Balmoral would be transferred to the ownership of the state which would pay for its upkeep and open it up to the public.[7] The fact that no more was heard of this populist plan in subsequent years suggests it might have been a trial balloon but that does not prevent it from being aired again if Charles ever decided that the cost of running both Sandringham and Balmoral was prohibitive and that one had to go.

If he postponed streamlining his private estates, then he could always save money by slimming down the number of working royals. If nothing else it would cut down on the estimated £100m annual bill for their security. Most European houses – such as the Swedish and Danish royal families – have been reduced to only a handful of active members and Charles is likely to follow their example. Over the last decade, Clarence House has made it clear that it supports a "core family" of around half a dozen working royals – what the press soon dubbed the Magnificent Seven. This was given visual representation in the Thames river-borne pageant during the Diamond Jubilee celebrations in 2012 when the Queen and Prince Philip were seen on the royal barge accompanied only by Charles, Camilla, William, Kate and Harry. Andrew, Anne, Edward and their families travelled in a separate boat.

Their exclusion is believed to have caused a rift between Charles and Andrew who feared that this was a foretaste to the side-lining of his two daughters when the Queen died. The Duke of York reportedly wrote to his mother in 2016 demanding that Beatrice and Eugenie be allowed to carry out full-time royal duties and be funded from the public purse.[8] When this caused a media storm, he then issued a remarkably blunt statement denying any "split between the Prince of Wales and I over my daughters' participation as Members of the Royal Family" and expressing his wish for them to be "modern working young women."[9]

Some commentators saw this last point as a tacit acceptance that the two princesses wouldn't be working royals. But since then they have increased their profile on the royal stage – Eugenie had a very public wedding at Windsor Castle with taxpayer-funded security and Beatrice has been seen in the Royal Box at Ascot and at many official family gatherings – and it is now far from clear whether Charles will be able to cut them adrift when he accedes. As for Andrew himself, he claimed to be relaxed about any future downgrading: "The family flexes in size dependent on generational changes and shifts and ideas among the family. It's not a problem."[10] Those remarks were made before the Jeffrey Epstein sex trafficking scandal erupted in August 2019 with allegations that Andrew had had sex with a 17-year-old girl, but despite his strenuous denials, the fallout from the legal case led to mounting pressure for him to take a diminished role in royal life. The climax came in November of that year when after his disastrous interview to BBC-2 *Newsnight* where he failed to express any concern for Epstein's victims or remorse over his own friendship with the convicted sex-offender, he agreed "to step back from royal duties for the foreseeable future." Many commentators, including royal biographers Robert Hardman and Robert Lacey, believed that Andrew's unprecedented decision to withdraw from a public role came after pressure from Charles. Just two months later, the monarchy was further streamlined when it was decided after the "Sandringham Summit" in January 2020 that the Duke and Duchess of Sussex should step down from all public duties and pursue a life of financial independence in North America.

Money from the Duchies of Lancaster and Cornwall has long been used to bankroll junior royals and that too may be subject to change under Charles. He will have to review the practice of using the Lancaster profits to pay for Anne, Edward and to a lesser extent Andrew – as well as the Gloucesters and the Kents. It would be difficult to stop the support entirely but the threat to turn off the tap does give him considerable leverage over his immediate family, particularly if they misbehave in which case he would probably prove less indulgent than his mother. There is little danger then that Edward would repeat the mistake of incurring his elder brother's wrath as happened in 2001 when a crew from his television company illicitly filmed William at college in St Andrews causing Charles to go "ballistic."

The switch of funding from the Duchy of Cornwall to the Duchy of Lancaster will also have personal financial implications. On the one hand, he will probably lose money in that Lancaster's profits have in most recent years been lower than Cornwall's and he will also now have to fund a larger coterie of royals. But on the other hand he will no longer have to support William (who will inherit the Duchy of Cornwall with which he can fund Kate and if absolutely necessary, Harry and Meghan too) or indeed pay for all his official household overheads since he will now benefit from the ever-escalating Sovereign Grant which rose to £82.4m in 2019-20 and is set at £85.9m in 2020-21.

Although since the early nineties the Duchy of Cornwall has been more profitable than the Duchy of Lancaster, the gap has been steadily closing in recent years. It was down to £1.5m in 2017-18 and in 2018-19 the figures were almost tied on £21.7m. What we have witnessed in the last two decades is an inexorable increase in Lancaster profits, with a jump of more than £15m between 2000-2019.[11] As a result, the Duchy is now the wellspring of the Queen's wealth.

This spectacular profit growth when coupled with the increase in the value of her other assets forces one to revise upwards any estimate of her total private wealth. With the rise in property prices, Balmoral and Sandringham must now be worth over £100m. Her collection of British and Commonwealth stamps – the best of its kind in the world – would boost the inventory by another £100m and using the same ballpark figure the combined value of her jewellery and art collections could well be pushing £100m. The precise value of her private investments remains a mystery (and may have been hit by the post-Covid-19 market crash in 2020) but they are still likely to be worth tens of millions of pounds. The same could be said of all the private gifts she has received over the last 70 years and there is also her collection of antique cars thought to worth £10m or more.

A few caveats are in order, though. We do not know the long-term financial consequences of the coronavirus, with the Duchy's rental income being particularly vulnerable to any economic slowdown. The prices cited above include the added value of the royal name which can go up or down according to the changing popularity of the royals (for instance, Princess

Margaret's art treasures would probably not fetch as high a price at auction now as they did in her heyday in 2006). The valuations would have to be lowered if all the property was placed on the market at the same time (for instance, her stamp collection would not be worth as much as £100m if the market was flooded through a sale in one go rather than through a controlled release over a long period of time). There is also the issue of whether any money she may have put in a family trust is still technically hers (the Queen Mother made her estate millions of pounds poorer by putting aside cash for her great-grandchildren). But if you include the trust funds and make allowances for the effect of the royal name, her total wealth could well be in the region of £400m. This may not put her in the super-rich category but it certainly makes her wealthier than the palace would like us to believe.

When it comes to managing her money – whether private or public – the Queen has a reputation for being pragmatic. When in 1986 Lord Airlie proposed to overhaul the financial management of the royal household, she assented to his reforms without putting up a fight and when in 1992 she was told by courtiers that it was time that she paid income tax, she agreed without a fuss even though it must have significantly reduced revenue from her investments.

But over some issues she has put her foot down. One sticking point is control over her personal household since – as we have just seen – she likes to be able to appoint staff with whom she feels comfortable. Recruitment is regarded as an essential part of her private domain. When in 1971 it was suggested that the royal household might be run as a government department with civil servants choosing its employees she issued a stern rebuke, via the Lord Chamberlain, threatening to leave Buckingham Palace if it happened and when in 1986 Mrs Thatcher hinted at bringing in a similar reform she managed to pre-empt the move by putting her house in order.

Another red line appears to be personal transport. She prefers to travel in privacy. She cried when the costly Royal Yacht was decommissioned after 44 years as "her country house at sea" and one suspects that the Royal Train – "Buckingham Palace on wheels" – has only been saved from a similar fate by its sentimental significance to its infrequent passenger.

But enjoying even greater ring-fencing is the Duchy of Lancaster. It has always seemed untouchable. At the start of her reign in 1952 when a new Civil List was being worked out, the Treasury and the palace agreed not to alter its status. In 1971 during the review of the Civil List which entailed the most thorough scrutiny ever of the royal finances, the palace again succeeded with help from the government to keep the Duchy out of harm's way (although the Treasury's lawyer let the cat out of the bag by revealing that "one of the things the palace has insisted on is that there should be no surrender of the Duchy revenues"). And in 2011 when the Sovereign Grant was set up as part of "the greatest reform of the royal finances in 250 years," the Queen's private estate somehow escaped unscathed.

At the time a few lone voices wondered whether the Duchy could play a part in a more comprehensive settlement that considered the royal finances in the round. Instead of financing the monarchy solely from a slice of Crown Estate revenue, why not include the Duchy of Lancaster profits too? The pot could be made bigger still by also throwing in the income from the Duchy of Cornwall. From this combined pool of cash the monarch, the Prince of Wales and a core group of working royals could be paid a fixed salary. This alternative settlement would provide better value for money for the taxpayer since for the first time the funding going to the monarch and their heir would be based on their actual requirements rather than how well the property market happened to be doing. The public could get a bonus too if the monarch were persuaded that one of their two country estates was now surplus to requirements and should be handed over to the state.

Is it conceivable that Charles when king might be open to such ideas? As a public advocate of a leaner monarchy he could not object to having half a dozen fewer working royals (particularly in a post-Covid world of greater public belt-tightening) and as someone who has opened up Clarence House and Highgrove to general visitors he would almost certainly support extending public access to Balmoral and Sandringham. But that might be the limit to his royal revolution. By nature he is a spender rather than a saver. As someone whose affluent lifestyle for the past 50 years has been based on the ever-rising revenues of the Duchy of Cornwall, he would be reluctant to dispose of it or its sister cash cow the Duchy of Lancaster. By the time he is king he may be pushing eighty and his zeal for change may then have lost its edge. Will the longest standing royal heir in British history really want to downsize his inheritance when he at last gains the crown?

We may have to wait a generation for a real break with the past. Having witnessed the mistakes of his mother and father in dealing with the media and the overall public pressures of being a modern royal, William might be more amenable to ringing the changes – if only to have a quieter life himself. So far, he has shown a liking for keeping the lifestyle of his family and friends out of the public eye. By the time he is king he could be well into his fifties, by which time he may no longer see the need to hold on to the private residences of Sandringham and Balmoral or the ancestral estates of the Duchies of Cornwall and Lancaster. So, change may happen but not soon. More than likely it will take another decade or two before a new broom sweeps away the last vestiges of royal privilege.

Notes

Prologue: Monetising the Monarchy

1 *BBC News* website 08.01.2020
2 *NBC News* website 19.01.2020
3 *Globe and Mail* news website 14.01.2020
4 *Daily Mail* 21.02.2020
5 Ibid. 19.01.2020
6 See Chapter 14: Counting the cost of divorce
7 Dimbleby, Jonathan *The Prince of Wales* Warner Books, 1994, p615
8 *Mail on Sunday* "Royal Rich Report" 2001, p38
9 The Annual Review 2018-19, Income and Expenditure of the Prince of Wales
10 *Sky News* website 18.01.2020
11 *Guardian* 23.01.2020
12 *Financial Times* 09.01.2020
13 *Daily Mail* 22.01.2020
14 *BBC News* website 22.01.2020
15 *Observer* 21.01.2007

Chapter 1: Handing over Control of the Purse Strings

1 *The Times* 16.09.2017 + 18.09.2017
2 *BBC News* website 16.09.2017
3 Bates, Stephen *Royalty Inc* Arum Press 2015, p263

4 Interview with Richard Palmer 11.12.2017

5 Ibid

6 Email from Steve Kingstone 20.06.2018

7 Palmer op. cit.

8 Hardman, Robert *Our Queen* Hutchinson 2011, p130

9 Ibid p131

10 Somerville, Robert *History of the Duchy of Lancaster Vol II 1603-1965,* p469

11 Rhodes James, Robert *Memoirs of a Conservative: J.C.C. Davidson's memoirs and papers 1910-37* Weidenfeld & Nicolson, p413

12 Somerville op. cit. p469

13 *Sunday Times* 17.09.2017

Chapter 2: Trouble in Paradise

1 *BBC News* website 06.11.2017 "Paradise Papers: Queen's private estate invested £10m in offshore funds"

2 Facebook Online discussion on Panorama programme 09.11.2017

3 Ibid

4 *New Yorker* "Paradise Papers… and the German newspaper" by Elizabeth Zerofsky 11.11.2017

5 Ibid

6 *The Guardian* 04.05.2018

7 Op. cit. *BBC News* website 06.11.2017

8 Ibid

9 "The magazine interview" by John Arlidge, *Sunday Times* 03.12.2017

10 Private conversation with author 06.11.2017

11 "Queen's private estate invested millions of pounds offshore" by Hilary Osborne, *Guardian* 05.11.2017

12 Interview with Graham Smith 15.12.2017

13 Clarke, Kenneth *Kind of Blue* Macmillan, 2012, p169

14 "What were the Queen's moneymen thinking?" by Richard Kay *Daily Mail* 06.11.2017

15 Palmer interview op. cit.

16 *Daily Mail* 05.11.2017

17 *The Times* 05.11.2017

18 Smith interview op. cit.

19 *The Guardian* 05.11.2017

20 *The Economist* 11.11.2017

21 *The Financial Times* 06.11.2017

22 Interview with Dame Margaret Hodge MP 13.12.2017

23 *Daily Mail* 05.11.2017

24 See Duchy of Lancaster annual report 2018-19

25 Somerville, Robert *History of the Duchy of Lancaster Vol II 1603-1965,* p483

26 Oral evidence, Report from the Select Committee of the Civil List 1971-72

27 Letter from Charles Hill to Enoch Powell 18.11.1957 in NA T219/584

28 *The Guardian* 05.11.2017 "Revealed Queen's private estate" + Op. cit. *BBC News* website 06.11.2017

29 *BBC News* website 07.11.2017 "Paradise Papers: Prince Charles lobbied on climate policy after shares purchase"

30 Ibid

31 Ibid

32 Ibid

33 Bedell Smith, Sally *Prince Charles* Michael Joseph 2017, p36

34 *BBC News* website 07.11.2017

35 Palmer op. cit.

36 Hodge op. cit.

37 *BBC News* website 07.11.2017 op. cit.

38 Hodge op. cit.

39 "Paradise Papers deal a blow to the Queen's approval ratings" *Daily Express* 11.11.2017

40 Hodge op. cit.

41 "Paradise Papers: Tax haven secrets of ultra rich exposed" *BBC News* website 06.11.2017

42 Hodge op. cit.

43 Smith op. cit.

Chapter 3: Is the Palace Public or Private?

1 *The Royal Rich Report* (*Mail on Sunday*, 14.10.2001) p11

2 *The Sunday Times Rich List* 07.05.2017

3 Email from Philip Beresford 01.12.2018

4 *Sunday Times Rich List* 2011 07.05.2011

5 Message from Roberts Watts to the author 17.05.2020

6 Brand Finance *Monarchy 2017* report

7 Interview with Konrad Jakgodzinski 19.01.2017

8 Brand Finance op. cit.

9 "Buckingham Palace to undergo essential £370m refurbishment" *Guardian* 18.11.2016

10 Eade, Philip *Young Prince Philip* HarperCollins, 2011, p264

11 NA T326/1321 Letter from Lord Cobbold to Anthony Barber 30.06.1971

12 *Daily Telegraph* 31.05.2002

13 NA T233/734 Memo from Rab Butler 20.03.1952

14 NA T233/734 Letter from Ulrick Alexander to Eric Bridges 06.03.1952

15 NA Work 19/1193 Letter from Sir Burke Trend to Sir Harold Emmerson 21.05.1952

16 NA Work 19/1193 Select Committee on the Civil List note on the maintenance of the royal palaces 26.05.1952

17 Hansard 09.07.1952 debate on the 1952 Civil List Bill

18 NA Work 19/1193

19 Obituary David Eccles *Independent* 29.02.1999

20 *Guardian* 05.04.2016

21 Royal Collection annual report 2018-19

22 Ibid

23 Hardman, Robert *Our Queen* Hutchinson, 2011, p94

24 Hansard 11.02.1993

25 Email from Sophie Lawrenson, Royal Collection Press office 11.10.2018

26 Ibid

27 Email from Lucy Whitaker, senior curator of pictures, Royal Collection 16.07.2014

28 NA T628/176 *Report on the future of the Civil List* November 1989

29 Andrew Graham-Dixon BBC-4 Television "*Art, Passion and Power: the Royal Collection*" 17.01.2018

30 *BBC News* website "King of the Collectors" 10.01.2018

31 Hardman op. cit. p261

32 *Royal Rich Report* op. cit. p71

33 Interview with Dickie Arbiter 21.09.2018

34 Notes

Chapter 4: Stabilising Sandringham

1 Ridley, Jane *Bertie – The Life of Edward VII* Vintage, 2013, p91

2 Titchmarsh, Alan *The Queen's Houses* BBC Books, 2014, p195

3 Rose, Kenneth *King George V* Weidenfeld & Nicholson, 1983, p38

4 Bahlman, Dudley (ed) *The Diary of Sir Edward Hamilton* Clarendon Press, 1972 entry for 01.06.1904

5 Rose op. cit. p98

6 Treasury papers for the 1936 Civil List NA T171/331

7 Curtis, Sarah (ed) *The Journals of Woodrow Wyatt vol II* Macmillan, 1999 entry for 09.07.1991, p546

8 Hugh Gaitskell Papers UCL 1951-2 C/63

9 Hugh Gaitskell Papers UCL 1951-2 M7

10 1952 Report of the Select Committee on the Civil List p4

11 NA T233 2027 Treasury memo on the Civil List to Mr Hunt (marked "secret")

12 NA T233 2027 Confidential memo "Civil List" dated 28.02.1957 from EAS

13 Brandreth, Gyles *Philip and Elizabeth* Century, 2004, p305

14 Gaitskell Papers op. cit. C/G/63 Treasury briefing documents on the 1952 Civil List "Salary Bill 1951"

15 NA T326/1319 Treasury memo of meeting with Lord Cobbold for the preparation of the Civil List 11.06.1971

16 See oral evidence of Lord Cobbold to the Select Committee on the Civil List July 1991

17 Hall, Phillip *Royal Fortune* Bloomsbury, 1992, p205

18 CAP payments DEFRA website

19 "Brexit threatens subsidies for Britain's landed gentry, and Queen" *New York Times* 03.09.2017

20 *Independent* 25.10.2016

21 Pope-Hennessy, James *The Quest for Queen Mary* (ed. Hugo Vickers) Zuleika 2018 location 1358

22 "Charles put his green on royal warrants" *The Times* 20.01.2018

23 *Daily Mail* 03.11.2017

Chapter 5: The High Cost of a Highland Home

1 Shawcross, William *Queen Elizabeth* Macmillan, 2009, p799

2 Registers of Scotland: Application 16ABN26773 01.11.2017

3 See Registers of Scotland, Title Information: ABN130387 search 21.09.2018

4 Email from Steven Davie, Registers of Scotland 13.02.2018

5 Wightman, Andy *The Poor had no lawyers* Berlinn, 2013, p113

6 McClure, David *Royal Legacy* Thistle Publishing 2014/second edition Lume Books, 2020, p341

7 *Daily Telegraph* 09.07.2000

8 *Royal Rich Report* op. cit. "Prince Andrew"

9 See company entry in Companies House online records

10 See Land Registry records for Sandringham estate

11 Picknett, Lynn (et al) *War of the Windsors* Mainstream, 2002, p135

12 Wightman op. cit.

13 Diary entry cited in Titchmarsh, Alan *The Queen's Houses* BBC Books, 2014, p143

14 BBC Radio 4 *In Our Time* 08.03.2018

15 Clark, Ronald *Balmoral: Queen Victoria's Highland Home* Thames and Hudson, 1981, p30

16 Hall, Phillip *Royal Fortune* Bloomsbury, 1992, p14

17 Registers of Scotland, Sasine records for Balmoral estate SS 26689

18 Titchmarsh op. cit. p150

19 Clark op. cit. p44

20 Kuhn, William "Queen Victoria's Civil List: what did she do with it" *Historical Journal* vol 36 1993, p655

21 Ibid p656

22 Lacey, Robert *Majesty* Hutchinson, 1978, p384

23 Clark op. cit. p89

24 Ridley op. cit. p359

25 Titchmarsh op. cit. p166

26 Ridley op. cit. p360

27 NA T171/131 Treasury papers on the 1936 Civil List

28 NA T171/338

29 Shawcross op. cit. p367

30 Titchmarsh op. cit. p168

31 Shawcross op. cit. p797

32 Hall op. cit. p151

33 *Royal Rich Report* op. cit.

34 Gaitskell Papers op. cit. C/G/63 Treasury briefing documents on the 1952 Civil List "Salary Bill 1951"

35 Titchmarsh p171

36 Lacey, Robert *Royal* Little Brown, 2002, p284

37 Crossman diary entry 20.09.1966 quoted in Bradford, Sarah *Elizabeth* William Heinemann, 1996, pp322-3

38 Quoted in Marr, Andrew *The Diamond Queen* Macmillan, 2011, p214

39 Crossman, Richard *The Crossman Diaries vol III* Hamish Hamilton, 1977, p283

40 Pimlott, Ben *The Queen* HarperCollins, 2001, p430

41 Bradford op. cit. p380

42 Marr op. cit. p303

43 Cameron, David *For the Record* HarperCollins, 2019, p373

44 *Daily Telegraph* 19.09.2019

45 Hoey, Brian *At Home with the Queen* HarperCollins, 2002, p66

46 Blair, Tony *A Journey* Hutchinson, 2010, pp148-9

47 Op. cit. Lord Cobbold oral evidence to the 1971-2 Select Committee Report on the Civil List

Chapter 6: The Shape Shifting Estate

1 Oral evidence in the *Public Accounts Committee Report on the Accounts of the Duchies of Cornwall and Lancaster 2004-05*

2 Duchy of Lancaster Annual Report 2018-19

3 Somerville, Robert *History of the Duchy of Lancaster Vol II 1603-1965*, 1970, p52

4 Ibid p52

5 Hall, Phillip *Royal Fortune* Bloomsbury, 1992, p188

6 Oral evidence by Ernest Wheeler, 21.07.1971, *Report of the Select Committee into the Civil List 1971-72*

7 Ibid

8 NA T227/3380 Treasury memo on the hereditary revenues and the Civil List

9 Somerville op. cit. p288

10 *Public Accounts Committee Report on the Accounts of the Duchies of Cornwall and Lancaster 2004-05,* p3

11 *Hansard* Standing Committee G 17.11.1987

12 Brennan, Laura *A Passion for the Past*, WordPress, p4

13 Wilson, A.N. *Victoria: A Life* Atlantic Books, 2014, p342

14 Somerville op. cit. p385

15 Kuhn op. cit. p656

16 *Fortnightly Review* March 1901 "The Civil List and the Hereditary Revenues of the Crown" by 'G Percival'

17 Somerville op. cit. p444

18 Hall op. cit. pp60-61

19 *Hansard* 07.05.1936 debate on the Civil List Bill

20 Gaitskell Papers op. cit. C/G/63 Treasury briefing documents on the 1952 Civil List Statement VI

21 NA T233/734 Memo from Rab Butler 20.03.1952

22 NA T233/804 Memo from Sir Burke Trend 13.05.1952

23 NA T233/804 Letter from Rab Butler to Sir Clement Attlee 14.05.1952

24 Somerville op. cit. p482

25 NA T227/2085 Memo from Sir Jack Rampton 19.11.1964

26 NA T227/3380 Letter from Whalley to Armstrong 18.12.1969

27 NA T227/3380 Sir Robert Wheeler-K. Whalley letter 09.01.1970

28 NA T326/1310 Sir John Fiennes Taylor letter to Mr Taylor 01.09.1970

29 See T326/1319 Memo by Treasury official LJ Taylor dated 10.03.1971

30 NA T227 2085 "Duchy of Lancaster" memo by D. Shepherd dated 25.11.1964

31 See Wheeler oral evidence to the 1971 Select Committee on the Civil List op. cit.

32 NA T227/380 Treasury memo dated 03.03.1971

33 NA T326/1328 Treasury memo "Duchy of Lancaster and the Queen's private fortune"

34 See Chapter 11 for full discussion of the plan

35 *Hansard* 14.12.1971

36 Oral evidence to 1971-72 Select Committee on the Civil List op. cit. 27.07.1971

37 Barton, Cassie *Finances of the Monarchy* House of Commons Library Briefing Paper 25.07.2017 [the figures are given at 2016 prices]

38 Interview with Graham Smith op. cit.

39 Interview with Richard Palmer op. cit.

40 Interview with Dame Margaret Hodge MP op. cit.

41 Interview with Chris Bryant MP 09.10.2018

42 Notes

Chapter 7: Geeks and Greeks Bearing Gifts

1 Interview with Richard Palmer op cit

2 *Report to his Royal Highness the Prince of Wales* by Sir Michael Peat and Edmund Lawson March 2003

3 ITV1 television documentary *A Very Royal Wedding* 30.10.2017

4 *Marriage of her Royal Highness the Princess Elizabeth and Lieutenant Philip Mountbatten* Gifts Catalogue 1947

5 Duff, David *Hessian Tapestry* Muller, 1967, p88

6   Ibid p88
7   Menkes, Suzy *The Royal Jewels* Granada, 1985, p142
8   Menkes op. cit. p141
9   Field Leslie *The Queen's Jewels* Guild, 1987, p56
10 Ibid pp30-33
11 *Royal Rich Report* pp32-33
12 Menkes op. cit. p33
13 Lord Cobbold oral evidence to the Select Committee on the Civil List 1971-72 op. cit.
14 Hall op. cit. p31
15 Field op. cit. p39
16 Shawcross op. cit. p653

Chapter 8: Savings from State Subvention

1   Eade, Philip *Young Prince Philip* HarperCollins, 2011, p195
2   Ibid p175
3   Ibid p191
4   Oral evidence of Lord Cobbold 21.06.1971 in the *Report of the Select Committee on the Civil List 1971-72*
5   Diary of Hugh Dalton 18.10.1947 (Dalton Papers, from LSE Library, Dalton 1/35)
6   Ibid entry for 19.10.1947
7   Marr op. cit. p110
8   Ibid entry for 22.10.1947
9   Pimlott, Ben *The Queen* HarperCollins, 2001, pp128-9
10 Pimlott, Ben *Hugh Dalton,* Cape, 1985, pp416-7
11 See record of meeting NA PREM 8/652
12 Pimlott, Ben *The Queen* HarperCollins, 2001, p130
13 Bradford, Sarah *Elizabeth* William Heinemann, 1996, p124
14 NA T171/331 1936 Civil List papers
15 Hall, Phillip *Royal Fortune* Bloomsbury, 1992, p25 [NA T160/631]
16 Ibid p107 [NA T171/329] + NA T160/631
17 NA T171/329 p25 Appendix E of Select Committee on the Civil List 1936

18 Gaitskell Papers UCL C/ G /63 Statement I, Draft Report of the Select Committee on the Civil List 1952

19 Ibid see final report p7

20 NA T233-734 Letter from Sir Ulrick Alexander 06.03.1952 (see para 16 of final report p9)

21 NA T233/734 Letter from Sir Ulrick Alexander 20.03.1952

22 NA T233/804 Letter from Sir Ulrick Alexander 12.05.1952

23 NA T233/734 Memo dated 21.02.1952

24 NA T233/734 Memo from Sir Burke Trend 15.03.1952

25 Williams, Philip *Hugh Gaitskell* Cape, 1979, p251

26 NA T233/804 Treasury memo by Sir Burke Trend 09.05.1952

27 Ibid

28 Gaitskell Papers C/G/63 Memo by Sir Ulrick Alexander on the Duchess of Kent's finances

29 Gaitskell Papers C/G/63

30 *Hansard* debate on the 1952 Civil List Bill 09.07.1952

Chapter 9: Inheriting the Earth and More

1 NA T171/338 "Taxation Questions" memo from the Treasury papers for the 1937 Civil List p2

2 Pope-Hennessy, James *The Quest for Queen Mary* (ed. Hugo Vickers) Zuleika, 2018, location 2873

3 NA T233/734 Treasury memo 15.2.1952

4 Cannadine, David *The Decline and Fall of the British Aristocracy* Penguin, 2005, pp641-2

5 Hall op. cit. p79

6 Oral evidence of Lord Cobbold 21.06.1971 in the *Report of the Select Committee on the Civil List 1971-72*

7 Smithsonian Institution lecture by Michael Sefi 16.10.2004

8 Courtney, Nicholas *The Queen's Stamps* Methuen, 2004, p73

9 Ibid p132

10 Ibid p86

11 Ibid p151

12 Rhodes James, Robert (ed) *Chips – The Diaries of Sir Henry Channon* Weidenfeld & Nicolson, 1967 entry dated 28.04.1947

13 Courtney op. cit. p136

14 Hart-Davis, Duff *King's Counsellor: Abdication and War: the Diaries of Sir Alan Lascelles*, Weidenfeld & Nicolson, 2006, p422

15 *The Times* 20.04.2017

16 *Royal Rich Report* op. cit. "One of the Queen's stamps is worth £2m"

17 Wilson, Sir John, *The Royal Philatelic Collection* Dropmore Press, 1952, pp36-37

18 Field, Leslie *The Queen's Jewels* Guild, 1987, p16

19 Pope-Hennessy, James *The Quest for Queen Mary* (ed. Hugo Vickers) Zuleika, 2018 location 4132

20 Menkes, Suzy *The Royal Jewels* Granada, 1985, p52

21 Roberts, Hugh *The Queen's Diamonds* Royal Collection Publications, 2012, p113

22 Menkes op. cit. p67

Chapter 10: Milking the Cornwall Cash Cow

1 Gaitskell Papers UCL C/63 papers on the 1952 Civil List

2 NA T233/804 Treasury preparatory papers for the 1952 Civil List

3 Gaitskell Papers op. cit.

4 NA WORKS 19/1193

5 Ibid

6 Ibid letter from Rab Butler to David Eccles 16.04.1952

7 NA T233/734 Treasury memo 15.02.1952

8 NA T233/734 Chadwick-Burke memo 27.02.1952

9 NA T233/734 Trend-Bridges memo 24.03.1952

10 NA T233/734 Chadwick-Trend memo 23.02.1952

11 *Hansard* 09.07.1952

12 NA T233/734 Rab Butler memo 20.03.1952

13 NA T233/734 Sir Burke Trend memo 05.03.1952

14 Dimbleby, Jonathan *The Prince of Wales* Warner Books, 1994, p293

15 Kuhn, William "Queen Victoria's Civil List: what did she do with

it" *Historical Journal* vol 36 (1993) p654

16 NA T171/338

17 *Report of the Select Committee on the Civil List 1952* statement VIII Duchy of Cornwall

18 *Clarence House Annual Review 2018-19*

19 Gaitskell Papers op. cit. statement on the Duchy of Cornwall

20 *Duchy of Cornwall Annual Report 2018-19*

21 Barton, Cassie *Finances of the Monarchy* House of Commons Library Briefing Paper July 2017 Appendix on the Duchy of Cornwall

22 *Duchy of Cornwall Annual Report 2019-2020* [including pension contributions]

23 NA T628/174 1989 Treasury report "Taxation and the Civil List" p9

24 *Report of the Public Accounts Committee on the Duchy of Cornwall*, 2013-14 Oral evidence

25 Ibid

26 *Report of the Public Accounts Committee on the Duchies of Cornwall and Lancaster* 2005

27 Bradford Sarah, *Elizabeth* William Heinemann, 1996, p70

Chapter 11: Playing Hide and Seek with her Private Fortune

1 *Report of the Select Committee into the Civil List 1971-72*

2 Lacey, Robert *Majesty* Hutchinson, 1978, p326

3 Barry, Stephen *Royal Service*, Macmillan 1983, p29

4 Pimlott, Ben *The Queen* HarperCollins, 2001, p381

5 Hardman, Robert *Our Queen* Hutchinson, 2011, p213

6 Lacey op. cit. p220

7 Pimlott op. cit. p.382

8 Bradley, Ian *God Save the Queen* Bloomsbury, 2012, p202

9 NBC *Meet the Press* 09.11.1969

10 Crossman, Richard *The Crossman Diaries vol III* Hamish Hamilton, 1977, p666 + Castle, Barbara *The Castle Diaries 1964-70* Weidenfeld & Nicolson, 1984, p728

11 Crossman op. cit. p666

12 Ibid pp666-7

13 NA T326/1319 Treasury memo 12.05.1971

14 Ziegler, Philip *Mountbatten* HarperCollins, 1988, p684

15 *Daily Telegraph* 10.06.1971

16 Hall, Phillip *Royal Fortune* Bloomsbury, 1992, p165

17 NA T326/1325 Memo from Bill Ryrie of the minutes of the meeting 11.06.1971

18 *Report of the Select Committee on the Civil List 1971-2* oral evidence of Lord Cobbold 21.06.1971

19 Ibid evidence of Lord Cobbold 27.07.1971

20 NA T326/1310 Fiennes-Taylor memo 01.09.1970

21 NA T326/1328 Boyd-Carpenter to Barber letter 04.08.1971

22 NA T326 1329 Treasury memo dated 20.09.1971

23 NA T326/1319 Barber to Whitelaw letter dated 20.09.1971

24 NA T326/1330 Middleton to Airey memo dated 01.10.1971

25 *Hansard* debate on the 1971-2 Civil List Report 19.01.1972

26 Hamilton, William *My Queen and I* Quartet Books, 1975, p65

27 *Financial Times* 03.12.1971

28 *Report of the Select Committee on the Civil List 1971*-2 minority report p xlvii

29 Ibid appendix 12 p109

30 Ibid evidence of Sir Douglas Allen p43

31 *Royal Rich Report,* the *Mail on Sunday,* 2001, p13

32 NA T233/1490 Treasury report "Taxation questions" 25.05.1959

33 Pimlott, Ben *The Queen* HarperCollins, 2001, p425

34 *The Times* 12.02.1993

35 *Royal Rich Report* p14

36 Bates, Stephen *Royalty Inc* Arum Press, 2015, p259

37 Hardman, Robert *Our Queen* Hutchinson, 2011, p94

38 *Independent* 22.10.2014

Chapter 12: Tacking around Thatcherism

1 Hall, Phillip *Royal Fortune* Bloomsbury, 1992, p107

2   Pimlott, Ben *The Queen* HarperCollins, 2001, p399

3   Ibid p399

4   Bradford, Sarah *Queen Elizabeth II: Her life in our times,* Viking, 2012, p180

5   Morgan, Kenneth *Callaghan: a Life*, OUP, 1997, p511

6   Donoughue, Bernard *Downing Street Diary, Vol II*, Jonathan Cape, 2008, p443

7   See Dimbleby, Jonathan *The Prince of Wales* Warner Books, 1994, pp277-78

8   Bradford, Sarah *Queen Elizabeth II: Her life in our times,* Viking, 2012, p183

9   Moore, Charles *Margaret Thatcher Vol I* Allen Lane, 2013, p117

10 Ibid p453

11 Pimlott, Ben *The Queen* HarperCollins, 2001, p460

12 Moore op. cit. p453

13 Moore, Charles *Margaret Thatcher Vol II* Allen Lane, 2015, p577

14 Thatcher, Margaret *The Autobiography* William Collin, 2013, p256

15 Pimlott op. cit. p501

16 Hall op. cit. p140

17 Ibid p140

18 Hardman op. cit. p75

19 Pimlott op. cit. p532

20 Hardman p77

21 Ibid p80

22 Bates, Stephen *Royalty Inc* Arum Press, 2015, p286

23 Hardman op. cit. p78

24 Strong, Roy *Scenes and Apparitions: the Roy Strong Diaries 1988-2003* Weidenfeld & Nicolson 2016, p430

25 Wyatt, Woodrow *Journals of Woodrow Wyatt Vol I* Macmillan, 1998, p174

26 *Sunday Times* 20.07.1986

27 Moore vol II op. cit. p576

28 Ibid p577

29 Wyatt op. cit. p174

30 Hennessy, Peter *Having it so Good,* Penguin, 2007, p235

31 NA T628/174 *The Future of the Civil List* report December 1989

32 Ibid paragraph 28

33 Pimlott, op. cit. p531

34 NA CAB 128/97 Cabinet meeting 19.07.1990

35 *Hansard* Civil List debate 24.07.1980

Chapter 13: Making a Major Tax Concession

1   *The Times* 24/26.11.1972

2   Pimlott, Ben *The Queen* HarperCollins, 2001, p533

3   NA CAB 128/103

4   Ibid

5   Hardman, Robert *Our Queen* Hutchinson, 2011, p88

6   Wyatt, Woodrow *Journals of Woodrow Wyatt Vol III* Macmillan, 2000, p88 [19.08.1992]

7   Ibid entry for 28.11.1992 p133

8   Ibid entry for 26.11.1992 p132

9   *The Times* 26.11.1992

10 Ibid 12.02.1993

11 Wyatt op. cit. p133

12 Shawcross, William *Queen Elizabeth* Macmillan, 2009, p894

13 Email to the author 10.12.2017

14 NA T171/338 Memo to Neville Chamberlain dated 10.04.1937

15 Hall, Phillip *Royal Fortune* Bloomsbury, 1992, p81

16 Bradford, Sarah *Elizabeth* William Heinemann, 1996, p70

17 Hall op. cit. p81

18 NA T171/338 "Report on taxation questions"

19 Kuhn, William "Queen Victoria's Civil List: what did she do with it" *Historical Journal* vol 36 (1993), p653

20 Bahlman, Dudley (ed) *The Diary of Sir Edward Hamilton* Clarendon Press, 1972, entry for 07.05.1901, p406

21 Ibid p398

22 Ibid p406

23 NA T171/331 Report on taxation questions

24 Bahlman op. cit. entry for 21.10.1903, p444

25 Hall op. cit. p34

26 NA T171/338 Lloyd George 02.07.1910 Tax Questions report

27 Hall op. cit. p35

28 NA T626/176 Treasury note December 1989 *"Taxation and the Civil List"* p3 + p7 (above)

Chapter 14: Counting the Cost of Divorce

1 *The Times* 13.07.1996 article by Sarah Bradford

2 Sarah, Duchess of York "My Story" Pocket, 1997, p178

3 Ibid p162

4 Ibid p171

5 Bradford, Sarah *Elizabeth* William Heinemann, 1996, p471

6 Sarah, Duchess of York op. cit. p11

7 *The Daily Telegraph* 12.03.2011

8 Brown, Tina *Diana Chronicles* Century, 2007, p359

9 *The Daily Telegraph* 12.03.2011

10 *The Guardian* 03.07.2016

11 *The Daily Mail* 22.05.2018

12 *The Times* 10.12.1992

13 NA CAB 128/103 Cabinet minutes 10.12.1992

14 Bower, Tom *Rebel Prince: The Power, Passion and Defiance of Prince Charles* Collins 2018 Kindle book location 231

15 Bedell Smith, Sally *Elizabeth the Queen* Random House 2012, p374

16 Anthony Julius interview to *Chambers Student* Newsletter website January 2017

17 Brown op. cit. p359

18 *The Times* 08.07.1996

19 Sarah, Duchess of York op. cit. p195

20 Seward, Ingrid *William and Harry* Carlton, 2008, p190

21 *The Times* 13.07.1996

22 *Chambers Student* op. cit.

23 Brown op. cit. p363

24 Bradford, Sarah *Diana* Viking, 2006, p305

25 *Daily Telegraph* 25.07.2004

26 Howard, Anthony *Rab: The Life of R. A. Butler* Cape, 1987, p356

27 Bates, Stephen *Royalty Inc* Arum Press, 2015, p124

28 *Royal Rich Report* op. cit. p114

29 *The Times* 27.11.1992

30 Tweet by BBC Royal Correspondent Peter Hunt 21.07.2016

Chapter 15: Looking a Gift Horse

1 *Royal Rich Report* pp24-5

2 ITV1 *The Royal Wives of Windsor* 30.04.2018

3 Paxman, Jeremy *On Royalty*, Viking, 2006, p48

4 Curling, Bill *All the Queen's Horses* Chatto and Windus, 1978, p13

5 Smith, Sean *Royal Racing* BBC books, 2001, p18

6 Ridley, Jane *Bertie – The Life of Edward VII* Vintage, 2013, p317

7 Ibid p270

8 Bahlman, Dudley (ed) *The Diary of Sir Edward Hamilton* Clarendon Press, 1972, p324

9 Ridley op. cit. p353

10 Bahlman op. cit. p428

11 Smith p18

12 Ibid

13 Ibid p23

14 Ibid

15 Ibid p26

16 Ibid p28

17 Shawcross, William *Queen Elizabeth* Macmillan, 2009, pp50-51

18 Lacey, Robert *Majesty* Hutchison, 1978, p395

19 Curling op. cit. p109

20 Bedell Smith, Sally *Elizabeth the Queen* Random House 2012, p350

21 Smith op. cit. p224

22 Shawcross op. cit. p790

23 Ibid p708

24 *Royal Rich Report* pp24-25

25 *Daily Mail* 24.10.2017

26 Interview with Dickie Arbiter 21.09.2018

27 *Daily Telegraph* 19.10.2008

28 BBC-1 *Countryfile* 10.06.2018

29 Ibid

Chapter 16: Cheating Death Duties

1 Strong, Roy *Scenes and Apparitions: the Roy Strong Diaries 1988-2003* Weidenfeld & Nicolson 2016, p377

2 Bedell Smith, Sally *Elizabeth the Queen* Random House 2012, p435

3 Wilson, AN *The Queen* Atlantic Books, 2016, pp144-5

4 Ibid location 1485

5 Interview with Richard Palmer 11.12.2017

6 *Guardian* 11.11.2011

7 *Daily Telegraph* 14.01.2007

8 *Sunday Telegraph* 12.06.2006

9 Brown, Craig *Ma'am, Darling* Fourth Estate, 2017, p403

10 *Daily Telegraph* 18.06.2006

11 Shawcross, William *Queen Elizabeth* Macmillan, 2009, p688

12 *Daily Telegraph* 31.03.2002

13 *Daily Telegraph* 03.05.2016

14 *Royal Rich Report* p51

15 *Sunday Times* 07.04.2002

16 Mullin, Chris *Decline and Fall* Profile 2011, pp55-56

17 *Times* 06.05.2002

18 *Guardian* 09.05.2002

19 *Daily Telegraph* 12.05.2002

20 *Sunday Times* 05.05.2002

21 See McClure, David *Royal Legacy* Thistle Publishing 2014/second edition Lume Books, 2020

22 Email to author from Lucy Whitaker 16.07.2015

23 *Sunday Express* 15.03.2015

24 *Hansard* 11.02.1993

25 Commission, *Report on the Future of the Monarchy* Crowes, 2003, pp.129-130

26 *Royal Rich Report*

27 From November 2018 a "virtual tour" of Clarence House was made available to the public online, although the paintings were not the main feature. See *Evening Standard* 13.11.2018

Chapter 17: Trains and Boats and Planes

1 Cowper Coles, Sherard *Ever the Diplomat* HarperPress 2012, p260

2 *Car Keys* "What car does Her Majesty drive?" 21.04.2016

3 Castle, Barbara *The Castle Diaries 1964-70* Weidenfeld & Nicolson, 1984, entry for 03.04.1968, p421

4 Bedell Smith, Sally *Elizabeth the Queen* Random House 2012, p21

5 *Car Keys* op. cit.

6 Ridley, Jane *Bertie – The Life of Edward VII* Vintage, 2013, p323

7 *Royal Rich Report* pp28-29

8 *Car Keys* op. cit.

9 Bedell Smith op. cit. p417

10 Ibid p416

11 Bradford, Sarah *Elizabeth* William Heinemann, 1996, p218

12 *Royal Rich Report* p132

13 Marr, Andrew *The Diamond Queen* Macmillan, 2011, pp195-96

14 Hardman, Robert *Our Queen* Hutchinson, 2011, pp68-69

15 *The Daily Telegraph* 12.07.2010

16 *Report of the Select Committee into the Civil List 1971-72* Annex D Royal Yacht *Britannia*

17 Clarke, Kenneth *Kind of Blue* Macmillan, 2012, pp322-23

18 Ibid p323

19 NA BD 41/457 Letter from Sir Kenneth Scott to Richard Williams 05.05.1995

20 Ibid memo from Mark Powell 10.05.1995

21 Hardman op. cit. p176

22 Ibid p177

23 *Public Accounts Committee Report on the Sovereign Grant 2013-14* oral evidence by Sir Alan Reid
24 National Audit Office Report *Royal Travel by Air and Train* 2001-02
25 *The Guardian* 17.03.2017
26 *Public Accounts Committee* Report op. cit.
27 *Daily Mail* 19.02.2017
28 National Audit Office Report op. cit.
29 *The Sovereign Grant Report 2017-18* Travel Annex
30 Bates, Stephen *Royalty Inc* Arum pp287-288
31 Ibid p287
32 National Audit Office Report op. cit.
33 *The Sovereign Grant Report 2018-19* Travel Annex
34 Ibid

Chapter 18: Giving the Sovereign a Generous Grant

1 *Daily Mail* 30.03.2018
2 *Evening Standard* 31.03.2017
3 *Forces TV* 14.03.2016
4 *Sovereign Grant Annual Report 2018-19*
5 *The Times* 25.06.2019
6 Interview with Richard Palmer 11.12.2017
7 See *Hansard* debate on the Civil List 30.06.2011
8 Ibid
9 *Financial Times* 02.07.2011
10 Cameron, David *For the Record* HarperCollins, 2019, p370
11 Interview with Chris Bryant MP 09.10.2018
12 *Hansard* debate on the Civil List 03.10.2011
13 NA T628/175 *Future of the Civil List* meeting
14 *Hansard* debate on the Sovereign Grant 2011 14.07.2011
15 *BBC News* website/*The Guardian* 18.11.2016
16 Interview with Dickie Arbiter 21.09.2018
17 Interview with Dame Margaret Hodge MP 13.12.2017
18 *BBC News* website 18.11.2016

19 *Independent* 21.11.2016

20 *Public Accounts Committee Report on the Sovereign Grant* 2013-14

21 Dickie Arbiter op. cit.

22 Strong, Roy *Scenes and Apparitions: the Roy Strong Diaries 1988-2003* Weidenfeld & Nicolson, p379

Chapter 19: Ditching the Duchy for a New Deal

1 *The Guardian* 17.03.2017 "London Bridge is down" by Sam Knight

2 Ibid

3 Bedell Smith, Sally *Prince Charles* Michael Joseph 2017, p454 [interview with NBC anchor Brian Williams, 17.06.2010]

4 Interview with Richard Palmer 11.12.2017

5 Interview with Dickie Arbiter 21.09.2017

6 Arbiter, Dickie *On Duty with the Queen* Blink, 2014 e-book location 404

7 *Daily Express* 05.10.2008

8 *Sunday Express* 24.10.2016

9 *BBC News* website 09.12.2016 "Prince Andrew denies rift over daughters"

10 *Sunday Times* 03.12.2017

11 See Barton, Cassie *Finances of the Monarchy* House of Commons Library Briefing Paper July 2017

Bibliography

Allfrey, Anthony *Edward VII and his Jewish Court* Weidenfeld & Nicolson, 1991

Arbiter, Dickie *On duty with the Queen* Blink, 2014

Bahlman, Dudley (ed) *The Diary of Sir Edward Hamilton* Clarendon Press, 1972

Barry, Stephen *Royal Service*, Macmillan, 1983

Bates, Stephen *Royalty Inc* Arum Press, 2015

Bedell Smith, Sally *Prince Charles* Michael Joseph, 2017

——*Elizabeth the Queen* Random House, 2012

Blair, Tony *A Journey* Hutchinson, 2010

Bloch, Michael *The Secret File of the Duke of Windsor* Bantam Press, 1988

——*The Duchess of Windsor* Weidenfeld & Nicolson, 1996

Boyd Carpenter, John *Way of Life* Sidgwick & Jackson, 1980

Bower, Tom *Rebel Prince: The Power, Passion and Defiance of Prince Charles* Collins, 2018

Bradford, Sarah *Diana* Viking, 2006

——*Elizabeth* William Heinemann, 1996

——*George VI* Weidenfeld & Nicolson, 1989

——*Queen Elizabeth II: Her life in our times,* Viking, 2012

Brandreth, Gyles *Philip and Elizabeth* Century, 2004

Bryan, J & Murphy, Charles *The Windsor Story* William Morrow, 1979

Brown, Craig *Ma'am Darling* Fourth Estate, 2017

Brown, Ivor *Balmoral* Collins, 1966

Brown, Tina *Diana Chronicles* Century, 2007

Burgess, Colin *Behind Palace Doors* John Blake, 2006

Burrell, Paul *A Royal Duty* Thorndike, 2004

——*The Way We Were* HarperCollins, 2006

Cameron, David *For the Record* HarperCollins, 2019

Campbell, Alastair *The Alastair Campbell Diaries Vol III* Hutchison, 2011

Cannadine, David *The Decline and Fall of the British Aristocracy* Penguin, 2005

Castle, Barbara *The Castle Diaries 1964-70* Weidenfeld & Nicolson, 1984

Clark, Ronald *Balmoral: Queen Victoria's Highland Home* Thames and Hudson, 1981

Clarke, Kenneth *Kind of Blue* Macmillan, 2012

Courtney, Nicholas *The Queen's Stamps* Methuen, 2004

Crawford, Marion *The Little Princesses* St Martin's Press, 2002

Crossman, Richard *The Crossman Diaries vol III* Hamish Hamilton, 1977

Curling, Bill *All the Queen's Horses* Chatto and Windus, 1978

Curtis, Sarah (ed) *The Journals of Woodrow Wyatt vol II* Macmillan, 1999

——*The Journals of Woodrow Wyatt vol III* Macmillan, 2000

Dalton, Hugh *The Political Diary of Hugh Dalton* Cape, 1986

Dean, John *HRH Prince Philip, Duke of Edinburgh* Robert Hale, 1954

De Courcy, Anne *Snowdon* Orion, 2009

Dimbleby, Jonathan *The Prince of Wales* Warner Books, 1994

Donoughue, Bernard *Downing Street Diary*, vol II, Jonathan Cape, 2008

Duff, David *Hessian Tapestry* Muller, 1967

Eade, Philip *Young Prince Philip* HarperCollins, 2011

Fabian Commission *Report of the Future of the Monarchy* Crowes, 2003

Field Leslie *The Queen's Jewels* Guild, 1987

Frankland, Noble *Prince Henry, Duke of Gloucester* Weidenfeld & Nicolson, 1980

Goodman, Jean *Seago – A Wider Canvas* Erskine Press, 2002

Hall, Phillip *Royal Fortune* Bloomsbury, 1992

Hamilton, William *My Queen and I* Quartet Books, 1975

Hardman, Robert *Our Queen* Hutchinson, 2011

Hart-Davis, Duff *King's Counsellor: Abdication and War: the diaries of Sir Alan Lascelles*, Weidenfeld & Nicolson, 2006

Haslam, Nicholas *Redeeming Features* Jonathan Cape, 2009

Heald, Tim *Princess Margaret* Orion, 2008

——*The Duke, A Portrait of a Prince* Hodder & Stoughton, 1991

Heffer, Simon *Power and Place* Weidenfeld & Nicolson, 1998

Hennessy, Peter, *Having it so Good,* Penguin, 2007

Hobhouse, Sir Charles (ed. Edward David) *Inside Asquith's Cabinet* John Murray, 1977

Hoey, Brian *At Home with the Queen* HarperCollins, 2002

——*Mountbatten* Sidgwick & Jackson, 1994

Holden, Anthony *Charles – A Biography* Bantam Press, 1998

Howard, Anthony *Rab: The life of R. A. Butler* Cape, 1987

Jephson, Patrick *Shadows of a Princess* HarperCollins, 2001

Lacey, Robert *Royal* Little Brown, 2002

——*Majesty* Hutchison, 1978

Lees-Milne, James *Ancestral Voices* Faber & Faber, 1984

Magnus, Philip *Edward VII* Penguin, 1964

Mail on Sunday Royal *Royal Rich Report* Associated Newspapers, 2001

Marr, Andrew *The Diamond Queen* Macmillan, 2011

Mayer, Catherine *Charles: the heart of a king* Penguin, 2015

McClure, David *Royal Legacy* Thistle Publishing 2014/second edition Lume Books, 2020

Menkes, Suzy *The Royal Jewels* Granada, 1985

Moore, Charles *Margaret Thatcher Vol I* Allen Lane, 2013

——*Margaret Thatcher Vol II* Allen Lane, 2015

Morgan, Kenneth *Callaghan: Life* OUP, 1997

Mullin, Chris *A Walk on Part* Profile, 2012

——*Decline and Fall* Profile 2011

Nicolson, Harold *George V* Constable, 1952

Nicolson, Nigel (ed) *Diaries and Letters 1907-1964 Harold Nicolson* Weidenfeld & Nicolson, 2004

Paxman, Jeremy *On Royalty* Viking, 2006

Picknett, Lynn (et al) *War of the Windsors* Mainstream, 2002

Pimlott, Ben *The Queen* HarperCollins, 2001

——*Hugh Dalton* Cape, 1985

Pope-Hennessy, James *Queen Mary* George Allen & Unwin, 1959

——*The Quest for Queen Mary* (ed. Hugo Vickers) Zuleika, 2018

Rappoport, Helen *Queen Victoria* ABC-Clio, 2003

Rhodes, Margaret *The Final Curtsey* Birlinn, 2011

Rhodes James, Robert (ed) *Chips – The Diaries of Sir Henry Channon* Weidenfeld & Nicolson, 1967

——*Memoirs of a Conservative: J.C.C. Davidson's memoirs and papers 1910-37* Weidenfeld & Nicolson, 1967

Ridley, Jane *Bertie – The Life of Edward VII* Vintage, 2013

Roberts, Andrew *Eminent Churchillians* Phoenix, 1994

Roberts, Hugh *The Queen's Diamonds* Royal Collection Publications, 2012

Rose, Kenneth *King George V* Weidenfeld & Nicholson, 1983

Sarah, Duchess of York "My Story" Pocket, 1977

Sebba, Anne *That Woman* Weidenfeld & Nicolson, 2011

Seward, Ingrid *My Husband and I* Simon and Shuster, 2017

——*William and Harry* Carlton, 2008

Shawcross, William *Queen Elizabeth* Macmillan, 2009

Somerville, Robert *History of the Duchy of Lancaster Vol I 1265-1603,* 1953

——*History of the Duchy of Lancaster Vol II 1603-1965* [privately printed], 1970

Strong, Roy *Scenes and Apparitions: the Roy Strong Diaries 1988-2003* Weidenfeld & Nicolson, 2016

Temple, Jon *Living off the State* Progressbooks, 2008

Thatcher, Margaret *The Downing Street Years* HarperCollins, 1995

Titchmarsh, Alan *The Queen's Houses* BBC Books, 2014

Van der Kiste, John *Queen Victoria's Children* History Press, 2009

Vickers, Hugo, *Behind Closed Doors* Hutchison, 2011

——*Elizabeth, the Queen Mother* Random House, 2006

Wightman, Andy *The Poor had no lawyers* Berlinn, 2013

Williams, Kate *Young Elizabeth* Orion, 2015

Williams, Philip *Hugh Gaitskell* Cape,1979

Wilson, A.N. *Victoria: A Life* Atlantic Books, 2014

——*The Queen* Atlantic Books, 2016

Wilson, Sir John, *The Royal Philatelic Collection* Dropmore Press, 1952

Ziegler, Philip *Mountbatten* HarperCollins, 1988

——*King Edward VIII* HarperCollins, 2012

Journals & Parliamentary Reports

Barton, Cassie *Finances of the Monarchy* House of Commons Library Briefing Paper July 2017

Hall, Phillip et al *Royal Rich Report,* the Mail on Sunday, 2001

Kuhn, William *Queen Victoria's Civil List: what did she do with it* Historical Journal vol 36 (1993)

Report of the Public Accounts Committee on the Duchies of Cornwall & Lancaster, 2005

Report of the Public Accounts Committee on the Duchy of Cornwall, 2013

Report by the Comptroller and Auditor General on the Royal Household, 2013

Report of the Public Accounts Committee on the Sovereign Grant, 2014

Archives

National Archives: Treasury papers for the 1911, 1936, 1952,1971 and 1989 Civil List reviews and Prime Minister's Office/Cabinet papers for 1992

Royal Archives: private correspondence of Queen Victoria and George VI

University College London, Special Collection: private papers of Hugh Gaitskell
London School of Economics Library: private papers of Hugh Dalton
British Library: the papers of William Gladstone

Acknowledgements

I am grateful to Phillip Hall who wrote the pioneering book *Royal Fortune: Tax, Money and the Monarchy* (Bloomsbury, 1992) and was a principal contributor to the equally grounding breaking study *The Mail on Sunday's The Royal Rich Report,* 2001. This excellent report has been an invaluable source of material for my own study. A special thanks too to Robert Hardman for his insightful *Our Queen* Hutchinson, 2011.

I would also like to thank for agreeing to talk to me: Dame Margaret Hodge, MP, Chris Bryant, MP, Crispin Blunt, MP, Dickie Arbiter, Richard Palmer, Graham Smith, Konrad Jagodzinski, Philip Beresford, Robert Watts, and many other palace sources who did not want their names revealed.

I thank too the archivists at the British Library, the Royal Archives, the National Archives, the UCL Library Services, Special Collections, and the LSE Library Special Collections – as well as Steven Davie at the Registers of Scotland who was especially helpful.

I am also grateful to several royal biographers who were granted access to the Royal Archives: Sarah Bradford (*Elizabeth,* 1996) Jonathan Dimbleby (*The Prince of Wales,* 1994). Robert Lacey (*Majesty,* 1978) Jane Ridley (*Bertie – The Life of Edward VII,* 2013) Philip Eade (*Young Prince Philip,* 2011), William Shawcross *Queen Elizabeth,* 2009) and Philp Ziegler (*King Edward VIII,* 2012).

I also owe a large debt to the work of Dudley Bahlman, Stephen Bates, Michael Bloch, Gyles Brandreth, Tina Brown, Paul Burrell, David Cannadine, Anne de Courcy, Jo William Hamilton, Tim Heald, Anthony Holden, Andrew Marr, Chris Mullin, Andrew Roberts, Hugo Vickers and Philip Ziegler.

I wish to thank the following copyright holders: Macmillan's for *Queen Elizabeth: the Queen Mother* by William Shawcross; David Higham for the use of extracts from *The Castle Diaries 1964-70* by Barbara Castle, Weidenfeld & Nicolson, 1984; and Penguin books for use of "one hundred and twenty-eight (128) words from *Margaret Thatcher* by Charles Moore (Penguin Book 2019) Copyright © Charles Moore, 2019."

I would like to thank my indefatigable agent Andrew Lownie who oversaw the project from conception to birth. I am also grateful to James Faktor and all his team at Lume Books for expertly getting the work to publication in record time.

All efforts have been made to trace the copyright holders to quote from their books and diaries. I apologise to any copyright holders who I have been unable to reach and I promise to rectify the situation in future editions.

CPSIA information can be obtained
at www.ICGtesting.com
Printed in the USA
LVHW041142250920
667084LV00002B/99